IN DEFENCE OF CANADA

In Defence of Canada

APPEASEMENT AND REARMAMENT

◆◆

JAMES EAYRS

UNIVERSITY OF TORONTO PRESS

Printed in the United States of America

To Elizabeth

STUDIES IN THE STRUCTURE OF POWER:
DECISION-MAKING IN CANADA

Editor: JOHN MEISEL

STUDIES IN THE STRUCTURE OF POWER:

DECISION-MAKING IN CANADA

The series "Studies in the Structure of Power: Decision-Making in Canada" is sponsored by the Social Science Research Council of Canada for the purpose of encouraging and assisting research concerned with the manner and setting in which important decisions are made in fields affecting the general public in Canada. The launching of the series was made possible by a grant from the Canada Council.

Unlike the books in other series supported by the Social Science Research Council, the studies of decision-making are not confined to any one of the disciplines comprising the social sciences. The series explores the ways in which social power is exercised in this country: it will encompass studies done within a number of different conceptual frameworks, utilizing both traditional methods of analysis and those prompted by the social, political, and technological changes following the Second World War.

In establishing the series, the Social Science Research Council has sought to encourage scholars already embarked on relevant studies by providing financial and editorial assistance and similarly to induce others to undertake research in areas of decision-making so far neglected in Canada.

J. M.

PREFACE AND ACKNOWLEDGMENTS

Too often prefaces are "writ . . . for filling" (as Swift said of Dryden's): a book should speak for itself. This preface is therefore written with some reluctance. It is intended not as filling, only as clarification of two or three matters which the reader might otherwise find puzzling.

In Defence of Canada: Appeasement and Rearmament is a companion and sequel to my *In Defence of Canada: From the Great War to the Great Depression* (Toronto, 1964). I can now refer fearlessly to Volume I and Volume II of this study; and while I hesitate to tempt the fates by referring to an as yet unwritten Volume III, it is my intention to offer a third book dealing with Canada's national security policies in the age of the atom, the long-range bomber, and the inter-continental missile.

Like Volume I, Volume II rejects as outmoded and misleading the traditional division of national security policy into two compartments, one called foreign policy, the other, defence policy. Like Volume I, Volume II is meant to demonstrate that the military and diplomatic components of national security policy are, and ought to be, indissolubly combined, in study and analysis as well as in formulation and execution. If in Volume I the emphasis was mainly on the military, in Volume II it is mainly on the diplomatic: the tempo and importance of Canadian diplomacy steadily increase during the period with which it is concerned.

That period opens with the Italian war of aggression against Ethiopia in 1935. It closes in the late summer and early fall of 1940, as the twilight war becomes a total war. An alternative closing date would have been 10 September 1939: it has been avoided deliberately, to emphasize that policy does not change just because a country acquires the legal status of belligerency.

Within this chosen period there has been no attempt to deal with everything of importance. In some cases the gaps are due to insufficient

evidence. In other cases they are due to the existence of work in progress elsewhere. Thus, a forthcoming volume of the official history of
Canadian military policy during the Second World War relieves me of
the obligation to deal, for example, with the control and deployment of
the Army overseas. In the same way I have refrained from commenting
as fully as I might have done upon the personality of the central figure
of this book, knowing that this intriguing theme will be amply and well
treated in the forthcoming biography of W. L. Mackenzie King.

◆◆

It is with no reluctance, however, that I acknowledge my indebted-
ness to the people who in different ways have helped me with the writing
of this book.

My greatest debt is to H. Blair Neatby, of the Department of History,
Carleton University, Ottawa, and the official biographer of Mackenzie
King. The reader of this book will quickly discover how much of it
derives from material in the King Papers; he would not know, however,
that only the generosity of Professor Neatby has made it possible for
me to use this material. Having for the time being put to one side his
work on the second volume of his biography, he graciously volunteered
to waive a previous arrangement whereby my own work had to await
the appearance of his before being brought to publication. My gratitude
for this exceptionally generous act is in no way lessened by my expectation that the revelations in my own book will add to, rather than
diminish, interest in his. I am grateful, too, to the Literary Executors of
W. L. Mackenzie King for giving their consent to this agreement between
us.

I am again indebted to Professor John Meisel, of the Department of
Political Studies, Queen's University, Kingston, and Editor of the series
"Studies in the Structure of Power: Decision-Making in Canada" in
which both Volume I and Volume II make their appearance. His editorial counsel has been invaluable, not least because he has refused to
allow our friendship of over twenty years to stand in the way of the
sternest critical comment.

No less valuable (and certainly no less stern) a critic of my work is
Dr. C. P. Stacey, now Director of the Historical Section, Canadian
Forces Headquarters. Once again he has placed at my disposal his
unrivalled knowledge of military history and his wise judgment.

I wish to record my thanks to the Directors and personnel of the
three Historical Sections of the Armed Forces, and to wish them well

in the new integrated order of things; and to the Dominion Archivist and his staff, and to wish them well in their new building.

For permission to make use of the various collections of private papers on which much of the book is based, I am grateful to their various custodians (who are listed in the Note on the Sources).

My thanks are due to Brigadier G. P. Loggie, who was kind enough to provide me with a written account of his experiences as Ordnance representative of the Department of National Defence in London, England, before the Second World War; to Mr. F. J. Hatch (formerly F/L, R.C.A.F.), who allowed me to read his unpublished memorandum on the origins of the British Commonwealth Air Training Plan; to Mr. E. C. Beer, Archivist of the Douglas Library, Queen's University, for helping me peruse the Norman Rogers Papers at short notice and in short order; and to Maj.-Gen. T. V. Anderson, D.S.O., Mrs. H. E. Bates, Mrs. Loring Cheney Christie, Dr. Paul Christie, Mrs. A. R. Menzies, and Mrs. W. A. Riddell, who were good enough to help me secure photographs.

The University of Toronto Press has provided expert help and friendly encouragement at every stage of the production of my book. Again I thank, and marvel at the patience of, Miss Francess Halpenny, Managing Editor of the Press, and Mr. R. I. K. Davidson, of its Editorial Staff.

This being my sixth book, it is about time I expressed my appreciation of the contribution to my work of my wife. A youthful Cyril Connolly once attacked a happy marriage and a happy home as enemies of promise in writers. I have not found them so.

J. E.

July 1965
Toronto

◆◆

CONTENTS

IN DEFENCE OF CANADA

I

War in Africa

DE BONO'S CAMPAIGN, AND BENNETT'S

Emilio de Bono—Mussolini's marshal, minister of colonies, and master planner of the conquest of Ethiopia—revealed in his memoirs that the Italian fascist regime had determined upon war in East Africa as early as 1933. Efforts were made the following year to provoke internal revolution in Ethiopia as a pretext for intervention. The intended victim's refusal to be provoked made cruder methods necessary, and Mussolini's legions accordingly girded themselves for invasion. As the dry season, when the armour could manoeuvre, drew closer, the tempo of diplomacy quickened. But diplomacy did not dissuade the Duce from his aggression. On 3 October 1935, Italian airmen bombed the Ethiopian town of Adowa, and Italian troops crossed the Ethiopian frontier.

These momentous events occurred while Canadians were more than usually distracted from international affairs by what was happening at home. The Great Depression still lay like a blight across the land. The failure of five years of Conservative rule to solve the country's economic problems and alleviate the suffering of the unemployed had thrown up radicalism of the left and of the right. A new party of socialism, calling itself the Co-operative Commonwealth Federation, came out of Regina. A new movement, calling itself Social Credit, came out of Calgary. "People," wrote the Under Secretary of State for External Affairs in August 1935, "are immensely more interested in Alberta than in Abyssinia."[1] And while Marshal de Bono's campaign ran its brutal course in East Africa, R. B. Bennett was campaigning across Canada. A general election had been called for 15 October.

For its knowledge of Mussolini's activities in East Africa, the Canadian Government, lacking its own diplomatic representation in

Italy, was largely dependent upon the Foreign Office. On 22 May, Anthony Eden told the Canadian Advisory Officer at Geneva that the fascist regime was "engineering for war." The Canadian High Commissioner in London, inquiring at a meeting between the Foreign Secretary and dominion representatives on 29 July whether Mussolini was likely to press on "jusqu'au bout," was told that this seemed "most probable." It did not take a very penetrating intelligence to see that this was so.

Italy's intentions were plain enough. So was the injustice of her cause. The real question was what should be done if it came to war.

This question arose during the general election campaign in Canada, but briefly and without much consequence. The Leader of the Opposition raised it for the first time in a speech at London, Ont., on 15 August: "If there comes a war in Abyssinia who will say where the situation is likely to end? . . . If it should come that a decision should have to be made in Europe, so far as the Liberal Party is concerned no decision will be made until a new Government has been formed and Parliament assembled together and until the voice of Parliament is heard." Here was the famous formula: let Parliament decide, without indicating what it was to decide. At Quebec City, on 9 September, Mackenzie King hinted at what its answer might be: "I believe the people of Canada would be strongly opposed to war connected with economic interests in the Near East." But it was his political lieutenant, speaking from the same platform on the same occasion, who gave the answer straight out: "No interest in Ethiopia, of any nature whatever, is worth the life of a single Canadian citizen. No consideration could justify Canada's participation in such a war, and I am unalterably opposed to it."[2] Ernest Lapointe spoke for French Canada; and on this issue French Canada was to speak for Canada.

R. B. Bennett was under strong pressure to exploit the crisis in East Africa for electoral advantage. From Washington, the Canadian Minister —the energetic and erratic W. D. Herridge who, as brother-in-law to the Prime Minister, was accustomed to addressing him with candour— advised him to speak up. That was not his earliest advice. Herridge had described Mackenzie King's speech at London, Ont., as "an unbelievable blunder," adding that "it is very difficult for Billy King to go right on this war business. He is sensitive about the last one."[3] But he was soon to change his mind about the wisdom of keeping silent.

The Council of the League is now preparing its report [which] . . . will in all probability recommend sanctions under Article 16. Where then will Canada stand? Before you can justly and patriotically make answer to this question, you must have clearly in mind the consequences of the application of sanctions. . . . Sanctions mean war. When once sanctions are applied, the only real chance that war may be averted is that Italy will surrender. You gamble on that chance. If you guess wrong and Italy does not surrender, then Canada is at war. . . . No Government has the right to gamble with the life of this country. . . .[4]

This is probably the most important letter you will ever receive. . . . Tomorrow . . . the League will take action upon the Council's recommendations on sanctions. . . . If I were the Prime Minister, I would take this line: . . . that hereafter, no compulsion will be put upon any Canadian to leave the shores of Canada to engage in a war in Europe or elsewhere. . . .

If the Prime Minister takes the position I have indicated, . . . he will succeed in doing several things: He will succeed in hoisting the Conservative Party out of the ruck . . . ; he will succeed in subordinating every other issue now before the electorate to this paramount issue; and he will succeed in obtaining the support of sober and decent people, French and English, from one end of the country to the other. . . .[5]

Herridge was not now thinking of Ethiopia, or even of the fate of Europe; he was thinking of the election. It was as a master-stroke in Bennett's faltering campaign, a roorback of monumental proportions and, hopefully, of electrifying results, that he wanted his country's external policies to be shaped. "It must of course be apparent to you," he had written in a letter destined for the Prime Minister's eye,

that the dead weight of opposition to the Government can only be shattered by the fiercest kind of counter-attack. To get up, in these circumstances, and babble about the Government's record, however noble that may be, and talk about what you have done in the last few years, and try to wriggle out of the promises which have not been literally fulfilled, and try to prevail upon the electorate to seriously regard the promises which must now be made— all this is just waste of breath. You will not only be defeated—you will be annihilated. But if you can devise some dynamic force, powerful, as I say, to pierce this dead wall of hostility, it is conceivable that you may still get through. . . .[6]

Only a drowning man could clutch at such a straw. Bennett, though in danger of drowning, was not so desperate as to take his brother-in-law's advice. "I am making no statement," he wrote to a friend, "until after Italy has an opportunity to present her case to the League. I cannot express a public opinion while the case is *sub judice* and the evidence is incomplete."[7]

So far as the voters could tell, there was little difference between the leaders of the two main parties in their attitudes towards the East African crisis and the part Canada should play. Both hoped it would not get worse; both hoped that if it did get worse it would not mean general war; both hoped that if it meant general war Canada would keep out. On this point, indeed, Bennett was if anything more emphatic than

Mackenzie King. "I do not believe," he wrote, "this country will permit, in your lifetime or in mine, Canadians to fight as an army in a foreign country, nor will it make any difference if the League in Geneva (as it at present functions) designates a particular nation to be an 'aggressor.' "

But between Bennett and King there really lay a fundamental difference of approach. At the heart of Mackenzie King's political philosophy was the notion that force and coercion rarely if ever play constructive roles. That thought was alien to Bennett. While he had no liking of violence for its own sake, he would not shrink from violence if he thought it could do good; and sometimes he thought it could. Tariffs might blast a way into the markets of the world; armies might keep the peace of the world. "So long as nations continue to arm and train men by hundreds of thousands to fight, there will be no such thing as peace. If nations will agree together to maintain an international police force, it might serve a very useful purpose." There was nothing wrong (contrary to King's view) with collective security as such; what was wrong was that nations were not prepared to act collectively for their security. There was nothing wrong (contrary to King's view) with sanctions as such; what was wrong was that nations refused to apply them, leaving their application to a faithful few.

We perhaps expect too much of poor old England. Four times she has saved the world. . . . and now, with her army reduced to a skeleton, with her navy so weakened as not to be able to protect her trade routes, and a wholly insufficient air force, it is suggested she might "lead the world." But where? Into war? Her moral leadership is still the hope of mankind. I am satisfied she will do everything that can be done, but I do not believe that alone she can enforce peace upon Italy. . . .

The purpose of the Covenant was to secure an organization every member of which would be pledged to take specified action under indicated circumstances. The fact that so many members of the League decline to live up to that obligation has placed countries like England in a false position. Certainly where the Covenant contemplates united action by all the members, it would be idle to expect two of the number [Great Britain and Canada] to discharge an obligation that rested upon all. . . .[8]

GROPING FOR A POLICY

As the leader of a political party seeking re-election, R. B. Bennett might hope to get away with saying nothing about Ethiopia in his speeches across the country; but as Prime Minister of Canada he could not expect to get away for long with saying nothing about Ethiopia in his despatches overseas. On 3 September he sent a lengthy cable to the

Dominions Office, the first to set out a Canadian position. Canada's delegates at the forthcoming Assembly, the despatch stated, would be ready to discuss the question of the application of sanctions against Italy. But it also indicated that Canadians, immersed in domestic economic crisis, had no taste for sanctions, any more than they had had at the outset of the League of Nations when they saw how gravely collective security was weakened by the absence from its membership of certain powerful states. On the other hand, the despatch declared, they did recognize the importance of preserving the League from that loss of authority which would follow from a failure to carry out the obligations of the Covenant; and recognized, too, the "undoubtedly aggressive character of declared Italian policy."

But was this really so? Might it not have been more helpful, as well as more candid, to admit, in the brutally frank language of a French-Canadian intellectual, that "the League of Nations as it now exists is not highly prized in the Province of Quebec"? That French-speaking Canadians of the Roman Catholic faith were not persuaded of the wisdom of making economic warfare against the home of the Papacy? Or that they showed even less enthusiasm for running the risk of war on behalf of "a certain tribe of negroes"?[9] To have expected the Government of Canada thus to address the Government of the United Kingdom would have been to have expected too much by way of plain speaking. But the despatch did observe that the isolationist sentiment then making headway in the Dominion could only be encouraged by the "unfortunate concessions" recently granted by Ethiopia to Great Britain for the construction of a high dam at Lake Tana.

This broad hint that the East African crisis could be interpreted as a clash of rival imperialisms rather than as a test of principle betrays very clearly the hand of the Under Secretary of State for External Affairs. For the formulation of Canadian policy towards the crisis, at least until the change of government late in October 1935, O. D. Skelton must bear major responsibility. When in the capital the Prime Minister made policy by himself, untroubled by what his "so stupid cabinet" (as his brother-in-law described the Bennett Government) might think. But as the campaign reached its climax, Bennett was not often in the capital; Skelton ran the Department and drafted its despatches.

Skelton opposed Canadian participation in any scheme of collective security. He had always been strongly isolationist in his attitude towards European problems; he had always felt that the sanctions provisions of the Covenant were both unwise and unfair. "I am frankly prejudiced against their use," he wrote to a friend in 1932. "In general I doubt the possibility of fighting the devil with fire, or of ending war by going to war—for an economic boycott could with difficulty stop short of war; in particular I doubt whether France & the other European countries which are always demanding sanctions against European 'aggressors' (i.e., disturbers of the *status quo*) would lift a finger in a non-European dispute."[10] And three years later: "The application of sanctions involves much of the manoeuvring and rousing of national hatreds, and the gliding into positions from which questions of national prestige will allow no escape, that are characteristic of wars of a more old-fashioned type."[11] That in the East African crisis the United Kingdom Government appeared to be more favourable towards the application of sanctions than it had been during the Manchurian crisis served only to reinforce Skelton's suspicions. For, in the words of one who worked closely with him in the Department, "he had a strong and lasting suspicion of British policy and an unchanging coldness towards Great Britain. . . . He was anti-British."[12]

On 4 September, the Italo-Ethiopian dispute came formally before the Council of the League of Nations. As Mussolini moved closer to war, the movement for sanctions acquired new impetus and urgency. That week Skelton set to work on a paper setting out the pros and cons of Canadian participation in sanctions against Italy at the direction of the League of Nations. Skelton's memorandum was destined to serve two Canadian governments.

It began with the pros. Canada had pledged her word to support the Covenant; not to support it now would be dishonourable. If the League failed in this test of strength with Mussolini, the world would move closer to anarchy, and to war. A firm stand against Italy might retrieve the sorry performance in the Manchurian crisis. By remaining aloof from sanctions Canada might come into conflict with British foreign policy. Italy was more vulnerable to sanctions than most countries: the proposed remedy was not just mock-heroics, it would really work. Finally, Canadian public opinion would support a pro-sanction policy, just as it would be critical if the Government refused to comply with a League of Nations directive or recommendation.

When he came to the con side of his position paper, Skelton wrote at greater length and with greater conviction, for he was now speaking his mind. Canadian governments and publics had always stood opposed to the punitive parts of the Covenant, just as they had sought to emphasize its conciliatory and preventive procedures; neither in 1920 nor in 1935 had they any desire to turn the League into an armed alliance in defence of the *status quo*. By 1935, moreover, the sanctions provisions of the Covenant had become obsolete, and enlightened delegations at Geneva had been working consistently to turn the League into an instrument for publicity and conciliation; "the present wave of extreme nationalism" was not a juncture at which to try to move in the other direction. Nor was it evident that sanctions against Italy would deter her imminent aggression: "her theatrical ruler has gone too far to draw back" and "he will trust to loopholes being found and to dissension and half-heartedness in the application of the sanctions." Sanctions mean war. "Throttling a country by cutting off its whole trade and financial relations with the rest of the world is war, or next door to war. Passions rise, incidents multiply out of embargoes and blockades of this stringent character, and recourse to arms is difficult to avoid." If economic sanctions proved ineffective, the League would be discredited and the peace of the world threatened for nothing. If they proved effective Mussolini might turn in desperation to the Nazis, while Japan would take advantage of the preoccupation elsewhere of the powers by completing her conquest of China. It was by no means certain that the British Government was enamoured of the sanctions solution: "in any case, each member of the League must decide for itself." Application of sanctions created for Canada peculiar and probably insurmountable difficulties; under the Covenant she would be obliged to prevent the movement of goods and persons between the United States and Italy: "To attempt to carry out such a pledge would be suicide." Finally, it was not at all obvious that public opinion favoured sanctions. "Canadians are not expecting or demanding intervention. The public have been mildly interested in the dispute—from the sidelines. . . . The League of Nations Society contains many fine members, but the attitude of a few of its leaders or officers does not reflect any widespread and informed public opinion."[13]

II

The day had long sinced passed when a British foreign secretary could assume, or even ask for, a common British Commonwealth front on major international issues. The most that Sir Samuel Hoare thought it fit to do was to request of the dominion governments statements of their views on the crisis in East Africa, as a guide in framing British policy. The variety of their responses hardly justified the confident assertion of the Imperial Conference ten years earlier that while every dominion necessarily remained the sole judge of the nature and extent of its co-operation in the Commonwealth, no common cause would suffer. There was no common cause. There were not even common attitudes. Traditional alignments—Australia and New Zealand firmly in Britain's footsteps, Canada, South Africa, and the Irish Free State in various postures of reluctant proximity—were no longer recognizable. What some called diversity might have been better called disarray.

In New Zealand, even before the election in November of the Labour Government of Michael Joseph Savage—unique among the governments of the British Commonwealth in its consistent opposition to the appeasement of the European dictators—an observer was able to report that "it seems universally accepted that the League of Nations must be justified and supported by all nations even at great cost"; and in September the National party Prime Minister, G. W. Forbes, declared that "the League of Nations is the hope of the future," and that "its testing time had come."[14] South Africa was less consistent than New Zealand: its government picked and chose among the aggressions to which it was opposed. But if Hitler's invasion of the Rhineland was welcomed as a partial righting of the wrongs imposed by an unjust treaty, Mussolini's designs upon Ethiopia were viewed with undisguised alarm; if they proved successful, a European militarist power would be brought to the borders of Kenya and Uganda, and even if unsuccessful would have a profound and disquieting influence upon the "natives." The Irish Free State presented at this time the remarkable spectacle of Eamon de Valera exerting all his powers of leadership in support of collective security and sanctions against any aggressor, even Italy; but his countrymen were not behind him. Australia, ever apprehensive about the Suez lifeline, was determined to prevent an armed clash between Britain and Mussolini; the High Commissioner at London, Stanley Bruce (a former prime minister), was a tireless apostle of appeasement. And no dominion was more irresolute than Britain herself. There, in a curious reversal of roles, radical pacifists urged militancy and the militants urged peace.*

For the moment ignoring these discordant voices, the British Foreign Secretary delivered his eagerly awaited statement in the Assembly. Samuel Hoare's declaration—"the League stands, and my country stands with it, for the collective maintenance of the Covenant in its entirety, and particularly for steady and collective resistance to all acts of unprovoked aggression"—created a sensation among the delegations. Howard Ferguson, representing Canada, was caught up in the new spirit of Geneva. Obviously keen to add to the general enthusiasm, he cabled to Ottawa for permission to speak. Permission was refused. But

*For a perceptive analysis of this paradox, see R. B. McCallum, *Public Opinion and the Last Peace* (London, 1944), pp. 144 ff.

—perhaps after reading the editorials effusively praising Hoare's speech —Skelton changed his decision, and Ferguson was authorized to deliver the following remarks:

Canada believes the League of Nations is an indispensable agency for world peace. We cannot agree that any member is warranted in resorting to war to enforce its claims, in violation of its solemn pledges to seek and find a peaceful settlement of every dispute. We hope that an honourable and peaceful solution of the Ethiopian controversy will yet be reached. If unfortunately this proves not to be the case, Canada will join with the other Members of the League in considering how by unanimous action peace can be maintained.

Ferguson incorporated this statement into his speech to the Assembly on 14 September; the Canadian Advisory Officer reported that it was well received and in keeping with other statements put forward by other delegations. All British Commonwealth delegations spoke in support of Hoare's speech, with the exception of the Australian.

The speakers in the Assembly were not stating the views of their governments upon the dispute, but the positions their governments would adopt should the Covenant be violated. Violation was not long in coming. While the Council worked on peaceful settlement, Mussolini secretly put the finishing touches upon his military plans. The Council's proposal was advanced on 18 September, accepted by Haile Selassie, rejected by Mussolini. Thereupon the Council, acting under Article XV of the Covenant, met on 26 September and reached the ineluctable conclusion that conciliation had failed. A report was issued on 5 October, two days after Italian troops had invaded Ethiopia. In swift succession, Council and Assembly accepted its verdict that Italy had resorted to war in disregard of its Covenants under Article XII. The acceptance of that verdict legally obliged states that were members of the League to apply sanctions against the aggressor. A Committee of Co-ordination was appointed to consider how this should be done; on 11 October it took its first decision, to prohibit immediately the export of all arms to Italy. A sub-committee of the Co-ordinating Committee—known as the Committee of Eighteen—was created by its parent to expedite its work. Such was the machinery improvised by the League of Nations in its first and only attempt to put down aggression by force.

III

These events coincided with the last stages of the general election campaign in Canada. As a consequence they were not closely followed by the Government whose members, including the Prime Minister, were crossing and re-crossing the Dominion in the throes of exhortation. On 7 October, the Canadian Advisory Officer, Walter Riddell, cabled from Geneva to report that delegations to the Assembly would be required in the very near future to declare themselves on the Council's decision that Italy had resorted to war in violation of the Covenant, and requested "explicit instructions." He also asked whether Canada should accept membership on any committee created by the Assembly to draw up plans for the collective imposition of sanctions. This appeal elicited no response from Ottawa. On 8 October Riddell repeated his request for instructions, emphasizing that Canada's abstention through lack of instructions would be most unfortunate as the country would be grouped with others which abstained because of instructions. Later that day, Riddell cabled Ottawa once more, stating that the Council's report on Italian aggression would probably come before the Assembly on the afternoon of 9 October and requesting instructions—for the third time.

Only then was a reply received from Ottawa; it was not helpful. "We cannot believe," Skelton cabled, "that it is proposed to take vote on question of such vital importance tomorrow without opportunity for full consideration and for making statement of position if considered advisable." He asked for information on this point, and for an indication of the attitude of various other countries. The Prime Minister was speaking that night at Cornwall, Ont., and Skelton wished to talk over the whole question with him. As the result of the discussion between Skelton and Bennett, two further telegrams were sent from Ottawa to the Canadian delegation at Geneva. One instructed it not actively to seek membership on any Assembly committee involved with sanctions, but not to refuse membership if offered. The other instructed it to abstain from the Assembly vote on the Council's report on Italian aggression, and to explain its abstention in the following words:

The Canadian delegation is instructed to refrain from voting at the present juncture. The Canadian Government consider the decision to be taken is one of the greatest moment for the future relations of Canada and the League. In view of fact that the Canadian Parliament has been dissolved and that a new Parliament is to be elected next Monday, it is not considered advisable to anticipate in any way the action of that new Parliament.[15]

The Canadians at Geneva were dismayed when they received this message. "Hope you realize," Riddell cabled to Skelton, "Canada's abstention . . . will without question be misinterpreted here and its importance magnified."[16] Ferguson immediately put in a long distance telephone call to the Prime Minister, who was eventually reached at

Lindsay, Ont., on the evening of 9 October (Canadian time). He was able to talk the Prime Minister into allowing him to use his own judgment whether or not to support the declaration of Italian aggression. The vote in the Assembly, which was to have been taken on the afternoon of 9 October, was postponed to the morning of the following day. The procedure then followed was that delegations were considered to have voted in favour of the declaration unless they specifically stated otherwise. Ferguson, by remaining silent, committed Canada to the overwhelming majority—all save the delegations of Albania, Austria, Hungary and Italy—concurring in the Council's findings against the fascist regime. Skelton notified Bennett of the news by telegram that afternoon.

While the voting was taking place in the Assembly, Skelton spoke on the telephone with the Prime Minister, then in Toronto. The conversation, recorded by Skelton, discloses a sharp difference of opinion between them over the wisdom of applying sanctions, Skelton being opposed, Bennett in favour:

R.B.B.   Any further word from Geneva? Understood further telegram was to come.

O.D.S.   Only telegram today refers to procedure in voting. . . .

R.B.B.   Have talked [by trans-Atlantic telephone] with Ferguson—agree with him that can decide only one question at a time—that question now before League is whether Italy is guilty and that only one answer can be made to that: so we will give our verdict of "guilty".

O.D.S.   Certainly no question as to Italy's guilt, and we should say so; but to say without explanation or qualification under circumstances involves commitment to apply sanctions. Ferguson's statement emphatically not a correct or honest picture.

R.B.B.   No commitment as to kind of sanctions, and if it did require such commitment, cannot evade that. No doubt we signed the Covenant; no doubt of Italy's guilt; we must take the consequences. Talk about honesty! Can you deny we gave our pledge in the Covenant?

O.D.S.   No. But I also insist we repeatedly and publicly declared our opposition to sanctions and that whole League development since then re sanctions, disarmament, etc., must be considered; not change our position without fullest consideration, merely because Britain has changed.

R.B.B.   Chasing moon-beams—hair-splitting—King's old letters—brains-trust business—must be practical men—every part of Empire sees it clearly. We went into League, took benefits, must assume responsibilities or get out, not try to hornswoggle ourselves out. We will vote guilty and make no further statement now. Ferguson says will cable later when question of sanctions comes up.

O.D.S.   Must insist question is up now, and is decided by this vote if not qualified.

R.B.B.   Well, it will be so decided then.

O.D.S.   Quite understand your position, but do not understand how you reconcile it with your instructions Tuesday night [8 October] and your definite statement you would not seek to commit next Parliament.

R.B.B.   No inconsistency—deal with one thing at a time—whatever Government in power next week can deal with next point. No one in Canada is going to deny Italy guilty or object to our saying so. If they did, not going to wriggle out if it meant I didn't get one vote. . . .[17]

IV

On 10 October, Riddell cabled Ottawa that the Co-ordinating Committee would be holding its first meeting on the following day and that, subject to instructions—which he urgently requested—Ferguson would provisionally accept membership for Canada. The Acting Prime Minister, Sir George Perley, replied that as the Committee would consist of all members of the Assembly (with the exception of the four states, including Italy, which had refused to accept the report of the Council), there was no objection to Canadian membership. He explained that because of the absence of nearly all members of the cabinet from Ottawa, he was not able to furnish the delegation with any instructions, and informed it that it should not for the present express any views in the Co-ordinating Committee.

The Co-ordinating Committee met next day, and created its subcommittee (originally of sixteen delegations, later of eighteen, so that it became known as the Committee of Eighteen). The Canadian delegation accepted membership on the Committee of Eighteen, without seeking permission of Ottawa to do so. This action annoyed Skelton, and produced an acrimonious exchange of correspondence between him and Riddell.[18] The episode was of no importance in itself, but it shows that the lines of communication between Ottawa and Geneva had become impaired well in advance of the breakdown to come.

At the first session of the Committee of Eighteen, on 11 October, some delegations tried to delay the formulation of practical sanctions proposals by embarking upon a technical discussion of the legal implications of Article XVI of the Covenant in relation to the Assembly resolutions of 1923.* The Swiss and Argentine delegates, Riddell later recalled, "appeared ready and willing to split any number of legal hairs."[19] The Rumanian delegate, M. Titulescu, was strongly opposed

*On the 1923 resolutions, and Canada's attitude towards them at the time, see my *In Defence of Canada*: Vol. I, *From the Great War to the Great Depression* (Toronto, 1964), pp. 8–10.

to these tactics, and said so; and the Canadian delegate, Howard Ferguson, did the same. He thought (the League records report)

that a stage had been reached at which, if the League was to be taken seriously by the world, it was absolutely essential that it should take some definite progressive action and not allow technical difficulties, if there were any, to stand in the way. The delegations had already stated their position with great unanimity and emphasis in the Assembly. They had declared who was the aggressor, and the proceedings that must be taken followed as a matter of course.[*]

The sole problem before the Committee was to decide what sanctions the delegations could all agree upon that afternoon and put into application immediately. Let them show the world that the League was no longer to be scoffed or laughed at, but that it meant business, and that when a breach of its Covenant took place it proposed to deal with the aggressor in the proper way. Otherwise the League and the Assembly would lose prestige and influence in the world, and might as well be dissolved. If the delegations were not at Geneva to see that the Covenant was carried out, there was no purpose in their being there at all. . . .[20]

Geneva had never heard a stronger plea in support of collective security from a Canadian delegate; by the same token it had never heard a speech less typically Canadian. Ferguson spoke in the same vein on 14 October. His interventions thrust the Canadian delegation to the front and centre of the stage, where its unaccustomed presence heartened the supporters of collective security. A Canadian on the Secretariat wrote at the time: "Ferguson has been very useful in the Co-ordinating Committee. He has price-cut across rambling apologias and withdrawings, and has made it clear to everyone that the Canadians are determined to see the collective system put in motion in this case."[21]

In Ottawa, however, Ferguson's activities were not favourably received. Bennett had by this time veered round to a position of unqualified support of strong League action against Italy, even if it should involve Canada. But Skelton remained highly critical. "In spite of instructions that no definite attitude should be taken until a further communication was received," he wrote afterwards to Riddell, "the Canadian delegation actually took the initiative in making the first proposal for the application of sanctions."

*By putting forward this argument, Ferguson contradicted his assurances to the Canadian government contained in his telegram of 9 October, in which he had stated that "it should be appreciated that this is merely a declaration as to who is aggressor and that actual form of application of sanctions which may be recommended by Committee that will be appointed may be accepted or modified by individual states members of the League." Skelton had also insisted that to declare Italy an aggressor was in the circumstances tantamount to declaring support for sanctions. See above, p. 14.

By the morning of 15 October, the extent of Mackenzie King's tremendous victory in the general election (171 seats in the House of Commons out of 245) became known. Bennett instructed the delegation at Geneva to take no further positions on any League of Nations matters until instructions had been received from the new Government. The Secretary-General of the League inquired of a Canadian member of his Secretariat what the policy of the new Administration was likely to be.[22] M. Avenol was not alone in awaiting, with interest and anxiety, the reaction of the Mackenzie King Government to the great experiment under way in the committee rooms of the Palais des Nations.

THE RIDDELL INCIDENT

Between 11 October and 19 October, the Economic Sub-Committee of the Committee of Eighteen, on which Canada was represented by Walter Riddell, had under consideration various possible measures of economic warfare which might be applied as sanctions against Italy. One of these, which eventually became what was called Proposal IV (being the fourth of five sanctions proposals eventually adopted by the League), called for the placing of an embargo upon exports to Italy of certain key products. Two features of this proposal in its original form disturbed the Canadian representative. One was its division into two separate lists: List I, composed of those products which were controlled by states members of the League, and List II, composed of those products not so controlled. The embargo was in the first instance to apply only to the products on List I. This would have had the result that certain materials of great strategic importance to the prosecution of Mussolini's campaign —iron, steel, coal, and oil—would slip through the embargo net. The proposal, Riddell recalled afterwards, "came after M. Laval had been in telephone communication with Signor Mussolini; I somehow associated this in my mind as part of a deal between the two men, since France exported a considerable tonnage of iron and steel to Italy and Italy was dependent upon imported oil and coal."[23] It was a fair and, as events were to show, accurate inference.

Nickel was initially placed on List II, on the grounds that while its production was practically a Canadian monopoly, the ore was finished in the United States and exported from a country not a member of the League. On 17 October, Riddell cabled Ottawa that it had been decided in the Sub-Committee to transfer nickel from List II to List I. Neither then nor afterwards did Riddell accept responsibility for this important move (though he never denied it); but according to a close observer, it was in fact his work: "The Canadians themselves have taken the initiative in getting nickel placed on the list of raw materials to be withheld from Italy under economic sanctions. . . . This cheers people up from more than one standpoint—it is a reassuring indication of both the American and the Canadian attitude."[24]

The second feature of Proposal IV to which Riddell took exception was that, while it prohibited the export of certain key commodities, it permitted the export of their derivatives. Such a formulation placed raw material exporting countries, such as Canada, at a disadvantage, and in the Economic Sub-Committee on 18 October Riddell said as much. He proposed that a revision should be made in Proposal IV, so that the key commodities, together with their derivatives, would be subject to the proposed embargo. Having made this suggestion—not before—he cabled Ottawa, stating that the Drafting Committee was to take it up, and asking whether he should continue to support it. The Bennett Government, now a caretaker administration, promised to bring the matter before the incoming administration. Meanwhile, despite a powerful plea on its behalf by the Spanish delegate, the Canadian suggestion was not accepted. Its rejection, Riddell wrote later, "I felt . . . was very unsatisfactory to Canada, but lacking specific instructions I did not feel free to press my point."[25] He was to shed this inhibition soon enough.

By 19 October, four days before the Mackenzie King Government took office, the first phase of the Assembly's work on sanctions had been completed. The Co-ordinating Committee and its offspring had evolved five proposals on sanctions to be submitted to the fifty governments which had declared Italy to be an aggressor. Proposal I prohibited the export of arms and munitions to Italy. Proposal II prohibited the granting of loans and credits. Proposal III prohibited all imports from Italy. Proposal IV—in the framing of which the Canadian delegate had played so prominent a part—prohibited the export of certain products to Italy. And Proposal V provided for mutual support among the sanctions-applying states so that the burden would be as fairly distributed as possible. The text of the five proposals was communicated to the fifty governments, and replies stating what action they proposed to take were requested no later than 28 October.

II

In this way the new Mackenzie King Government was confronted at the very outset with a foreign policy problem of the utmost importance, on which an immediate decision was required. For this purpose, O. D.

Skelton resurrected the memorandum on sanctions that he had prepared in August for the Bennett Government. That document, it will be recalled, while canvassing both sides of the question, argued the case against sanctions more fervidly than it argued the case in favour. But Mackenzie King and Ernest Lapointe needed no convincing, as Bennett had needed convincing. Their minds were already made up.

The conclusions which they had reached were communicated to Riddell at Geneva just before the expiry of the 28 October deadline, and made public the following day. The statement began by setting forth briefly the manner in which the five sanctions proposals had emerged, and recited the texts of those proposals. It then continued as follows:

The Government has no doubt it expresses the overwhelming conviction of the people of Canada in declaring its continued and firm adherence to the fundamental aims and ideals of the League of Nations, and its intention to make participation in the League the cornerstone of its foreign policy in the general field. It regards the League as an indispensable instrument for organizing and strengthening the forces of peace and goodwill in the world, and for effecting the adjustment of conflicting national aims essential if the advance of science and the closer contact of peoples are to make for the advantage and not the destruction of mankind.

As regards the means to the advancement of these ends, successive Canadian Governments have opposed the view that the League's central purpose should be to guarantee the territorial *status quo* and to rely upon force for the maintenance of peace. In the proposals for the repeal or revision of Article X, in the rejection of the Geneva Protocol because of "its rigid provisions for the application of economic and military sanctions in practically every future war," in the discussions preceding the adoption of the Briand-Kellogg Pact, this position was taken repeatedly and publicly, without dissent from any appreciable section of parliamentary or public opinion. The absence of three great powers from the League, the failure of the repeated efforts to secure the disarmament contemplated in the Covenant, and the unwillingness of League members to enforce sanctions in the case of countries distant from the European scene, have increased the difficulty of making general commitments in advance to apply either economic or military sanctions.

In the present instance, when an earnest effort is being made with wide support to test the feasibility of preventing or at least terminating war by the use of economic sanctions, and when there is no room for doubt as to where the responsibility rests for the outbreak of war, and having regard also to the position taken by Canada at the recent Assembly, the Canadian Government is prepared to co-operate fully in the endeavour. The League authorities are being informed that the Canadian Government will take the necessary steps to ensure the effective application of the economic sanctions against Italy proposed by the Co-ordinating Committee. The Canadian Government at the same time desires to make it clear that it does not recognize any commitment binding Canada to adopt military sanctions, and that no such commitment could be made without the prior approval of the Canadian Parliament.

It is also to be understood that the Government's course in approving economic sanctions in this instance is not to be regarded as necessarily establishing a precedent for future action. In the future, as in the past, the Government will be prepared to participate in the consideration of the most effective means of advancing the aims of the League through the adjustment of specific controversies, the lessening of the rivalries based upon exaggerated economic nationalism, the renewal of the effort to stop the rising tide of competitive armament, and such other policies as are appropriate for a country in the geographic and economic position of the Dominion, and as will ensure unity and common consent in Canada as well as the advancement of peace abroad.[26]

This statement Riddell construed as an acceptance by the new government of the sanctions proposals agreed upon by the Co-ordinating Committee "without any reservations whatsoever"; it was, he wrote afterwards, "a heartening surprise."[27] Yet, so far from accepting sanctions without reservations, the Canadian statement fairly bristled with them. The proposals of the Co-ordinating Committee were accepted on condition that they were applied with an "earnest effort" and with wide support; on condition that acceptance in the present instance was not to create a precedent for the future; on condition that acceptance of economic sanctions was not to be taken as acceptance of military sanctions. Moreover, the statement indicated that the Government had taken up its position at least in part because it had been placed there by the previous activities of the delegation at Geneva. Quite apart from these specific reservations, the statement conveyed the impression that it had been drafted in a mood of grudging acquiescence—which indeed it had—not in a mood of enthusiastic support; much of it was devoted to a recapitulation of grievances against those who sought to impose "general commitments in advance to apply either economic or military sanctions." Nor did subsequent commentators fail to detect its reluctant and carping tone.*

That Riddell failed to grasp the import of what his Government was trying to say is evident both from subsequent events and from his subsequent recollection of them. "I must have misunderstood," he confessed later, "the significance of the Government's acceptance of the first four proposals and the Prime Minister's declaration to the Press."[28] How to account for his misunderstanding? The cabled despatch which reached him from Ottawa did not contain a full version of the

*See S. Mack Eastman, *Canada at Geneva* (Toronto, 1946), p. 98; and Nicholas Mansergh, *Survey of British Commonwealth Affairs: Problems of External Policy, 1931–1939* (London, 1952), p. 116.

statement; it summarized the first few paragraphs in two or three lines, reproduced *verbatim* the penultimate paragraph (beginning "In the present instance . . ."), and concluded with the first sentence of the final paragraph. Had the full version of the statement been placed before him, it is possible that he would have been less confused about its contents. But Riddell also misinterpreted its purpose. It was intended to be no more than general information; it was interpreted at Geneva as instructions. "This was the first information I had received," Riddell explained afterwards, concerning the attitude of the new government towards sanctions. "Since this statement had been sent to me by urgent telegram and I could not recall ever having received a Government press release even by deferred telegram, I at once concluded that the Government had sent it for my information and guidance until the new Cabinet could find time to send more definite instructions, and that it was intended to govern my actions in the Committee [of Eighteen]."[29]

The consequences of these misunderstandings may now be examined.

III

On 31 October the Committee of Eighteen resumed its meetings, as arranged previously, to consider the application of sanctions against Italy in the light of the replies received from governments to the five proposals communicated to them ten days before. Discussion began at once on the various exceptions and derogations requested by some of the governments. Led by the delegate of Switzerland, a number of delegations—among them Poland, Norway, and Rumania—demanded exemption from the operation of Proposal III (calling for prohibition on imports from Italy) in respect of existing contracts. Riddell was among those opposing this demand. "It seemed most unfortunate," he is reported to have said, "that there should be any reservations at all or that any exceptions should be made. . . . If there were going to be reservations, other Governments would have to review their position."[30] The matter was referred to the Economic Sub-Committee of the Committee of Eighteen for further consideration.

The debate in the Economic Sub-Committee on 1 November was marked by acrimony. The attack on Proposal III was renewed by Switzerland, Rumania, Yugoslavia, and Norway; the British and French delegations came to its defence. Once again Riddell intervened, feeling (as he later wrote) "that the Canadian Government would not view with equanimity attempts to weaken and render ineffective a proposal to which they had so recently agreed without reservation."[31] He ended a lengthy statement on behalf of Proposal III with an impassioned defence of what he called "the biggest experiment ever yet tried among the nations." He had the impression (so the official record states him to have said)

that some nations wished to play their part at little or no cost to themselves; but as the Canadian representative (Mr. Ferguson) at a previous meeting had said, the thing could not be done without cost. Canada was a long way from the seat of trouble; but the Canadian Government was prepared to pay its share. . . . What were a few million lire against the attainment of real security?[32]

These remarks, Riddell recalled afterwards, "had some effect in taking the matter out of the field of petty trade manoeuvring and in recalling to certain delegates' minds the great responsibility they were taking in pressing their claims for special consideration if the granting of such claims would undermine the success of the whole system which we were pledged to maintain."[33] His statement was certainly an important and an impressive intervention. But it was one of which the Government would not have approved and, when it learned of it for the first time, strongly disapproved. On 2 November, word of Riddell's activities in the Economic Sub-Committee reached Ottawa through the newspapers. Mackenzie King (or Skelton) immediately despatched a message to Geneva, warning Riddell "regarding press despatches reporting your taking prominent part in committee discussions yesterday" that he should take no further position on any important matter "without definite instructions." But this message was too late.

Riddell arrived early for the meeting of the Committee of Eighteen scheduled for the morning of Saturday, 2 November. From informal discussion among the delegates he gathered that plans were on foot for the amplification of Proposal IV. The French delegate had come to the meeting armed with a proposal to add to those commodities already on the embargo list certain other strategic materials, namely, oil, coal, iron, steel, and copper. When Riddell learned of this plan, according to his later account, he

at once realized that with slight alteration here was an opportunity of placing both oil and coal, as a source of oil, on the list of key products which would do more to defeat Italy than all the other sanctions together. At the same time the inclusion of iron and steel strengthened the arguments I had made before the Committee for incorporating the derivatives of all key products. If I left off copper, as the inclusion of copper at the time was not important, it might be more acceptable to my Government as we were probably already as much affected as any other country by the key products proposal. Then, too, I could count upon the strong support of both the Spanish and Chilean delegates. As by this time it appeared certain that no one was going to take the initiative, I decided to make the proposal at the afternoon session. While I might act on the authority of the Prime Minister's press telegram [of 29 October] I preferred to obtain my Government's direct approval to my so doing.

I thereupon drafted and sent off at once two cablegrams, hoping to receive a reply in time for the late afternoon meeting at which it seemed probable the question would arise. . . .[34]

While awaiting a reply from Ottawa, Riddell drafted his proposal and busied himself trying to drum up support for it among the delegations. He spoke to Anthony Eden, who counselled him to go ahead, and to Coulondre, the French delegate, who regretted the omission of copper. The Committee got on with its business more quickly than Riddell had anticipated; the chairman had only two more speakers on his list, and it was not yet noon. Obviously there was no chance at all of instructions from Ottawa arriving in time. What was he to do?

I consulted my two advisers as to whether or not I should act at once. Their advice cancelled out.[*] As I was convinced action was urgent and that this would be the only opportunity during the session, I decided to make the proposal. It seemed a moment when an immediate decision had to be taken if sanctions were to become really effective and if I were to safeguard Canada's interests.[35]

And so he went ahead. When he returned to his office from the meeting, he found a message from Ottawa. It was a reply to the two cables he had sent to Skelton earlier in the day. It told him to make no further statement about sanctions; to drop his advocacy of his proposal; and to say nothing further in the committee without definite instructions from the Government.

IV

The news of what Riddell had done reached Mackenzie King in Ottawa from his Monday morning newspaper. He read it, as he later told the House of Commons, with "amazement."[36] He immediately got in touch with Skelton, who told him that Riddell's sanctions proposal was in direct violation of instructions sent to him within an hour of receiving his request for instructions. Mackenzie King thereupon drafted and despatched a strongly worded reprimand. Riddell replied by relating the circumstances causing him to act as he had done, and stressing that he had been motivated by the desire "to forestall extension of list to include

*Riddell's advisers were Jean Désy and L. B. Pearson of the Department of External Affairs. Mr. Pearson advised Riddell to act at once.

products of special importance to Canada," that is, copper. Despite his repeated requests for "advice and instruction," the only indication of the Government's policy at his disposal had been the Prime Minister's press statement of 29 October, which, he thought, sufficiently covered his initiative. "You will realize," his telegram concluded, "the difficulty of my position: with meagre instructions and no basic statement of policy to co-operate fully to secure effective application of economic sanctions while safeguarding Canada's interests. I regret exceedingly if I have caused the Government any embarrassment."[37] Riddell already knew he was in trouble; he did not yet know how deep.

"When we became aware of Dr. Riddell's statement and of what he had done," Mackenzie King told the House of Commons on 11 February 1936, "we considered very carefully whether we should not immediately publicly repudiate his act, and it was only because we were most anxious not to take any step which might possibly embarrass the situation in Europe or which might appear even remotely to indicate an exception on the part of Canada to what was being done by other parts of the British Empire, that we refrained. . . ."[38] The Government hoped that Riddell's initiative would be quickly forgotten in the onrush of other events. But, so far from that happening, it became the subject of mounting interest and debate; still worse (from the standpoint of the Government), it was increasingly referred to as "the Canadian proposal," or "the Canadian initiative," in the world's chancelleries and in the world press.* The Government was thus publicly identified with a policy which it had not originated and of which it disapproved; the temptation to disown it became strong, too strong to be resisted.

During most of November, Mackenzie King and O. D. Skelton were absent from the capital; they visited Washington, D.C. from 6 November to 9 November, and spent the remainder of the month on vacation at Sea Island, Georgia. In their absence, the Department was taken in charge by the Minister of Justice, Ernest Lapointe, and the Assistant Under Secretary of State for External Affairs, Laurent Beaudry.

On 28 November, Beaudry sent a cable to Skelton at the retreat on Sea Island. It reported that Lapointe was deeply concerned at the extent of the publicity being given in Canadian and foreign newspapers to "the Canadian proposal," and wondered whether something should not be

---

*It was so described in the 4 November editions of the London *News Chronicle*, *Observer*, and *Daily Telegraph*, the Montreal *Gazette*, the *New York Times*, and in news despatches from London and Geneva. A Canadian Press-Havas despatch of 26 November reported from Geneva that "League of Nations circles believed tonight an oil embargo against Italy will go into effect early in December, in conformity with Canada's proposal to the League sanctions committee."

done to make clear that Canada was not prepared to take an initiative in regard to imposing sanctions against Italy. Skelton conferred with the Prime Minister, and a reply was sent to Beaudry that day. Two things might usefully be done. The High Commissioner in London could be instructed to inform the British Government in confidence that Riddell had acted on his own and that his proposal did not have the support of the Canadian Government. Lapointe might arrange to be interviewed so as to make this clear to the public. A summary of points to be made in his statement was included for his guidance.

The statement drafted by Lapointe and Beaudry, and released by them to the press in time for publication on 2 December, was considerably more elaborate than the brief outline suggested by the Prime Minister. It began by reviewing the circumstances in which the Liberal administration found itself when confronted by the sanctions issue so soon after taking office; it quoted at length from the Prime Minister's public statement of 29 October; and it continued as follows:

With regard to the further application of the measures already adopted by the League and the possible extension of the scope of such measures, the Canadian Government has not departed in any way from the position as stated by the Prime Minister on the 29th October. The Government is not taking the initiative in proposing the extension of the measures with regard to the prohibition of exportation to Italy and does not propose to take the initiative in such measures. Canadian action and Canadian participation by the Canadian Government has been and will be limited to co-operation in purely financial and economic measures of a pacific character which are accepted by substantially all of the participating countries.

With regard to future developments, Canada will continue, with other Members of the League of Nations, to consider the changes in the situation as they arise, including any proposal for the revision of economic sanctions.

The suggestion which has appeared in the press from time to time, that the Canadian Government has taken the initiative in the extension of the embargo upon exportation of key commodities to Italy, and particularly in the placing of a ban upon shipments of coal, oil, iron and steel, is due to a misunderstanding. The Canadian Government has not and does not propose to take the initiative in any such action; and the opinion which was expressed by the Canadian member of the Committee—and which has led to the reference to the proposal as a Canadian proposal—represented only his personal opinion, and his views as a member of the Committee—and not the views of the Canadian Government.[39]

The statement created a furore. In Quebec, it was interpreted as an indication that the Government was ready to abandon sanctions altogether, and received with satisfaction. But by that small minority of Canadians who supported collective security, it was strongly resented, as it was by that larger group for whom the only test of Canadian policy was its fidelity to Downing Street's. The cabinet, which had not been consulted about the statement, was divided, T. A. Crerar, Minister of the Interior, expressing the feelings of James Gardiner, J. L. Ilsley, and Norman Rogers, when he wrote that "Lapointe's statement . . . was unfortunate in its phrasing."[40] The episode was widely commented upon in the international press. It did not go unnoticed in Italy, where the Foreign Ministry issued its own statement, remarking that "as the oil embargo has been repudiated by the Government supposed to have made it, we believe it must now be discarded."[41]

V

Mackenzie King and O. D. Skelton returned to the capital a day or so after Lapointe had given his statement to the world. Greatly concerned to discover how much controversy it had aroused, the Prime Minister sought to quiet the hubbub by meeting himself with the press —an unusual procedure for him, especially on so delicate a matter. The press conference took place on 6 December; "a battery of correspondents," according to the Ottawa *Citizen*, attended. Mackenzie King sought to make clear to them that the Government's policy towards sanctions had not changed from the policy outlined by his statement of 29 October. He did this at least to the satisfaction of his colleagues; Crerar thought that "King's statement to the press yesterday will . . . correct any wrong impression."[42] It unquestionably helped at home, but no one outside the country paid much attention.

For Mackenzie King, the Riddell affair had been awkward but not critical. It was an annoying way in which to begin the most promising of his administrations, and exasperating in that through no fault of his own (as he firmly believed) his Government had been unnecessarily exposed to criticism at home and abroad. But the situation could be retrieved. It was Mackenzie King's good fortune to have the public memory of the event all but erased by a wholly unexpected incident elsewhere. On 9 December, three days after his press conference, an astonished and, in the main, an outraged world read in its newspapers that Pierre Laval and Sir Samuel Hoare had proposed to purchase peace in East Africa by presenting Mussolini with practically all the territory so far overrun by his armies. Critics of the Canadian Government were either drowned out by or themselves became part of the chorus of denunciation of the British Government for its part in the Hoare-Laval deal.

According to the version of the Riddell affair which has passed into history, the predicament of the Canadian Advisory Officer at Geneva was very largely the work of Lapointe and Beaudry, who too zealously catered to the prejudices of their French-speaking compatriots. This interpretation circulated at the time,* and it was later offered by Riddell himself in his memoirs.† To the extent that this version suggests that Mackenzie King and Skelton felt any less strongly than their French-speaking colleagues that Riddell's intervention at Geneva had been both unwise and uncalled for, it is incorrect. Doubtless the Prime Minister felt that had he, rather than Lapointe, drafted the statement of 2 December, much of the ensuing clamour would not have occurred; given his very special talent for drafting statements least likely to cause offence, Mackenzie King was justified in his feeling. But this is not to say Mackenzie King did not share Lapointe's views. He thought Riddell had acted foolishly, rashly, and in a spirit of self-glorification. He suspected that Riddell was working side by side with Anthony Eden, to the detriment of Canadian policy. On 17 December Mackenzie King told an interviewer that he had been dumbfounded by Riddell's initiative: " 'I am certainly going to give him a good spanking', was the way he put it."[43] To Vincent Massey, he wrote on 26 December: "What a calamitous act was that of Riddell's at Geneva! Had we not made clear that it was Riddell speaking for himself, or the Committee of Eighteen acting on its own, Canada might for all time have come to be credited with having set Europe aflame, with what consequences to the rest of mankind no one can say."[44] He repeated this opinion in the House of Commons on 11 February 1936: had the Government not disavowed Riddell when it did, he declared, "the whole of Europe might have been aflame today."[45] After the speech Skelton ventured to suggest that the Prime Minister had gone too far by claiming that Riddell's repudiation had prevented a European war, but Mackenzie King stood his ground. "I told him I really believed what I had said. . . . I believe that the people generally will be relieved at my having said what I did, and will welcome the statement as a means of occasioning a pause in rash action at Geneva."[46]

Early in 1936 Riddell was instructed by his Government to represent it at a conference in Chile. Some months later, on his return, he called upon Mackenzie King at Ottawa. He found him to be "most gracious,"

---

*"Your friends in Canada," N. W. Rowell wrote to Riddell on 3 December 1935, "feel that you have been sacrificed in a measure to some political exigencies. . . ." (Rowell Papers).

†"The suggestion [for repudiation], I believe, did not originate with either the Prime Minister or with Dr Skelton. It is true that Mr King is on record as saying he was consulted and took full responsibility for it, but that is far different from being its author." W. A. Riddell, *World Security by Conference* (Toronto, 1947), p. 129. See also p. 140.

in contrast to the "cold, critical and overbearing" attitude of Ernest Lapointe who also was present; the meeting served to confirm Riddell's impression that Lapointe, not Mackenzie King, had been responsible for the reprimand of the preceding December.[47] But if anyone merited Riddell's grudge, it was the Prime Minister, not the Minister of Justice. Mackenzie King had wanted to dismiss him outright from diplomatic service, and it was only after some of his colleagues strongly protested this course that the compromise was agreed to of sending him as far away as possible from the scene of his misdemeanour. If that is what it was.*

THE COLLAPSE OF SANCTIONS

By 15 November 1935, the four sanctions recommended by the Co-ordinating Committee at Geneva had been put into effect by the Canadian Government.[†] After that date, Italy received no arms, credit, transport animals, bauxite, aluminum, iron ore, manganese, chromium, tin, molybdenum, tungsten, vanadium or nickel from the Dominion; while Canada received no imports from Italy of any kind, except for books and newspapers and those imports paid for before 19 October or in transit on that date.

Riddell's proposal, which had come to be known as Proposal IV(a), had not yet been referred to any government for consideration.[‡] The Committee of Eighteen was scheduled to meet on 29 November to discuss the possibility of doing so. To gain some respite—sanctions had

*The "Riddell incident" cast a long shadow upon the conduct of Canadian diplomacy in the years to come. Instructions prepared in 1948 for the guidance of the Canadian representative on the United Nations Security Council read in part as follows: "When issues of importance arise which involve commitments on the part of the Government, it is essential that the Canadian representative should secure specific instructions from the Government before participating in a decision. If time does not permit obtaining such instructions before a vote is taken, the Canadian representative should in such circumstances abstain. He should explain that his reason for such abstention is that time has not permitted him to receive instructions from his Government on the matter. . . ."

†By Order-in-Council P.C. 3594. The arms embargo had been in effect (under P.C. 3461, by virtue of Section 290 of the Canada Customs Act) since 31 October. Five proposals had been submitted to the Canadian Government, along with forty-nine other governments, by the Co-ordinating Committee; the fifth proposal was not, strictly speaking, a sanctions proposal but a provision for mutual aid among sanctions-applying states. Canada approved the proposal in principle, but let it be known that she did not consider the Canadian economic system, then lacking quota and exchange control mechanisms, suited to its application.

‡Proposal IV(a) was Riddell's original proposal slightly modified in committee; it contemplated the extension of the measures of embargo provided in Proposal IV to include petroleum and its derivatives, pig iron, iron and steel (cast, forged, rolled, drawn, stamped or pressed), coal, coke and derivatives thereof.

already begun to hurt—Mussolini turned to Laval, and Laval obliged. He asked for a postponement of the meeting to 12 December. During the fortnight thus secured, Italy replenished oil supplies by purchases from the United States, Soviet Russia, and Rumania. When the Committee of Eighteen finally met, it was informed by Laval and Eden that a new peace settlement was in process. The discussion on Proposal IV(a) was accordingly postponed for a second time.

On 13 December the Hoare-Laval plan was officially released to the public. A wave of resentment and revulsion swept through Britain, all but engulfing the government and dragging under the Foreign Secretary who, as the scapegoat, was made to resign.

The feasibility of oil sanctions finally came before a committee of experts in February 1936. It concluded without dissent that an embargo would exhaust Italy's petroleum reserves in three months and that, providing sanctions-applying states denied the regime the use of their tankers, its mechanized campaign in East Africa would have to be curtailed. The governments concerned read the report and asked for time to consider its implications. While they procrastinated, Italian troops, now under the command of Marshal Badoglio, were sweeping deeper into Ethiopian territory; a new feature of their campaign was its liberal employment of mustard gas. On 2 March, Anthony Eden, now British Foreign Secretary, announced at Geneva that the British Government would apply the oil embargo in company with other oil-producing and oil-transporting states members of the League. Before any definite decision was taken on Proposal IV(a), Hitler marched troops into the Rhineland in open violation of the Locarno Pact.

Hitler's aggression, itself caused by Anglo-French irresolution, increased that irresolution ten-fold. With consummate skill Mussolini allowed Britain and France to believe they could purchase his support against Germany by allowing him a free hand in East Africa. These tactics enabled him to complete his conquest before action on the oil sanction was taken. On 6 May Badoglio entered Addis Ababa; on 9 May Mussolini acclaimed the founding of the Fascist Empire; on 10 June Neville Chamberlain declared that the continuation of the existing sanctions against Italy was "the very midsummer of madness."

II

The reaction of the Canadian Government to these events was mute and inglorious. On 10 and 11 February, its role in the crisis was discussed in Parliament. The discussion was largely confined to the Riddell affair. Mackenzie King defended the statement of 2 December with the arguments employed by him at his press conference on 6 December, adding to these one of which he had become particularly fond: "There is such a thing as a sense of proportion in international affairs as in all else. Do hon. members think that it is Canada's role at Geneva to attempt to regulate a European war?" He would not be drawn into any discussion of the merits of the oil sanctions proposal; that proposal, he reminded his listeners, was still before the League of Nations and had not yet been referred to member governments for their consideration. When and if it was, "it will be considered on its merits."[48]

For the next four months, despite the attempts of J. S. Woodsworth and one or two others to force a debate on the general question of sanctions, collective security, and the League of Nations, the Government maintained a stubborn and unbroken silence. It was Mackenzie King's conviction that that silence was golden. The public's interest, he wrote to a fellow member of Parliament, was "that as little discussion as possible should be raised in our House of Commons with respect to the present European situation, either as regards the violation by Italy of the League of Nations Covenant, or the violation by Germany of the Treaties of Versailles or Locarno. It is sometimes well to allow sleeping dogs to lie. This, I believe, is especially true where they happen to be the dogs of war."[49] The policy of reticence did not go uncriticized,* but for the time being it was successfully maintained.

Behind the scenes, the Government kept a close watch on events in Ethiopia and Europe. The question of what to do about the oil sanction was canvassed by Skelton in a memorandum prepared for the Prime Minister's perusal in advance of the meeting of the Committee of Eighteen on 2 March. Of the three possibilities—to press for it, to drop it, to go along with the crowd—the first was dismissed without comment. Whether Canada should take the lead in abandoning sanctions was seriously considered, but rejected, mainly because of the consideration "that if the sanctions experiment fails, the United Kingdom and Europe and sections of our own people will be only too eager to seek an alibi and throw the blame on Canada for breaking the front." And so, Skelton concluded, Canada should do what the Committee of Eighteen might decide which, he predicted correctly, "will probably be against present action on oil."

By May 1936, it had become more difficult for the Mackenzie King

*See, for example, F. H. Underhill, "Parliament and Foreign Policy," *Canadian Forum*, June 1936, pp. 6–7; Edgar McInnis, "A Nation in the Dark," *Queen's Quarterly*, Autumn 1936, pp. 241–9.

Administration to refrain from stating its own attitude. During the weeks following the reoccupation of the Rhineland, France had shown itself to be more strongly opposed than formerly to the maintenance of sanctions; opinion in Britain was sharply divided. In Canada there was mounting restiveness with reticence. "How can we uphold the hands of those who are endeavouring to maintain the peace of the world," inquired the Winnipeg *Tribune* on 14 May, "if we simply sit like a bump on a log and have nothing to say?" And Henri Bourassa, back from a tour of Europe, wrote to Mackenzie King: "For Heaven's sake, speak now, and speak clearly."[50]

It was a matter of timing. Chamberlain's reference on 10 June to the maintenance of sanctions as being "midsummer madness" indicated to Mackenzie King that the flight from sanctions was about to begin. Personally he was elated. He described the speech as "a happening which has done more to relieve my mind than anything this year," and as evidence "that I was right when I said that my action and Lapointe's in exposing Riddell's action, and thereby restraining the application of sanctions against Italy at the time we did, saved a European war, for which Canada would have been blamed. I am as sure of that as that I am alive." He felt as well that it vindicated his silence over the past few months: "Had we declared for the continuance of sanctions or against the continuance of sanctions, Britain would have jumped at using our attitude as an excuse for her own. She has now been obliged to pull her own chestnuts out of the fire."[51] The same phrase was employed by Skelton. "I have never felt," he wrote to Mackenzie King on 11 June, "that we should pull anyone's chestnuts out of the fire by being the first to propose the lifting of sanctions."

III

The speech which Mackenzie King delivered in Parliament on 18 June on Canadian foreign policy was one of the most carefully considered of his career. It was written almost entirely by Skelton, and is a fine example of the style and analytical power of the author. The day before delivering it, the Prime Minister read it aloud to his cabinet, apparently without dissent. A normally stern critic of the Government, F. H. Underhill, thought it "the best speech made by a Canadian Government leader since the Peace Treaties."[52] That was to judge it by lenient standards, but the speech was powerful by any standards.

Mackenzie King began by dealing with the charge that his Government had not sufficiently kept Parliament and the public informed of events abroad. "It is true," he said, "that the government has declined to make a statement at some critical stages when a statement would be premature, and would complicate rather than advance a solution." But he conceded that there had not been much discussion of Canada's external relations, whether within the House of Commons or outside. "That has been due," he asserted, "to our slow emergence from the colonial attitude of mind; our relative immunity from any serious danger of war on our own account; the real difficulties inherent in our pre-occupation with the tremendous, absorbing and paramount tasks of achieving economic development and national unity, which with us take the place of the preoccupation with the fear of attack and the dreams of glory which beset older and more crowded countries; and the unparalleled complexity of our position as a member of the British Commonwealth of Nations and one of the nations of the American continent."

Next, Mackenzie King reviewed the development of Canadian policy towards the conflict between Italy and Ethiopia. The sanctions agreed to had been strictly imposed: "special care," the Prime Minister told the House, "was taken to ensure against not only direct but indirect shipment of Canadian nickel." On the Government's attitude towards the controversial Proposal IV(a) he had this to say:

The criticisms of the Canadian Government's attitude on these proposals [to add coal, iron and steel, and oil to the list of prohibited exports] which were voiced in some quarters last December did not survive a clearer appreciation of what the Canadian Government's attitude was and of the position taken by other countries. These commodities have not hitherto been included in the prohibited list for two reasons. In the early stages of the conflict, the prohibited exports were confined to articles which were substantially controlled by members of the League and trade in which therefore could not easily be diverted to non-sanctionist countries. When at a later stage their inclusion came up for review, a second consideration came into play, namely, whether their application would or would not lead to war. . . . The difficulty arises from the inevitable dilemma which the application of sanctions presents: if moderate, they may fail to deter or to halt the aggressor; if extreme, they may drive an aggressor to prefer the gamble of sudden battle to the prospect of slow strangulation. There is no blinking the fact that economic sanctions may lead to war. They mean the application of force. They are no mere commercial measures. They are in intention and reality a means of imposing the will of one nation or group upon another nation or group. . . .

Whether the enforcement of an oil sanction would, in fact, have led to war is . . . in dispute; the Italian threats may or may not have been genuine. In any case they were sufficient to cause some great countries to conclude that enforcement of oil sanctions might invoke new wars or at least make impossible a peaceful settlement of the existing war.

The Canadian Government, Mackenzie King pointed out, had not opposed the oil sanction on principle; it had in fact instructed its representative to support the sanction, if others supported it. But it saw no reason to take the lead in so dangerous and controversial a measure.

Why, Mackenzie King then asked, "has the League failed, thus far?" To this question he supplied his own answer: "In brief, collective bluffing cannot bring collective security, and under present conditions most countries have shown they are not prepared to make firm commitments beyond the range of their immediate interest." What should be done next? Should sanctions "be increased, continued at their present level, or discontinued"? They should, he believed, be discontinued; and the Canadian delegation at the forthcoming Assembly would be instructed to support their discontinuance. What, finally, was there left for the League of Nations to do? "It is of great value," Mackenzie King concluded,

to have at Geneva a world-wide organization where the machinery for conference and conciliation is always available, not having to be improvised in the midst of crisis; where representatives of fifty countries meet periodically and come to have some appreciation of the difficulties and the mentality of other lands, and slowly develop the habit of working together on small tasks leading to greater; where, in spite of all the criticisms we often hear as to vaguely worded resolutions and hotel bedroom conversations, the statesmen of great countries are forced to come into the open and defend in public, before a world forum, the policies of their governments. It can press on to its task of disarmament, or at least to the halting of armaments. It can develop and apply the instruments of conciliation and of arbitration in settling specific disputes before they lead to open challenges and entrenched positions. It can provide a forum for the discussion of economic grievances. . . .[53]

Damning the League of Nations by the faintness of its praise, Mackenzie King's speech was exceptionally well received by Parliament, by the press, and by the public at large. He was perfectly right in thinking that what he had said articulated exactly the consensus of his countrymen. The dissenters were few and scattered. Conspicuous among them was J. W. Dafoe of Winnipeg. His *Free Press*, as usual, did not mince its words:

Ever since the Manchurian episode the League has been dying from a mortal wound. Direct consequences of this demonstration that collective security, the foundation stone of the League, was a sham were the failure of the disarmament conference; the Nazi defiance of the League; and the determination of Italy to attack Ethiopia. . . . The repudiation has now come after a farcical pretence at supporting League authority. . . . Notwithstanding Mr. King's comfortable words the other day, time will show that, taking the long view, Canada had a much greater interest in collective security than the government of this country had any idea of when it fell in with the grand idea that the time had come to put the League out of business.[54]

The final scene of the Ethiopian tragedy was enacted at Geneva. On 30 June 1936 there assembled a special Assembly in what the League's historian has described as "a mood of ill humour, discouragement and anxiety."[55] Technically, the question of whether to continue sanctions or to end them was to be decided; practically, as everybody knew, the issue had already been decided. Vincent Massey headed the Canadian delegation. "Morning session of Assembly," he wrote in his diary on Dominion Day. "A great spate of speeches full of golden phrases." He announced on behalf of the Canadian Government its decision to support the ending of sanctions against Italy. Meeting for the last time as the Co-ordinating Committee, the delegates voted to bring to an end all measures taken under Article XVI by 15 July. The great experiment was over, and had failed.

II

Innocence Abroad

IN GENEVA

The special Assembly of the League of Nations which met at Geneva in June and July 1936, having decided to abandon sanctions against Italy, decided further to embark upon a reconsideration of the principles of the Covenant. On 4 July it adopted a resolution inviting member governments to proffer their suggestions, and instructing the Secretary-General to have a report ready for the consideration of the Seventeenth Assembly to meet that fall. It is important to understand the reality behind this procedural facade. The real purpose was not to "reform" the League; it was, in the words of the League's historian, to allow "each Member to consider its own situation, and to decide its own policy, in the light of the breakdown of collective security; and, having made its decisions, to announce them and to justify them, both to its own public opinion and to its fellow members of the international community."[1]

These were by no means trivial tasks to be performed in a perfunctory manner. As O. D. Skelton wrote to Mackenzie King in May 1936, the question of what changes, if any, in the organization and powers of the League were necessary in the light of the Italian experience was stirring up considerable controversy in the United Kingdom. The matter would doubtless come before the next Assembly. That session, therefore, would be of "extreme importance" and, Skelton felt, "it would be difficult for anyone except the Prime Minister to represent Canada adequately on that occasion."[2] By the middle of June, Mackenzie King had come to the same conclusion. "I have definitely decided about going to the League of Nations in the Fall," he wrote on 15 June, "and making a study of international relations in the interval. . . . Above all, I feel the necessity of Canada making her voice heard with respect to a

situation which threatens to engulf her in world war and which, by being
heard, may prevent such an appalling possibility."³

It was not Mackenzie King's intention, in deciding to go to Geneva,
to put forward any Canadian proposals concerning the "reform" of the
Covenant. The time for that had not yet come. "I feel that the present
Assembly," he wrote to Lord Robert Cecil, "is not the one at which
any attempt at the revision of the Covenant should be made."⁴ Moreover, for Canada to have taken too prominent a part in the formulation
of such proposals would have marred that "sense of proportion in
international affairs" of which he had spoken earlier in Parliament,*
and to which he was coming to attach ever greater importance. New
Zealand served as an example of how exactly not to go about it. The
Labour government of M. J. Savage had been the only government in
the British Commonwealth to have responded to the Assembly Resolution of 4 July by offering a detailed plan of League reform designed to
strengthen the machinery of collective security. Its proposals, Skelton
remarked after reading them over, "are clearly wholly out of line with
Canada's position, and with reality. It is somewhat nervy for a country
whose influence on either the economic or military situation is so negligible to propose . . . [such] suggestions."⁵ Mackenzie King agreed.

What he did want to do was to make his presence in Geneva felt by
delivering to the Assembly a firm lecture on Canada's conception of
how the League of Nations ought to go about its business. He was also
anxious to learn what he could at first hand about the European crisis.
The worsening of the political relations of the Old World—the Spanish
civil war had broken out in July—filled him with apprehension. What
was happening in Europe seemed to him to bear out his earliest views
on the nature of conflict in society. These he had always conceived as a
struggle between the powers of light and the powers of darkness; and
that is how it struck him now. "It seems to me," he wrote to a correspondent in August 1936, "that there is no more misleading term
than that of 'collective security'. At bottom, the struggle seems to be
not so much between nations as between conflicting ideas and ideals.
The materialist world with its belief in force seeking to conquer the
world's spirit with its belief in invisible realities. It is an appalling struggle,
one which, sooner or later, will engulf mankind."⁶ He made this the
theme of a broadcast address on Armistice Day:

Fundamentally, the world struggle of today is one between the contending
forces of good and evil. It is a part of the never-ending conflict between the
forces actuating those who, by their thought of others, and their unselfish

*See above, p. 29.

acts, are seeking to further "the law of Peace, Work and Health", and the forces actuating those who, by their greed and selfish ambitions, are furthering "the law of Blood and Death". Good and evil forces do not belong to different nations, to different races, to different classes, to men and women of different faiths. Within each nation, each race, each class, and each individual, these forces contend for supremacy.*

Such a way of looking at the world could only be comforting to a statesman; for if its ills were really the responsibility of ordinary people, statesmen could not fairly be blamed by them when things went wrong. Mackenzie King did not hesitate to draw this conclusion: "If another war comes, it will not be because governments have been unequal to their tasks, but because individuals, in their combined national efforts and daily lives, have greatly failed."

II

Mackenzie King left Ottawa on 12 September and arrived at Geneva a week later. He had selected his delegation with customary care. It included the faithful Skelton; Senator Dandurand (government leader in the Senate); and the Minister of Labour, Norman Rogers. Dandurand was French Canada's representative; Mackenzie King had picked him in preference to Lapointe, possibly because the latter's outspoken hostility towards collective security might have made a poor impression at Geneva, while Dandurand was an old League hand. Norman Rogers, Mackenzie King's protégé, had displayed in cabinet meetings a tendency to advocate sanctions and to look favourably upon the League of Nations; the Prime Minister brought him to Geneva not that this tendency might be encouraged but that it might be subdued. Present as an observer was a young member of Parliament named Paul Martin.

Mackenzie King did not address the Assembly until 29 September. He used the ten days beforehand to work on his speech, to listen to the speeches of other delegates, and to hold lengthy conversations on international affairs with various leaders, among them Malcolm MacDonald, Anthony Eden, and Lord Halifax. He even sought out Haile Selassie.

*"Address by the Rt. Hon. W. L. Mackenzie King, M.P., Prime Minister of Canada, on the occasion of the Canadian Legion Remembrance Day Broadcast, November 11, 1936." The quotations in this paragraph are from his favourite passage from Pasteur, which he had quoted in 1918 in *Industry and Humanity*: "Two contrary laws seem to be wrestling with each other nowadays: the one, a law of blood and death, ever imagining new means of destruction, and forcing nations to be constantly ready for the battlefield—the other, a law of peace, work and health, ever evolving new means of delivering man from the scourges which beset him."

The proceedings did nothing to overcome his distaste for the League of Nations and for its coteries. Shortly before setting out for Geneva, he had written to a friend: "Instead of the centre of the world's peace, the League seems to me to be becoming increasingly a Tower of Babel,"[7] and this impression was confirmed by the first day's session. "One felt," Mackenzie King wrote when it was over, "the absurdity of entrusting the affairs of one's country directly or indirectly to an aggregation of the kind which one sees in the Assembly Hall. Countries named by the dozens of which one has seldom or never heard. . . ."[8]

Mackenzie King had addressed the Assembly once before, at its ninth regular session. His speech on that occasion had been something less than a triumph; it had been for him "an agonizing ordeal" and he feared, with reason, that he had "really no message" for the statesmen of Europe.[9] This time he had a message. His speech of 29 September 1936 was as much a success as that of 7 September 1928 had been a failure. It set out many of the ideas contained in his speech to the House of Commons in June, and ranks with it as the most lucid and forthright statement on external affairs delivered by any Canadian statesman between two world wars. Skelton wrote them both.

Mackenzie King's speech to the Assembly began, as most Canadian speeches to the Assembly began, by contrasting the Dominion's "friendly relations with our neighbours" favourably with the politics of Europe— "the violent nature of the propaganda and recriminations hurled incessantly across the frontiers, the endeavours to draw all countries into one or other extremist camp, the feverish race for armament, the hurrying to and fro of diplomats, the ceaseless weaving and unravelling of understandings and alliances, and the consequent fear and uncertainty of the peoples." He made the comparison not in the expectation "that Europe at the moment can be expected to follow a similar course"— Canadians at Geneva had learned something since the 1920's when it was their habit to use the rostrum of the Palais des Nations as a pulpit from which to exhort Europe to emulate the example of North America —but "rather to explain a difference in national outlook, which has its bearing upon policies which some may feel the League should adopt." It was unreasonable, he pointed out, to expect "a North American state to have the same international outlook, the same conception of interest, or of duty, as a European state facing widely different conditions." But Canada was not only a North American state; it was also a Commonwealth state and as such concerned about many questions, particularly "questions of automatic obligations to the use of force in international affairs." The Commonwealth experience, he said, "has had an effect in convincing Canadians of the possibility of preserving close and friendly co-operation without the existence of a central authority, or of military commitments." Finally, the Canadian outlook had been shaped by Canada's experience as a member of the League of Nations itself, and that experience had convinced Canadians that "emphasis should be placed upon conciliation rather than upon coercion."

Mackenzie King next proceeded to outline Canadian policy towards the League in the light of the experience of the Italo-Ethiopian conflict. In Canada's view, the first objective of the League should be to obtain "the universal acceptance of the principles of the Covenant," for "every vacant seat in this Assembly is a broken link in the chain of collective security." To bring in the outsiders, it was essential to stress "the mediation and conciliation aspects of the Covenant." It was not necessary to change the Covenant to do that. The Canadian Government, he declared, "does not believe that formal amendment of the Covenant now is either possible or necessary. The powers and duties of the League develop by usage and experience as well as by explicit amendment. What its members will and will not do can be read more clearly from what they have done and not done than from the text of the Covenant. What is now called for is to register in the light of actual facts the position which has developed during sixteen years of League history. . . ."

What was that position? It consisted in the blunt fact that "many provisions of the Covenant have not been observed, or have been applied unequally or ineffectively." The pledge to reduce armaments, contained in Article VIII, had not been honoured; the pledge to revise treaties, contained in Article XIX, was a dead letter; the undertakings to apply sanctions, set forth in Article XVI, "were tacitly recognized at an early stage as unworkable in their entirety." The states members of the League had failed to apply sanctions when conflict arose in Asia (over Manchuria) or in America (the Chaco war); "applied once in an Afro-European conflict, they failed and were abandoned because of general unwillingness under the conditions of the day to press force to its conclusion."

Such was the record. What conclusions might be drawn from it? First, that in the place of the still-born doctrine of collective security there might be substituted regional security arrangements; these would at least "show a closer approach to reality by linking the obligation with a definite contingency and a direct interest." There was, he conceded, the danger that such arrangements might "develop in practice into old-fashioned military alliances"; perhaps it was a risk to be run, but it should be guarded against. The Canadian Government would welcome an interpretation of Article XI such that in future disputes a party to it would not be able to rob a decision of the Council of its legal validity by voting against it (as Italy had done a year before). Finally, Mackenzie King proposed that a conference be held among those states which were members of the League and those which were not, to consider "anew how best the original purpose of universality of membership may be achieved."[10]

One could not justly complain of this speech by Mackenzie King, as one could of so many of his others, that it had been obscure or elliptical. He was perfectly correct in claiming, as he did soon afterwards, that no more unqualified statement of Canada's position had "been made at any time, in any place, than that made here at Geneva on Tuesday of this week."[11] To an American correspondent he confided: "I came to the League of Nations feeling that it was well there should be no doubt as to Canada's position. . . . I think I said the right thing, at the right time, and in the right place."[12] And to the Governor General:

It is perhaps a franker statement than some would have preferred. I have long felt, however, that in these inter-imperial or international matters involving commitments in time of war, no country can too frankly express in advance what its position at the moment of crisis is pretty certain to be. While those who continue to stress the sanctions article of the Covenant as its most important one may not altogether have liked what I said at the Assembly, I believe the feeling of the Assembly generally is that if the position stated was the true one, it was much better that it should be known and definitely affirmed. I believe people are coming to see that the real weaknesses of the League lie in accepting professions at their face value and not sufficiently seeking to discover actualities and realities.[13]

III

On the day following the delivery of his speech, Mackenzie King was pleased and relieved to receive a telegram from Ernest Lapointe expressing on behalf of himself and colleagues of the cabinet full approval of what had been said as "thoroughly representing Canadian views and sentiments." It must have been on the strength of this message that the Prime Minister wrote to the Governor General next day that "there is no doubt that what I have said represents the general opinion of Canada."[14] That was a correct assessment. The French-language press expressed unqualified approval.* Most of the English-language newspapers did likewise, although the Montreal *Gazette* criticized the speech as too "negative." Not, its editorial explained, that it desired the Prime Minister to add his voice to "bolstering up a wobbling League" but

*E.g., "Conciliation D'abord," *La Presse* (Montreal), 30 Sept. 1936; "Le Discours de M. King à Genève," *Le Droit* (Ottawa), 30 Sept. 1936.

rather because he had not placed "the country on record as a British nation with an active appreciation of its responsibilities as such."[15] There remained the perennial dissenter. On 1 October, J. W. Dafoe delivered in the editorial columns of his *Free Press* a tremendous philippic against Mackenzie King's speech and the attitude and policies for which it stood. He described it as "the last in a long series of acts by successive Canadian governments intended to circumscribe the League's powers; and it is the most discreditable of them all because it amounts to the rejection by Canada of the League." That it was rejected with such decorum only added insult to the injury: "the League of Nations," Dafoe insisted, "with assurances of the most distinguished consideration, was ushered out into the darkness by Mr. Mackenzie King."[16] Privately, Dafoe conceded that, while Canada had been in at the kill, it could not fairly be charged with the assassination. "While I am very critical indeed of Mr. King's course on the League of Nations," he wrote to a friend late in October, "I do not think that Canada's virtual withdrawal from the spirit of the Covenant has been a factor of any considerable moment in bringing about the present disastrous situation. If our attitude had been completely right at every stage of the development I very much fear that the situation today would be very much what it is, only our skirts would be clear instead of our being bracketed in the current judgment of the world and in history as one of the wreckers."[17] As things turned out, only New Zealand was to experience that satisfaction.*

Nothing further came of the movement to "reform" the Covenant. A Committee of Twenty-Eight was created to study the proposals for amendment submitted by various governments, and discussion on the matter continued in a desultory fashion for the next two years. But there was no action. The Seventeenth Assembly marked the disappearance of the League of Nations as a force in international affairs. Henceforth it played no part in the course of events or in the calculations of the powers. For his part, Mackenzie King begrudged it even the pitiful existence to which it had been condemned. "I wish the League of Nations could be gotten out of the way altogether," he wrote to his Governor General in July 1937. "Every feeling I had had about the mischief being wrought through the intrigues of that institution has been intensified by what I have seen and heard while abroad."[18] Travel can narrow the mind.

*Professor Mansergh has written: "In 1949 in conversation with the author a United Kingdom cabinet minister, reflecting gloomily on Commonwealth policies before the war, concluded more cheerfully: 'Thank God for New Zealand!' " Nicholas Mansergh, *Survey of British Commonwealth Affairs: Problems of External Policy, 1931–1939* (London, 1952), p. 202, n. 4.

IN WASHINGTON

The association of Mackenzie King and Franklin Roosevelt had not begun in student days at Harvard University—the bulk of King's graduate work was completed by 1899, while Roosevelt entered as an undergraduate in 1900. But that Mackenzie King allowed a popular belief to the contrary to persist suggests the infinite satisfaction he derived from his friendship with the President—a friendship he was wont to describe in terms that might seem extravagant to someone unfamiliar with what it was later to contribute to Allied victory in the Second World War.

Their relations as Prime Minister and President, which reached the apogee of achievement on 20 April 1941—that "grand Sunday" on which they worked out together the idea for the Hyde Park Agreement —began in October 1935,* when Mackenzie King and Skelton visited Washington briefly after the general election; it was renewed in the summer of 1936, when the President paid a state visit to Canada as a guest of the Governor General at the Citadel in Quebec City. Mackenzie King followed Roosevelt's campaign as closely as he could, and was elated by its result. "Certainly *our* friend has scored the most magnificent of victories," he wrote to Leighton McCarthy on 7 November. "He well deserved to do so. It is fortunate, not only for the United States, but for the world, that he made the sweep he did." McCarthy, who had come to know the President through their mutual philanthropic interest in the care and prevention of poliomyelitis, was on his way to visit him at Warm Springs, Georgia; and Mackenzie King sought, through McCarthy, to enlist the President's interest in the healing of nations as well as that of human beings. "Impress upon him," he wrote, "as strongly as you can, that it is not assuming too much to believe that some good offices, on his part at this time, towards bringing together, into more friendly relationships, the nations of Europe, might be a means not only of saving them from themselves, but of saving much of civilization itself. It is the healing touch of the political physician that Europe needs, not the iron heel or the mail fist."[19]

When an opportunity of influencing the President presented itself, it was eagerly grasped. It came in the form of a letter from Roosevelt inviting Mackenzie King to visit him in Washington to discuss matters of mutual concern, particularly the European situation.[20] Mackenzie

*Not, as incorrectly stated in my *The Art of the Possible* (Toronto, 1961), p. 139, in March 1937.

King announced the visit at one of his rare press conferences. According to a newspaperman who was present, "he bounced into the room [the Speaker's chambers in the House of Commons], and pulled from an inside pocket a handwritten letter signed by the President of the United States. The letter began: 'My dear Mackenzie.' "[21] That was as far as the Prime Minister read. He was going, he said, immediately.

Before meeting with the President, Mackenzie King had a lengthy conversation, on 5 March, with Cordell Hull, the Secretary of State. (Hull's record of the conversation is reproduced in his *Memoirs*.[22]) The Secretary described it as "one of the most comprehensive I engaged in with any visiting statesman or ambassador. . . . The talk was basic in that it sought to hit at the roots of the problems facing the world. And I knew that Mackenzie King would faithfully interpret to the British Government what I said."[23] Mackenzie King also, as always, kept a record. "The impression Mr. Hull's conversation left on my mind," he wrote afterwards, "was that of a man deeply concerned in the European situation, one who believed that war was inevitable within two years, or something about as bad as war. . . ." The Secretary, Mackenzie King observed, was "so kindly and benevolent in his appearance, so gentle in his way of speaking" that it surprised him when he "used the expression 'Christ Almighty' "; he interpreted the profanity as showing "how deeply he was feeling the whole situation."[24]

After the interview with Cordell Hull, the Prime Minister went directly to the White House, where he stayed the night. "I had exceptional opportunities of conversation with the President," he wrote afterwards, "as we were practically alone during the late afternoon, at dinner, and throughout the evening, quite alone, with a complete absence of formality of any kind. . . . Our conversation was mostly of the European situation, which is giving the President and Mr. Hull a good deal of concern."[25] The high point of the discussion, for Mackenzie King, came when he proposed to the President that the United States take the lead in convening, through the League of Nations, a world conference on economic and social problems—those problems which, as he later wrote, "lie at the root of national discontent, world unrest, and international strife—and which are the fundamental cause of war."[26] The President appearing to be taken by Mackenzie King's ideas, or by his presentation of them, the Prime Minister decided, the following morning, to leave with him a written summary, which the President promised to consider carefully. [It is reproduced below, as Document 2.]

Mackenzie King was well pleased by his talks with the President. He was sure they would have some tangible result. "I believe," he wrote to the Governor General on 15 March, "there is every probability of the President himself taking action of a kind which will make clear his desire to effect an appeasement of conditions in Europe by lending good offices toward that end."[27] It had been, he wrote to Roosevelt, "a high privilege to be able to co-operate in the cause of world peace."[28] And, again to the President:

May I, in saying 'au revoir' emphasize once more what I so strongly believe. The very foundations of civilization are threatened today by international warfare on the one hand, and by industrial warfare on the other. The two are inseparable. You, it seems to me, more than any other living man, are in a position to save the world situation, and, with it, civilization. The bringing together of hostile nations in round table conference, and gaining their acceptance of the principle of investigation before resort to hostilities, would, I believe, mark the dawn of a new era in the history of the world. It would give a fresh impetus to round table conference in industrial as well as international relations.

Only the substitution of an enlightened public opinion as more fruitful of justice than an appeal to force, can save the world of today from internal and international strife. I believe you have it largely in your power to render mankind this service.[29]

Of Franklin Roosevelt's reaction to all this there is unfortunately no evidence. At this stage of his presidency he was prone to entertain plans of various kinds for intervening in the European situation, and it seems likely that he heard out the views of the Canadian Prime Minister with genuine interest and enthusiasm. It may even be that he recalled them when, later in the year, he proposed to his advisers the project of assembling a conference of all the ambassadors at Washington to consider "the methods through which all peoples may obtain the right to have access upon equal and effective terms to raw materials and other elements necessary for their economic life."[30] But this spark, along with others described by Cordell Hull as "pyrotechnical," was considered dangerous by the State Department, which successfully extinguished it.

IN BERLIN

No conviction was more deeply cherished by Mackenzie King than his belief that personal discussion by leaders of antagonistic forces was bound to abate hostility and result in better understanding. It was in accordance with this belief that, soon after returning to power in 1935, he began to think that the international situation would be dramatically improved by means of private negotiations between the heads of government of the democracies and the dictatorships. He himself had visited and talked with Mussolini—finding in Il Duce's countenance "evidence of sadness & tenderness as well as great decision"[31]—but that had been in 1928. Since then another, more remote, and evidently more consequential, figure had come into world prominence. Clearly, of all the leaders of Europe, Hitler was now the man to see.

It had first been Mackenzie King's idea to try to persuade the Prime Minister of Britain to seek out the German Chancellor for a heart-to-heart talk. He had spoken of this project to Stanley Baldwin during a week-end spent at Chequers, in October 1936; and he repeated the suggestion in a message later in the year: "If you are not too tired out, I would suggest that now is the moment for you personally to see the individual we spoke of, even if it means your leaving England for the purpose. I believe you personally can save the world situation if you do. Now is the time."[32] But Baldwin, because he was "too tired out" or because he did not like the idea, did not respond.

In May 1937, when in London for the Imperial Conference, Mackenzie King met the German Ambassador. Ribbentrop had spent some years in Canada (as, among other occupations, a salesman for a continental wine company) before his meteoric ascent in the Nazi hierarchy. Mackenzie King had been born in what was then Berlin, Ontario, and in the summer of 1900 had spent two months as a student in Berlin, Germany. The two men exchanged pleasantries on the basis of these experiences and, at a further meeting (arranged by Ribbentrop) they exchanged confidences. It was at this second meeting, held on 26 May at the German Embassy in London, that Ribbentrop invited Mackenzie King to visit Germany on his return from the Imperial Conference. An interview with the Führer would, of course, be arranged. Mackenzie King accepted the invitation, though not before he obtained from Neville Chamberlain and Anthony Eden assurances that his mission met with their approval.

At the time of Mackenzie King's visit to Berlin, the Nazi regime had acquired whatever veneer of respectability it ever possessed. "The years 1936 and 1937," writes one of the historians of appeasement, "were comparable to the most halcyon period of the Weimar regime, the years 1924-9. The Nazi 'experiment', having begun with a burst of disconcerting bravura, now showed signs, at least outwardly, of settling down into an efficient form of government, with which other governments could live and let live, so long as the principles of totalitarian ideology were practised at home and not destined for export. . . . The two years from March 1936 to March 1938 were the 'respectable years' of the Nazi Revolution, and Hitler took full advantage of them."[33]

There were, however, lapses from even this kind of respectability. One of these occurred just as Mackenzie King was on the point of setting out on his adventure. On 19 June (according to a Berlin announcement), the German cruiser *Leipzig* had been attacked in the Mediterranean by submarines alleged by the Germans to be either Spanish Loyalist or Soviet. When the British and French refused to accede to Germany's demand that they join it in a demonstration of protest, the German Government withdrew its ships from the Mediterranean naval patrol and abruptly cancelled a scheduled state visit to Britain of its foreign minister. In view of this sudden deterioration in Anglo-German relations, Mackenzie King consulted with Chamberlain and Eden to see if they wished him to postpone his own visit. They advised him to proceed as arranged. He set off in high hope. "All is part of a great plan," he wrote to a close friend in Canada before leaving for Germany. "The forces that are at work for international good-will and peace are going to triumph in the end."[34]

II

Mackenzie King arrived in Berlin on 27 June. Anxious to demonstrate to his hosts Canada's freedom of action in international affairs, he declined the hospitality of the British Embassy, staying instead in splendid isolation at the Adlon Hotel. For two days he was whirled through a tour of the more presentable institutions of the New Order—youth camps, labour camps, the Olympic Stadium. On the morning of 29 June he talked with Göring. Shortly after noon that day, he was received by Hitler at the Reichskanzlei. An interview scheduled for thirty minutes lasted for two hours. Mackenzie King made a careful record of the conversation, copies of which he sent to Chamberlain and Eden. [It is reproduced below, as Document 3.]

The confrontation of Reich Chancellor and Prime Minister was not wholly harmful. Mackenzie King took the opportunity (as he had done when he had obtained an interview with Mussolini in 1928) to clarify the significance of dominion status. Canada was free to go to war or not, he told the Führer, as Parliament might decide. He also made it very plain that if Britain were attacked by some foreign power, Parliament would decide to fight at her side. Heeded or not heeded, this message was at least delivered; more valuable service (as Chamberlain wrote at the time[35] and Anthony Eden stated publicly in 1943[36]) could hardly have been rendered.

But its value was diminished by the way in which the Prime Minister fell victim, despite at least one warning,* to the Führer's remarkable capacity for mesmerizing his visitors. "There is no doubt that Hitler had a power of fascinating men," Churchill wrote in his memoirs; and added the sage advice: "Unless the terms are equal, it is better to keep away."[37] As between the Prime Minister of Canada and the perpetrator of the Nazi *Schrecklichkeit* the terms were far from equal. The extent of Hitler's advantage may be measured by the opinions with which Mackenzie King departed his presence. "He impressed me," he wrote in the memorandum prepared for Chamberlain and Eden, "as a man of deep sincerity and a genuine patriot. I felt increasingly in the course of my stay that there were conditions in Germany itself which accounted for much that had been done there which it was difficult to understand beyond its borders."[38] To Hitler he wrote: "You have helped to remove much of the fear that in common with others I have, in some measure, shared. I was deeply impressed," Mackenzie King added, "with the great constructive work you have achieved in Germany in bringing into the lives of those in humble circumstances the opportunities which each and all should possess. . . ."[39] He was no less deceived by other members of the Nazi gang. "Both Göring and von Neurath impressed me very much," he wrote to Eden. "I believe they are men with whom it should be possible to work with a good deal of trust and confidence."[40]

Misjudging the character of the Nazis, it was easy enough to misjudge their aims. "I feel infinitely more reassured about the whole European situation," Mackenzie King wrote to Eden, "than I did before visiting the Continent."[41] To Lord Tweedsmuir he wrote: "I am perfectly certain . . . that the Germans are not contemplating the possibility of war, either with France or with Britain."[42] And to the Canadian people their Prime Minister declared, three weeks after his talks with the Nazi leaders: "Despite every appearance to the contrary, I believe the nations of Europe have a better understanding of each other's problems to-day than they have had for some years past. Moreover, despite all appearances, they are prepared, I believe, in an effort to work out a solution, to co-operate to a greater degree than has been the case for a long while. . . . Of this I am certain . . . that neither the governments nor the peoples of any of the countries I have visited desire war, or view

*"I shall be much interested to hear your impressions of Hitler," Mackenzie King's close friend Violet Markham had written to him just before his departure for Berlin. "Apparently he has a very attractive personality and makes a considerable impression on nearly everyone who sees him. All the same don't let him hypnotize you! . . . He is the head of a detestable system of force and persecution and real horrors go on in Germany today for which he is responsible." Letter of 15 June 1937, King Papers.

the possibility of war between each other, as other than likely to end in self-destruction, and the destruction of European civilization itself."[43] That the destruction of European civilization was precisely the object of the man he had so recently talked with in the Reichskanzlei was a thought unlikely to have crossed the mind of the Canadian Prime Minister; for, as was remarked of him in a different connection, "Mr. King never quite got it into his head during his economic studies at Toronto and Harvard that our civilization is dominated by carnivorous animals."*

*Frank H. Underhill, "The Close of an Era: Twenty-Five Years of Mr. Mackenzie King," *Canadian Forum*, vol. XXIV (Sept. 1944), p. 125.

Mackenzie King was not the only Canadian to undertake an inspection of the Reich at this time. In August 1936, W. D. Euler, Minister of Trade and Commerce, talked with Hitler in Berlin; no record of the interview is available. Shortly before the Prime Minister's visit in June 1937, the Director of Military Operations and Intelligence, Col. H. D. G. Crerar, visited Berlin with the object of obtaining some first-hand impressions of the nature of the regime. "From what I saw and heard," he wrote afterwards, "I should judge that it will be one, or perhaps two years before the military organization of the country will be sufficiently ready for [a major European war]. At the same time, not even the 'Leader' is infallible and in his aggressive pursuit of external objectives, which appear to him obtainable by the means at his disposal, he may miscalculate. The step from international blackmail to international blood-shed is all too easily accomplished. . . . The overriding impression which I took away from me . . . was that of a highly dynamic nation, determined before long to break its present bounds, and, consequently, increasingly dangerous to European and, indeed, to world peace." "Notes on Visit to Germany, 16–21 June 1937," Crerar Papers.

III

Appeasement

AT THE RHINELAND

"Her appeasement now may have the effect of turning her into a bulwark against the on-coming Bolshevism of eastern Europe." The words are those of Jan Christiaan Smuts, in a letter to Lloyd George of 26 March 1919 protesting the terms of the Treaty of Versailles, and urging upon the British the wisdom of applying to Germany the same "political magnanimity" which they had displayed at Vereeniging seventeen years before. It was an early appearance of the word "appeasement" in the vocabulary of politics. "Appeasement" figured (though without result) in the diplomacy of the peace settlement. It was revised at the time of Locarno and, as Smuts' biographer has noted, "from that time onwards was Briand's favourite word, the symbol of a policy towards Germany entirely opposed to that which Poincaré had been pursuing. In the Briand-Stresemann era the word, both in its French and English versions, signified reconciliation. Unfortunately, the word can also signify the satisfaction of immoderate appetites. During the 1930's statesmen like Simon and Halifax continued to intend the first meaning while Hitler and Mussolini were intending the second."[1] Only after it became evident that the appetites of the dictators had grown with feeding did appeasement acquire its present pejorative connotation and become not so much a description as an epithet.

The attempt to appease Hitler began in the days following 7 March 1936, when the Nazi leader made good his earlier threat to violate the Locarno agreements if France ratified her pact with the Soviet Union. A scanty detachment of the *Wehrmacht* was ordered by Hitler into the demilitarized zone of the Rhineland. It was prepared, we know now, to beat a hasty retreat in the event of determined military resistance by France; Hitler's generals were fearful about the enterprise, sure that so grave a provocation to the peace of Europe (involving the violation of Versailles and Locarno alike) would precipitate a fierce engagement for which their forces were ill-prepared. But Hitler had taken the measure of his opponents. Not a shot was fired, scarcely a voice was raised, by any of them. The Führer's timing was superb. Having seized his booty by force, he offered, in the form of a twenty-five year non-aggression pact with the West, what *The Times* of London called "A Chance to Rebuild" —a comment, notes an historian of the period, "which no doubt applies in a sense to any devastated area, provided the foundations have not been irremediably shaken."[2]

The Prime Minister of Canada received the grave news from an editor of an Ottawa newspaper, who called him on the telephone on the morning of 7 March. Mackenzie King relayed it to his cabinet. "There was complete silence," he wrote afterwards, "on the part of all. No one had anything to say."

Meanwhile, his High Commissioner in the United Kingdom had been meeting in more voluble company. Hitler's move—it was one of his "Saturday surprises"—had interrupted a week-end party at Lord Lothian's country home. "Off to Blickling after some work at Canada House," Vincent Massey recorded in his diary for 7 March. "We plunged into a house-party full of the German reoccupation of the Rhineland. The Waldorf Astors, Sir Walter and Lady Layton, the Norman Davises, Arnold Toynbee, Tom Jones, Sir Thomas & Lady Inskip. We found ourselves during the course of the weekend in extraordinary agreement. 'Don't get too excited about the technical breach of treaties, use Hitler's offer as a new foundation of peace.' "* These conclusions were relayed by the ubiquitous Tom Jones to the Prime Minister of Britain: the Blickling set was not used to wasting its time. The cabinet

*Massey Papers. A full account of the week-end meeting has been published by another of the guests:

"Immediately after dinner we listened to the news on the wireless and then, at my request, resolved ourselves into a shadow Cabinet with this agendum: 'Draft of Prime Minister's speech on Monday' . . .

I'll summarize our Shadow conclusions very much as I telephoned them early this morning for the P.M.'s enlightenment.

1. Welcome Hitler's declaration whole-heartedly.

2. . . . Palliate offence, as the last and least of the series of breaches of Part V of the Treaty. . . . Treat this as relatively *de minimus*: and not to be taken tragically in view of the peace proposals which accompany it. Versailles is now a corpse and should be buried. . . .

5. Accept Hitler's declaration as made in good faith. . . .

8. This is the 'last bus' and all turns on S.B. catching it tomorrow."

Thomas Jones, *A Diary with Letters, 1931–1950* (London, 1954), pp. 179–81.

agreed that the state of public opinion in England would not allow any useful resort to a threat or show of force; but there was some difference of opinion whether to move towards Germany or to France. Vincent Massey became alarmed at the extent to which a pro-French attitude was gaining ground, particularly at the Foreign Office where, thanks largely to Lord Vansittart, the Permanent Under Secretary, there was to be found "a narrow & precise interpretation on Brit. obligation which does not seem to be modified by British statesmanship. The letter of the contracts [Versailles and Locarno] is emphasized to the neglect of the spirit." He determined to bring Ottawa's influence to bear on the side of appeasement. "This is the moment when the point of view of the Dominions is of the greatest importance. Te Water [a fellow High Commissioner] has received from his government a document apparently drafted by Smuts calling for a constructive policy & dissociating S. Africa from the legalistic attitude which may well involve the country in war. We have suffered enough in the past from French vindictiveness against Germany and French pedantry in the interpretation of contracts. I have urged Ottawa to give me their views on the assumption that they too would help to counteract the French influence at present so powerful."[3]

But Mackenzie King, though favourable enough to the views of his High Commissioner that Germany's violation of her treaty obligations should not be allowed to develop into a *casus belli*, was strongly opposed to Canada taking any public or private initiative in the matter. To Massey's suggestion that a question might be asked in the Canadian House of Commons to which the Government could then respond with a statement of policy, the Prime Minister retorted: "Such a course would in our opinion only serve to provoke controversy from one end of Canada to the other. Our task in interest of Empire and of Canada is to keep Canada united." His message reminded Massey that Canada had declined to become a party to the Locarno arrangements at the time of their negotiation and, for his own information, that the Government felt it had no obligation whatsoever in regard to Germany's reoccupation of the Rhineland.[4] The High Commissioner received this rebuff with understandable dismay. "Canada seems to have resolved to be silent & await the consequences on the ground that the affair is not hers," he wrote that evening, "but she may [be] involved just the same in the cataclysm which an unwise & shortsighted although seemingly correct policy may lead G. B. into. Obscurantism is an unlovely policy at all times. . . . Who knows that a word said by the Government of a British Dominion with calmness and the perspective lent by distance and relative detachment might not [in] a crisis like the present when there seems to be an almost even balance between broad & narrow policies . . . tip the scales in favour of the former? The only thing is to obey orders at the present moment & hope for the best."[5]

Mackenzie King's estimation of the opinion of his countrymen was, as usual, wholly correct. The Rhineland reoccupation aroused none of the emotion produced by Mussolini's premeditated assault upon Ethiopia. On the contrary, there was a widely held conviction that in reoccupying the demilitarized zone Hitler was only avenging the wrongs of Versailles, taking possession of what rightfully belonged to Germany. "Why shouldn't a man walk into his own backyard?" In Canada, as in Britain, this rhetorical question was being asked everywhere. With the exception of Dafoe's *Free Press*, Monday's newspapers urged the acceptance without protest of Hitler's *fait accompli*. "Canadians who do not allow themselves to be swayed by a personal dislike for Hitler and his unpleasant colleagues," wrote the editor of the Vancouver *Sun*, "will feel a measure of sympathy for this new attitude of the German people. . . . Whatever morality lies in the scales seems to be, this time, on Germany's side of the balance." "After eighteen years," the Edmonton *Bulletin* suggested, "Europe can afford to restore Germany to full standing in the concert of nations." "Nothing can ever be gained," argued the Montreal *Gazette*, "by persistently treating Germany as though she were national enemy No. 1 in perpetuity. It would likewise be dangerous and futile to regard Adolf Hitler in no other light than as one whose designs are wilfully antagonistic to forces that hate war."

The reoccupation of the Rhineland posed a more troublesome issue for French-speaking Canadians. On the one hand, they were concerned for the safety of their mother country in the new confrontation with her old enemy. On the other, isolationism, a certain distrust of the politicians of the Third Republic, and an even greater distrust of British policy,* caused them to draw back. Perhaps the balance of informed opinion came down on the side of Henri Bourassa who, no Anglophile, wrote to Mackenzie King from Europe:

On the Rhine issue, will I shock you in saying that I side with the British against the French? Whether Hitler's peace proposals be sincere or not, they ought to be taken at their face value and Hitler *pousie au pied du mur* to deliver the goods. The French *nation*, I think, was prepared to emulate the British in that respect, but the third-rate politicians who then ruled France spoiled the game and acted foolishly. Whether the new gang [the Blum government] will do any better is very doubtful. And then, again, so long

*See for example, "Responsibilité de l'Angleterre," *Le Soleil* (Quebec), 9 March 1936.

as Britain and Italy are at loggerheads, Hitler can laugh at them all—which he does—and Mussolini as well—and I don't blame them.[6]

On 17 March the Canadian Government sent the first, and only, expression of its views on the reoccupation of the Rhineland to the Government of the United Kingdom. It served notice that the Canadian Government was not in sympathy with the French position, or those in the British Government inclined to favour the French position; and that if the United Kingdom were to embark, in the company of France, upon a venture to force German troops out of the Rhineland it could not expect to be joined by Canada, even if the operation were authorized by the League of Nations. All this was obliquely phrased. From South Africa, Hertzog had spoken more bluntly. If Great Britain could not restrain France, "she can at least keep out of this fatal mischief and decline to share the terrible responsibility before the world."[7] Vansittart was right in supposing that the dominions were no more ready to go to war over the Rhineland than they had been over Ethiopia. "One could not blame them, one could not admire them, one could not admire anybody."[8]

The Canadian Parliament was in session throughout the Rhineland crisis, but on only one occasion discussed it. On 23 March, R. B. Bennett, having previously given written notice of his question, asked the Prime Minister if he had any statement to make regarding the situation in Europe. Mackenzie King replied that any statement could only be unhelpful "to those who at the moment are involved in very critical and delicate negotiations on a matter of supreme concern to mankind," and he asked members of the House "to forbear, if they can see their way so to do, from proferring any request which might provoke discussion in our country at this time."[9] This reply satisfied Bennett, but not J. S. Woodsworth, the leader of the C.C.F. party. "What is the attitude of Canada?" he asked. "It seems to me that we cannot go on indefinitely without having some indication from the Government as to what the attitude of Canada is." To this Mackenzie King responded:

. . . in a word, the attitude of the Government is to do nothing itself and if possible to prevent anything occurring which will precipitate one additional factor into the all important discussions which are now taking place in Europe. I believe that Canada's first duty to the League and to the British Empire, with respect to all the great issues that come up is, if possible, to keep this country united. . . .[10]

His reply to Woodsworth's question, Mackenzie King wrote that evening, would "some day . . . serve to indicate the Liberal policy with respect to Imperial and Foreign Affairs."[11]

AT THE IMPERIAL CONFERENCE

In 1923, attending an Imperial Conference for the first time as Prime Minister of Canada, Mackenzie King had protested vigorously and decisively against the Conference attempting to assume "the rights of a cabinet in the determination of foreign policy, . . . expressing approval of the present [British] Government's foreign policy . . . , trying to shape the affairs of Europe."[12] By 1937, Mackenzie King's suspicions of "Downing Street domination" had been sufficiently allayed to allow him to do what he had never done before—to endorse at an Imperial Conference a united Commonwealth policy on international affairs. The policy for which the dominions (once more excepting New Zealand) offered their collective approval and support was the ill-fated policy of appeasement. "The settlement of differences that may arise between nations," asserted the official Report of the Proceedings of the Conference, "should be sought by methods of co-operation, joint enquiry and conciliation. . . . Differences of political creed should be no obstacle to friendly relations between Governments and countries. . . . Nothing would be more damaging to the hopes of international appeasement than the division, real or apparent, of the world into opposing groups."[13] Stated as generalities, in no political context and with no political intent, these maxims are inoffensive. Stated in the political context of the summer of 1937—"a great Commonwealth confronted with the shameless aggression of European tyrants unmatched for their cruelty and faithlessness since the Dark Ages"[14]—they may well be thought otherwise. Mackenzie King, as will now be shown, played a central part in their formulation.

II

As Mackenzie King made his preparations for the Imperial Conference to be held in London in May and June of 1937, two competing ideas of what the Canadian attitude ought to be were in his mind. One was the traditional attitude of isolationism and withdrawal. To remain aloof from Europe's turmoil, he felt, was no less wise and no less desirable than it had been fifteen years earlier, at the time of the Chanak crisis. "We are a fortunate people," he wrote late in 1936, "to be on this side of the Atlantic";[15] and he desperately desired to shield the fortunate people from what was going on on the other side. "I keep wondering," he confessed to Lord Tweedsmuir, "if some way cannot be found whereby if Europe is determined on war, she might not be left to herself, the British Empire standing outside. . . ."[16] O. D. Skelton was prepared to go a step further: should Britain determine on war, might not Canada stay outside? To a series of rhetorical questions, posed by him in a document subsequently read by Mackenzie King to the cabinet, and approved by the cabinet, his own answers were clearly in the negative:

Is the position that Canada is directly and inescapably tied to the European political process, particularly to the orbit of the ancient, unresolved feud between France and Germany—between Western and Eastern Europe? Is Canada to regard it as the normal thing that every generation (or less) she is to invade the Continent of Europe and join the European battle campaigns of the 20th century—so normal that she should now, in contradistinction to the 1914–1918 campaign, deliberately prepare in advance? Is it to be normal that this invasion and intervention from North America should be undertaken at the outset of each European campaign, regardless of what position the United States takes? Regardless, too, of the certainty that various "small" though important Powers in the complex of European civilization will not join in the campaign? Is the creation and maintenance of a Canadian nation feasible on such lines? Even if that were feasible, could such a programme be regarded as a contribution to European or world stability or appeasement, or to "civilization"?[17]

With all of this Mackenzie King was in strong agreement. But he was coming to believe that the traditional isolationist attitude, which he had himself espoused in the 1920's, would no longer suffice during the 1930's. He believed this because, unlike Skelton, he did not think that Canada could, or should, remain outside a general European war in which the United Kingdom became involved as a victim of aggression. "If the British Empire can be kept out of war," he wrote, "it will be able to take care of itself. . . . If drawn into war, I firmly believe disruptive forces will begin to operate which will lie beyond the control of all concerned."[18] A European war, with Britain a belligerent, was for him the ultimate catastrophe. No effort should be spared, nothing left undone, to try to prevent it. If that meant abandoning previous convictions about the unwisdom of attempting to influence British foreign policy, so be it. The Dominion could no longer afford detachment. It was time to become engagé. "I prayed very earnestly throughout the summer months that I might be of some service [in the cause of European peace]," Mackenzie King wrote to Tweedsmuir on 24 August 1936. "I am not without hope that in however slight a way, Canada may be helpful. . . ."

Not all members of his cabinet overcame so swiftly the isolationist impulse. "Whatever we do," wrote T. A. Crerar, one of its members accompanying Mackenzie King to the Imperial Conference as a member of the Canadian delegation, "I feel certain that Canada will keep out of that net [of a common Empire foreign policy] . . . The more I see of the whole thing, the more I am certain that our destiny is on the North American continent and that if Europe is going to insist on destroying itself, it is no part of our mission to destroy ourselves in attempting to prevent it in doing so."[19]

III

The largest delegation ever sent by a Canadian government to an Imperial Conference left Quebec on the *Empress of Australia* on 24 April 1937. It comprised five members of the cabinet (Mackenzie King, Ernest Lapointe, Ian Mackenzie, Charles Dunning, and T. A. Crerar); senior officials of the Departments of External Affairs (including Skelton, Loring Christie, and L. B. Pearson who acted as secretary to the delegation) and National Defence; and a retinue of lesser officials. The opening session of the Conference took place on 14 May. The Principal Delegates then moved into secret session. On the afternoon of 21 May, Mackenzie King delivered, on behalf of Canada, a statement on foreign affairs.*

He followed his practice at previous conferences of eschewing comment upon the *tour d'horizon* conducted by the British foreign secretary at the preceding session, confining his remarks to questions of foreign policy as they affected Canada only. But he did observe that Anthony Eden's statement had shown that "if there has not been any notable increase in friendliness or goodwill in Europe, at least there has been some lessening of tension." For that result the British government, by its patience and restraint, had been largely responsible. There followed a comprehensive survey of Canada's external affairs with various countries, particularly the United States; and the usual recital of the domestic difficulties of the Dominion. These, he said, could be overcome; but only if the task of maintaining national unity were not complicated by "the further strain that would be involved by present controversy as to participation in overseas wars or commitments so to participate."

This brought him to the League of Nations. Canadian opinion, he declared, was by this time overwhelmingly hostile to the concept of the League as a coercive instrument. "There are still elements which favour a policy of collective sanctions, but they are in a minority." The facts of international life made it impossible to regard either Article X or Article XVI of the Covenant "as having any real validity," and "we

---

*Of equal importance at the Conference was its discussion of defence, dealt with in chap. IV. See below, pp. 81–91.

have taken the view that this situation should be frankly recognized." On that, he said, most Canadians were agreed. "It is when we pass from the question of League to Empire war relations that we touch a really vital issue and face the possibility of definite cleavage." On the one hand there were many forces—"the strong pull of kinship, the pride in common traditions, the desire to save democratic institutions, the admiration for the stability, the fairness, the independence that characterized English public life"—which would make for Canadian participation in a war in which British interests had been placed in jeopardy through the actions of hostile powers. But on the other it had to be stated that "opposition to participation in war, any war, is growing." No one in Canada believed the Dominion to be in any danger of attack. It was widely held that it was because Canada had paid so dearly in the last war that she had been laid so low by the depression. There was impatience at Europe's seeming inability to keep its house in order, and a feeling that it was none of Canada's business to try where Europe herself had failed. The growth of isolationist sentiment in the United States inevitably produced a corresponding movement of opinion in the Dominion. "In some sections of the country"—he did not name them—"opinion is practically unanimous against any participation in either a League or a Commonwealth war." Any attempt by the Government to commit the country to war in advance of the circumstances which might justify resort to war would make participation impossible, for it would stretch to the point of rending the fabric of national unity. Whether Canada would fight in the event of war breaking out he would not venture to predict.* It would all depend on the circumstances—"upon the measures of conviction as to the unavoidability of the struggle and the seriousness of the outlook, and upon the measure of unity that had been attained in Canada." All this would show, he concluded, "why we consider peace so vital for the preservation of the unity of the Commonwealth as much as the unity of Canada."

After each of the delegations had finished declaring its views, the discussion on foreign affairs was suspended to allow Anthony Eden to proceed to Geneva on diplomatic business. When he returned, and the discussion resumed, the Conference had a new chairman. Neville

*It will be noted that Mackenzie King did not wish to disclose to the Imperial Conference what, a month later, he disclosed in Berlin, namely, that in the event of "a war of aggression, nothing in the world would keep the Canadian people from being at the side of Britain." Canada, H. C. Debates, 1944, vol. VI, p. 6275. See also above, p. 45.

Chamberlain replaced Stanley Baldwin as Prime Minister of Britain on 28 May. The transition was to prove significant. As chairman of previous imperial conferences, Baldwin had been somewhat indolent; "he intervened decisively in the proceedings only when a motion to adjourn was being entertained, and then usually in its favour."[20] Chamberlain was a different breed. "Masterful, confident, and ruled by an instinct for order, he would give a lead, and perhaps impart an edge, on every question."[21] So the delegates soon discovered. Mackenzie King found the change to be for the better. "It gave an opportunity," he wrote afterwards, "of coming to know Mr. Chamberlain and his attitude toward Empire and foreign affairs to a degree that would otherwise have been impossible and which, so far as he himself was concerned, was all to the good. Every member of our delegation has come away from the Conference with a feeling toward Mr. Chamberlain wholly different from what it was anticipated would be the case before we left. . . . Personally, I feel greatly reassured about the future."[22]

Back from Europe on 1 June, Anthony Eden gave the Delegates a résumé of the most recent turmoil. Spanish Government aircraft had attacked the German warship *Deutschland*, and Hitler ordered the bombardment of the undefended town of Almeria in retaliation. This alarming event greatly disconcerted the Prime Minister of Australia. In an impromptu and impassioned speech to the Conference, he pleaded that it should issue at once a declaration of the Empire's support of appeasement. Mackenzie King was the first of the Delegates to speak after Lyons had finished. He did not, he declared, object to the Commonwealth presenting a united front to the world, but it would be well for it to discuss somewhat more fully what it was proposed to unite upon. An argument broke out, to be ended by the chairman. The question raised by the Prime Minister of Australia, Chamberlain said, was whether the Conference might help the cause of peace by means of some public pronouncement. If they could agree on its terms it would, he was sure, "be a very impressive thing." He and his colleagues on the United Kingdom delegation were willing to try their hands at a draft, copies of which could then be circulated among the dominion delegations for deletions or amendments as required. A sub-committee could compose any differences that remained. To this procedure the dominions gave their consent.

In due course, on the afternoon of 4 June, Sir Maurice Hankey— that "institution indispensable to the stability of the State," as Chamberlain called him at the conclusion of the Conference—brought the British draft to Mackenzie King for his consideration. (Experience at the 1926

Imperial Conference had taught Hankey to seek out the Canadian Prime Minister before any of the others, not so much because he was Prime Minister of the senior dominion as because his approval was invariably the hardest to obtain.) It consisted of nine paragraphs, in content not unlike but by no means identical to the text of the paragraphs on foreign affairs eventually included in the published *Summary of Proceedings*. Over the three-day week-end much mimeographing and revision and exchanges of paper among the heads of delegations and their advisers produced by Monday morning, 7 June, a fifth or even sixth edition of the original for the consideration of the drafting committee. The committee took up the nine paragraphs one at a time. Most caused difficulty. Chamberlain took note of the various objections, and undertook to produce a fresh version by the following day.

Chamberlain's synthesis had been most skilfully executed; he had sought to offer something to placate each delegation, while including nothing that might be basically unacceptable. He almost succeeded. Skelton, who had looked over Chamberlain's draft, did not like the paragraph which referred to the "common agreement" of the dominions "in the cause of peace." "Still a good bit of common policy here," he minuted for the Prime Minister, "disguised under peace label; every Foreign Office says its foreign policy is directed to peace—on its own terms"; and: "Don't like this—it covers all foreign policy really." But Mackenzie King was no longer the opponent of a common front as such; all depended on the nature of the front.

When the Principal Delegates reassembled after a few hours' adjournment to consider the revision Chamberlain had laid before them that morning, all went well until they came to the third paragraph and the fourth. These affirmed, respectively, the members' determination to settle international disputes by means of conciliation, inquiry, and co-operation, and not by recourse to force; and their desire to base their policies upon the aims and ideals of the League of Nations. With the wording of Chamberlain's draft Mackenzie King was well content—he ought to have been, for he was mainly responsible for the wording; and he was disagreeably surprised when the Prime Minister of New Zealand declared that he was wholly unable to accept it. The words "not by recourse to force," M. J. Savage argued, should be deleted from the draft; some people, among whom he was proud to be numbered, *were* prepared to use force on behalf of peace and the League. He objected as well to the phrase "aims and ideals of the League of Nations"; it was too vague, too wishywashy. One thing his delegation could not agree to was any formulation which seemed to weaken the authority of the League of Nations. Chamberlain remarked that no one in the room wanted to do that. Savage retorted that it seemed to him that the Canadian delegation came pretty close to wanting to do it. Mackenzie King spoke up at once, and sharply. He could not agree to a declaration which proclaimed that the dominions based their policy upon "principles laid down by the League of Nations," as desired by the Prime Minister of New Zealand. Those principles included collective security, in the efficacy of which his Government did not believe.

It was a strange scene. Never in its history had the Imperial Conference come to so fundamental a dispute between two of the dominions. Fundamental disputes were familiar enough but they had been confined, hitherto, to disputes between the British Government and one or other of the dominion governments—usually the Canadian Government, and that usually represented by Mackenzie King—over questions of status. And here were two dominions quarrelling over a question of substance. It could be said that the British Commonwealth had come of age, but as things were going it seemed in danger of premature death. In vain did Chamberlain and Eden produce mollifying compromises; Savage would not have them. At one stage Mackenzie King remarked that if agreement could not be reached in reference to the League of Nations, there might be no resolutions at all. When Savage declared he would be quite content at that, Chamberlain hastily adjourned the discussion.

The way out of the impasse was eventually provided by the classical device of a footnote to the communiqué. The first suggestion was that the footnote express New Zealand's reservation. Savage was ready to accept this, but the British delegation were unhappy; so pointed an exclusion would indicate to a practised reader of the communiqué the existence of fundamental disagreement among the members of the British Commonwealth, whereas the whole purpose of the exercise had been to register their unity. There seemed nothing for it but to settle for a general reservation which any government, New Zealand's included, would be able to invoke in the event of there being objection at home to what had been agreed upon in London. And so it came about that in the published *Summary of Proceedings* there appeared as a footnote to the paragraph setting forth that the "representatives of the Governments concerned found themselves in close agreement upon a number of general propositions which they thought it desirable to set out," the following formulation:

It was understood and agreed that nothing in this statement should be held to diminish the right of His Majesty's Governments in the United Kingdom, Canada, Australia, New Zealand, South Africa, and India to advocate and support their statements of policy as submitted to the Assembly of the League of Nations in September, 1936.

New Zealand's submission to the Assembly had been wholly at variance with the document to which it now gave assent. On returning to Wellington, its embattled Prime Minister told the House of Representatives, in frank enough language, what had happened, and ruefully concluded: "To those who think it is a simple matter to reach a common understanding, even amongst the dominions that go to make up the British Commonwealth of Nations, I say to them to have another look. . . ."[23] Mackenzie King, from long and intimate experience, knew that to be the case. But then, his point of view customarily prevailed.

IV

It had prevailed once again, in 1937 not much less than in 1923 when, as Smuts grudgingly acknowledged, Mackenzie King had had his way in everything. In its endorsation of appeasement, and in its subtle repudiation of the League, the Report faithfully reflected his views; his victory in the section devoted to defence, as related below,* was even more complete. Mackenzie King wrote, as he could write after every meeting of its kind: "It was a difficult mission, but its results were much better than I had ever anticipated they could possibly be."[24]

The most important consequence of the Imperial Conference of 1937, from the standpoint of Canadian foreign policy, was that it removed from the mind of Mackenzie King any lingering feeling that a prime minister of Britain could not be entrusted with the task of keeping the world safe for the Empire. Nothing henceforth would shake his confidence in and admiration for Neville Chamberlain. "I am delighted with the manner in which Mr. Chamberlain has dealt with many of the baffling problems which have confronted him since attaining office," Mackenzie King wrote to a mutual friend in England after his return to Canada. "I marvel at the splendid manner in which he measures up to the exceptional obligations of his high office. He has my best of wishes and most sympathetic understanding in all that he undertakes. When you are again talking with him, tell him, at all costs, to keep the Empire out of war."[25] And a few months later: "I hope you will tell Mr. Chamberlain that I cannot begin to express the admiration I feel for the manner in which he has performed a task more difficult, I believe, than any with which any Prime Minister of Great Britain has ever before been faced. I approve wholeheartedly of the course he has adopted. . . . The one mistake that I see in British policy—and I believe it to be a very great one—is that Great Britain has been far too slow

*See below, pp. 87–91.

in taking the steps which Mr. Chamberlain himself has found it necessary to take within the past few weeks."[26] And, at the time of Munich: "Personally, I think Chamberlain has been magnificent. I came during the period of the [Imperial] Conference to have an entirely different opinion of him to that which I previously held. Following the situation from the inside from day to day, week to week and month to month, I have come to have entire confidence in the course he has pursued."[27]

AT MUNICH

Three events of critical importance altered the European crisis for the worse in the spring of 1938. The first was the resignation on 20 February of Anthony Eden as British Foreign Secretary. This event, which caused Winston Churchill one of his few sleepless nights, in which he lay, as he has himself recorded, "consumed by emotions of sorrow and fear," produced no comparable anxiety in Ottawa. Mackenzie King thought Eden's resignation was "all to the good," for "Halifax in this crisis will be a safer man than Eden," who had lost the confidence of the dictators.[28]

The second was the subjugation of Austria by Germany in March. The *Anschluss* too was accepted without demur or protest, even with satisfaction. "I felt all along," Mackenzie King wrote on 12 March, "that sooner or later the annexation of Austria was inevitable."[29]

The third was the conclusion, on 16 April, of an Anglo-Italian agreement—a complete triumph, in the view of Churchill at the time, for Mussolini. That was not the view of Mackenzie King. "When in England," he wrote to L. S. Amery, "I expressed to more than one member of the Administration the view that time should not be lost in seeking to bring about more immediate personal contacts between Ministers in the United Kingdom and those in authority in Italy and Germany. I was immensely relieved when Chamberlain set out to make the agreement he did in Italy. . . . There would have been war in Europe if Chamberlain had not adopted the course he did."[30]

These events came and went without any comment from the Canadian Government, either in the form of despatches to London or of speeches in Parliament. Speeches in Parliament Mackenzie King was determined to avoid. "The least that is said means the least being stirred up in the Commons and in the Press and in the minds of the people. To go on steadily as if all were proceeding satisfactorily is, I think, at times like the present, the best policy for the government of our country."[31]

He succeeded in deferring any discussion of foreign policy in Parliament until 24 May, when he delivered a comprehensive and carefully prepared statement of "Canada's Position with Respect to External Affairs" (the title given to the statement in the offprint which was subsequently produced). It contained, in addition to sections on Spain and the Far East, some revealing generalities concerning recent events in Europe and Canadian reactions thereto. There was, Mackenzie King noted, a "wide and violent conflict of opinion as to the policy that should be adopted" in regard to the "social and political revolution" which the nations of Europe were undergoing.

In the opinion of one group, Armageddon has already come, the forces of light and darkness are irrevocably swinging into battle line for the final test of destiny. Europe and liberty, it is contended, can be saved only if the democracies firmly and unitedly call a halt here and now.

The other widespread attitude is to recognise the situation as dangerous, but to insist that the policy of dividing Europe or the world into two antagonistic camps, organizing a holy alliance against communism, would be still more dangerous, and is neither possible nor necessary. There is no warrant, it is urged, for fighting a preventive war or for seeking to form a hard and fast alliance against the authoritarian states. If such an alliance could be formed, it would only drive the fascist countries into firmer alliance and put any possibility of peaceful settlement out of the question. The wiser policy, it is urged, is to try to bring all Europe back to sanity, to emphasize and strengthen the points of agreement, not of difference, to seek to adjust each specific difficulty in turn.

He would not admit that either of these views was his own; in stating them, he said, he was simply "stating the views which I believe are contending against each other in Europe today." But there is no doubt at all that the second accurately represented his own convictions. He did say that it represented the convictions of the Government of the United Kingdom; Britain, he declared, "has striven for peace." But he did not consider that Canadians were called upon "to pass judgment or to take sides in United Kingdom discussions." It was better to remain on the sidelines as silent spectators. Such had been the posture of the Canadian Government during the recent developments in the European crisis, and such it would continue to be. The Government does not consider, he said, "that it is in the interest of either Canada or of the Commonwealth to tender advice as to what policy the United Kingdom should adopt week by week, or become involved in British political disputes. We have expressed no opinion on that policy, and no one in London is authorized or warranted in interpreting us as doing so." (This last remark was a reminder, if not a rebuke, to the High Commissioner at Canada House, with whom Mackenzie King's official and private relations had become severely strained.) What the Government intended to do, Mackenzie King concluded, was to cultivate the Canadian garden, where plenty of hoeing and weeding remained to be done. "We shall try to keep in mind the difficulties and dangers that other countries are facing, but we shall not assume that it is our duty or within our power to work out their problems for them, to make over their social structure or their political ideas or their racial attitudes. In seeking within our own country, which constitutes half a continent, to build up a genuine democracy. . . . we shall be doing the task that lies to our hands, our Canadian task."[32]

II

Mackenzie King's conversations with the Nazi leaders in the summer of 1937 had left him with the impression that, while they did not wish to precipitate a general European war, they most certainly contemplated what he described as "expansion toward the East." Whether this eastward expansion, he wrote on 10 July, "can be effected without conflict remains to be seen; I rather believe that with confidence gradually established between Britain and Germany, such can be the case."[33]

He could hardly have been surprised, therefore, when, hard on the heels of the *Anschluss* came word of Nazi pressure upon Czechoslovakia. Acquisition of Austria placed German troops on three sides of the Czechoslovak frontier, and in position to turn Czechoslovak fortifications. It was evident to all that the integrity of the Czechoslovak state was now in deadly peril. What remained as yet uncertain were the methods of its intended destruction; and the price, if any, others were prepared to pay for its preservation. On 28 May, the Führer's directive to General Keitel proclaimed his "unalterable intention to smash Czechoslovakia by military action in the near future." 1 October was subsequently declared to be the deadline.[34] But Chamberlain had decided to abandon Czechoslovakia to its fate long before that.[35]

The appointment of Lord Runciman as a mediator between the Czechoslovak Government and the Sudetendeutsche Partei headed by the Nazi puppet, Konrad Henlein, was regarded with great satisfaction by Mackenzie King. "I am greatly pleased," he cabled to Runciman, "at your having been selected. . . . Please accept my best of wishes for the outcome of your efforts, which I feel sure will be of the greatest possible benefit to all."[36] Runciman, doubtless surprised at this word of encouragement from across the Atlantic, asked Mackenzie King if he might make it public; King replied that he was at liberty to show it privately "to any parties" if he thought it might be helpful to do so, but that he would prefer, "for reasons you will appreciate," not to publish his message.

The end of August brought the inevitable breakdown of the Runciman-Prague-Henlein "negotiations," and with it a feeling of despondency and alarm throughout the non-Axis world. "The chances are," J. W. Dafoe wrote at the time, "that between the fools & cowards in London and the madmen in Berlin the guns will go off."[37] Mackenzie King, while not assigning blame to either of these parties, was no less pessimistic. "I confess that, during the past few days, I have been very anxious with respect to the European situation," he wrote to his Minister of Finance on 3 September.

From official sources, it would seem that those who have most to do with the situation regard war not only as possible but probable, and that, before the present month is out. I have tried to anticipate what might be necessary in this eventuality with regard to the summoning of Parliament, measures to be introduced, etcetera. Most important of all would, of course, be the question of our participation in the event of Britain going into the war. . . . Should the worst come to the worst, I hope you will send me your own views confidentially on points you feel may have to be considered, and views which you feel ought to prevail. . . .[38]

And to the Governor General, three days later:

I have been deeply concerned during the past fortnight with the possibilities of war in the immediate future and what this would involve in the way of the immediate summoning of Parliament, etc., etc. I have everything in readiness, in case that step may have to be taken. I believe, however, that it will be found in the end that Hitler is for peace, unless unduly provoked. . . .[39]

On 13 September, widespread disorders broke out among the Sudeten Germans in Czechoslovakia. The Prague Government proclaimed martial law, whereupon the Sudeten leaders despatched an ultimatum stating that if martial law were not immediately withdrawn they would not be responsible for the consequences. That afternoon, the High Commissioner in London telephoned Skelton in Ottawa—the first time he had done so, Vincent Massey noted in his diary, since being posted in 1935; "Ottawa dislikes the telephone"—to inform the Government that the crisis was regarded with the utmost gravity by the Government of the United Kingdom. It was at this juncture that Chamberlain decided to resort to a "means of averting catastrophe" which he had described (some days earlier, in a letter to his sister) as "unconventional and daring."[40] He would go to see Hitler himself. A wire was despatched; Hitler replied that the British Prime Minister would be received. On 15 September, Neville Chamberlain began the flight to Berchtesgaden.

Duly informed of these events, Mackenzie King sought to do what he could to make the mission a success. He sent off a message of encouragement to the departing Prime Minister, expressing "my admiration for the vision and courage shown in your decision to have a personal interview with Herr Hitler." On the night of 14 September, he released the following statement to the Canadian press:

I have conveyed to Mr. Neville Chamberlain the deep satisfaction with which my colleagues and I have learned that his proposal for a personal conference with Herr Hitler, of which I was advised this morning, has been agreed to and that a meeting is being arranged tomorrow. I am sure the whole Canadian people will warmly approve this far-seeing and truly noble action on the part of Mr. Chamberlain. Direct personal contact is the most effective means of clearing away the tension and misunderstandings that have marked the course of events in Europe in recent months. Mr. Chamberlain has taken emphatically the right step. The world will hope that tomorrow's conference will create an atmosphere in which at last a solution may speedily be found of the problems which have threatened peace.

He sought as well to ensure the best possible reception for Chamberlain by the Führer; and for this purpose despatched the following message for Ribbentrop: "Should opportunity permit, I should be deeply grateful if you would let Herr Hitler know how thankful I am that he and Mr. Chamberlain are to meet each other tomorrow and to have a conference together, and how sincerely I hope and believe their joint efforts may serve to preserve and further the peace of the world and the wellbeing of mankind."[41] This message was sent through the British Embassy at Berlin; Nevile Henderson reported to Mackenzie King the next day that he had delivered it, and that it had been "most useful and timely."

Neville Chamberlain was not long ensconced with Hitler in the great chamber at Berchtesgaden before being made aware that the world was even closer to the brink than he had thought. He had set out with the object of exploring Hitler's mind and of arriving at some compromise which, while involving the Czechs in as slight a sacrifice as possible, would none the less preserve the peace of Europe. Hitler, however, seemed in no mood to compromise. He did agree to see Chamberlain once more, after the Prime Minister had consulted with his colleagues.

The rest of the world knew nothing of this when Chamberlain's aircraft returned to London on 16 September. A message intended to be reassuring was given to the newspapers, and the dominion governments were told only that Chamberlain felt the situation to be "enigmatical and must be so treated." After a meeting of the British cabinet, fuller information was transmitted to the dominion prime ministers. Chamberlain felt that Hitler had made up his mind to incorporate the Sudeten territories within the German Reich, if need be by force. Had he not gone to Berchtesgaden, they would already have been in possession of German troops. The cabinet had decided, therefore, to support a policy of self-determination for the Sudeten Germans. On receiving this information, Mackenzie King made public the following statement:

The Canadian Government have been giving unremitting consideration to the European situation, in the light of the confidential information which they are receiving. The position is changing from day to day. The present and essential task is to avert recourse to force by finding a peaceful and agreed solution to the present clash of interests in Central Europe. The Government of the United Kingdom have undertaken this task with a courage and vision which I have stated the people of Canada unanimously appreciate. If unfortunately that effort and other efforts to preserve the peace of Central Europe fail, it will become necessary for the governments and parliaments of all countries which may be directly or indirectly concerned to determine the course to be followed. The Canadian Government are examining all possible contingencies and will be prepared in accordance with the undertakings repeatedly given in Parliament, if occasion arises, to summon Parliament forthwith and submit their recommendations to it. In the meantime we do not consider in the light of all the circumstances known to us that public controversy as to action in hypothetical contingencies would serve the interest of peace or of Canadian or Commonwealth unity. It will have been noted that the Government of the United Kingdom, striving for peace, and knowing the situation, have considered it desirable to exercise restraint in any public statements at this stage regarding the course to be taken if peace fails. I am sure that all Canadians will join with me in the fervent hope that the fine endeavours of the British Government to preserve peace will be crowned with complete success.[42]

Privately, Mackenzie King remained optimistic. "Reading the despatches day by day," he wrote to the Minister of Finance, "and between the lines, I believe it will be found that Chamberlain has saved the day."[43] "How grateful I am," he wrote on 20 September to Lord Tweedsmuir, "that Chamberlain went to see Hitler! You may recall how strongly I urged these personal contacts. While it is not yet clear that war will be avoided, it is altogether certain that but for Chamberlain's meeting with Hitler we should all have been in the throes of a world war to-day."[44] And to Vincent Massey the next day: ". . . I do not see how Chamberlain and his colleagues could possibly have managed better than they have. . . ."[45]

III

Diplomatic activity during the days following Chamberlain's return from Berchtesgaden involved the delicate operation of dismembering a state at once an ally and a friend. On 19 September proposals were submitted to Prague by London and Paris suggesting the immediate transfer to Germany of all areas populated by Czechs more than half of whom were of German descent. Further pressure by Britain and France caused the Czechoslovak Government reluctantly to accept these proposals, and to authorize Chamberlain to place them before Hitler at their meeting at Godesberg on 22 September. But when the British Prime Minister confronted the Führer at the Hotel Dresden, he was astonished to find that Hitler now contemptuously rejected the Anglo-French proposals for the peaceful cession of German-speaking areas. He demanded the right to occupy the areas with his troops. In a letter sent across the Rhine to Hitler's quarters the next day, Chamberlain replied that public opinion in his own country and in France could never accept such an arrangement. Hitler's response was an abusive communication threatening war. Chamberlain thereupon asked for a memorandum embodying Germany's proposals which he could place before his colleagues in London. He received from the Führer that night a demand for the evacuation of Czechoslovak citizens from German-speaking parts of their country by 28 September. Chamberlain, apparently for the first time throughout this trying confrontation, lost his temper and, as he later reported to the House of Commons, told Hitler "with all the emphasis at my command" of "the risks which were incurred by insisting on such terms, and on the terrible consequences of war if a war ensued."[46] Hitler agreed to extend his deadline to 1 October, on which date, he declared, his troops would enter Czechoslovakia if the desired evacuation had not taken place. The next morning, on 24 September, Chamberlain returned to London.

Before meeting with his cabinet, the Prime Minister sought the views of the dominion governments. The high commissioners gathered with Malcolm MacDonald, Secretary of State for Dominion Affairs, on 24 September. "All four of the H.C.s (Jordan of N.Z. is at Geneva) take a view on the basic issue rather different from MacDonald's emphasis," Vincent Massey wrote after their meeting. "We are all prepared to pay a higher price for peace than he. The difference is because the Dominions are at the remove further away from Europe, not because our sense of honour is less acute. Bruce . . . feels very strongly that the German proposals *can't* be allowed to be a *casus belli* & says so on behalf of [the Australian] Govt. Te Water [South Africa] & Dulanty [Irish Free State] speak with great vehemence as well. I take the same line . . . as an individual."[47]

While the High Commissioners conferred in London, Mackenzie King was seeking the advice of his principal lieutenant in the cabinet. Ernest Lapointe was then in Geneva. Mackenzie King cabled him to ask his views on the wisdom of making a statement to the effect that the Canadian Government would recommend to Parliament that it should enter the war at Britain's side should Britain decide to fight. Lapointe's reply is of the greatest importance:

Cannot see that any statement should be made, prior to an outbreak of war. Situation in important parts of Canada extremely delicate and requires most careful handling. Public opinion will have to be prepared, not aroused by irrevocable steps. Australia and New Zealand stand in most different situation. Immediate cause of war namely minority problems in Central Europe not of a nature to enthuse our people. Submit that Parliament should be summoned, if war declared, and no definite commitment made meanwhile. Only yesterday in League of Nations I made statement based on our previous stands and constantly expressed policy that any decision on the part of Canada to participate in war would have to be taken by the Parliament of Canada in the light of existing circumstances.

I do not see how I could advise any course of action that would not only be opposed to personal convictions and sacred pledges to my own people but would destroy all their confidence and prevent me from carrying weight and influence with them for what might be essential future actions. Please consider these views and submit them to colleagues before reaching final decision. God help you. I still strongly feel that conflagration shall be avoided.[48]

The British Government was now not so optimistic. The Canadian High Commissioner, with other dominion high commissioners, met with Neville Chamberlain on the evening of 26 September. The Prime Minister, Vincent Massey reported to Ottawa, seemed to be convinced that Hitler's ambitions were more far-reaching than he had hitherto been led to believe. "I gathered," Massey wrote in his diary, "that he had reluctantly come to the conclusion that Hitler's profession of limited objectives was not sincere & that his ambitions were far wider than the boundaries of Sudetenland."[49] But still the dominions (always excepting New Zealand) continued to preach appeasement. "Chamberlain is as anxious as any of us," Massey wrote after the meeting, "not to allow a matter of method to be the cause of a world war but he has an inflexible sense of principle & a principle he feels is now at stake. Is it quite so clear as that?"[50] And at a meeting with the Dominions Secretary the next day, the high commissioners made it "clear for ourselves (& some spoke for their Governments) that there might be a dangerous reaction in the Dominions to a decision to plunge the Empire into war on the issue of how Hitler was to take possession of territory already conceded to him in principle."[51]

On the evening of 27 September, Neville Chamberlain spoke to the British people over the radio: "How horrible, fantastic, incredible it is that we should be digging trenches and fitting gas-masks because of a quarrel in a far away country. . . . However much one may sympathize with a small nation confronted by a big and powerful nation, we cannot in all circumstances undertake to involve the whole British Empire in a war simply on that account. If we have to fight, it must be on larger issues than that."[52] The issue of principle evidently had vanished overnight. The Canadian Government issued a statement expressing its "complete accord with the statement Mr. Chamberlain has made to the world today."

In the course of his radio address, Chamberlain had indicated his willingness "to pay even a third visit to Germany if I thought it would do any good." Hours later a letter from Hitler was delivered to him from the German Embassy, conciliatory in tone. Chamberlain drafted an immediate reply stating that he was prepared to negotiate in person to preserve the peace. Hitler's response was delivered in the most dramatic of all possible circumstances—in a note passed to the Prime Minister while he was recounting the events of the past few days to the House of Commons. The note announced an invitation to meet at Munich on the morrow. "Signor Mussolini has accepted," Chamberlain told the House, "and I have no doubt M. Daladier will also accept. I need not say what my answer will be."[53] During the next forty-eight hours, the policy of appeasement was to be consummated—to the almost universal acclaim of the people of Great Britain, the dominions, and the world.

The news of Chamberlain's invitation to Munich was received by Mackenzie King with feelings of joy and relief scarcely less than those experienced by Neville Chamberlain himself. He thought himself, indeed, in no small degree responsible for the fortunate outcome (as it then appeared) to the desperately anxious events of the past fortnight. "I cannot but believe," he wrote on 29 September, "that to-day's negotiation will open a path to appeasement of the European situation. I am not permitting my mind to entertain any other thought. . . . I shall always feel that that visit [Mackenzie King's visit to Hitler in 1937] was not without its relationship with subsequent interviews between Hitler and Halifax, and later, between Hitler and Chamberlain. I did my utmost at the time to remove distrust, and to establish confidence, in Hitler's mind, of the purpose of the British Government."[54] The message addressed by him that day to Chamberlain, and simultaneously made public, was more unstinting in its praise of British policy than any Canadian prime minister had ever been before:

> The heart of Canada is rejoicing tonight at the success which has crowned your unremitting efforts for peace. May I convey to you the warm congratulations of the Canadian people, and with them, an expression of their gratitude, which is felt from one end of the Dominion to the other. My colleagues in the Government join with me in unbounded admiration at the service you have rendered mankind. Your achievements in the past month alone will ensure you an abiding and illustrious place among the great conciliators whom the United Kingdom, the British Commonwealth of Nations and the whole world will continue to honour. On the very brink of chaos, with passions flaming, and armies marching, the voice of Reason has found a way out of the conflict which no people in their heart desired, but none seemed able to avert. A turning point in the world's history will be reached if, as we hope, tonight's agreement means a halt to the mad race of arms, and a new start in building the partnership of all peoples. May you have health and strength to carry your great work to its completion.[55]

It did not take long to complete. The terms by which peace was for the moment preserved required the dismemberment of the Czechoslovak state in a fashion not greatly different from that demanded by Hitler at Godesberg a fortnight earlier and at that time angrily rejected by Chamberlain. Hitler was allowed his military occupation, but on the instalment plan, not all at once. The boundaries were to be fixed by an international commission which, in the event, proved pliant enough to suit the Nazis' requirements. The word "Munich" has entered the vocabulary of politics as a synonym for a spineless and shameless surrender of the rights of small nations in the unenlightened self-interest of larger nations unwilling and unready to make the necessary sacrifices themselves. It is an entirely appropriate usage.

IV

The response of Canada to the Munich settlement was overwhelmingly favourable; and it is not hard to see why this should have been so. If it was "horrible, fantastic, incredible" for the British people to contemplate going to war in defence of "a far away country," how much more so for "a French-Canadian habitant, a Maritime fisherman, or a Saskatchewan wheat farmer"?[56] The acclaim which greeted Chamberlain on his return from Munich was shared by Mackenzie King for having helped keep his country out of war. "I have not met a single person," a French-speaking member of Parliament wrote to his Prime Minister after the terms of the Munich Agreement became known, "either French or English who did not approve the attitude you took in the crisis."[57] But again the voice of J. W. Dafoe struck a discordant note in the chorus of praise. The most famous of his editorials enquired, on 3 October 1938, "What's the Cheering For?"

The doctrine that Germany can intervene for racial reasons for the "protection" of Germans on such grounds as she thinks proper in any country in the world which she is in a position to coerce, and without regard to any engagements she has made or guarantees she has given has now not only been asserted but made good: and it has been approved, sanctioned, certified and validated by the governments of Great Britain and France, who had undertaken in this respect to speak for the democracies of the world. This is the situation: and those who think it is all right will cheer for it.[58]

History is hard enough without going in for hypothetical history. But one brief excursion may be taken here. Had Germany struck at Czechoslovakia, France marched to the aid of her ally, and Britain rallied to France, what would Canada have done in the fall of 1938?

It was rumoured at the time that had Britain become embroiled in war over Czechoslovakia, "Mr. King was prepared to call Parliament within two weeks and submit to it a policy of Canadian participation."[59] This report was accurate in all respects save the degree of unanimity with which it stated the members of the cabinet were prepared to endorse such a policy. Mackenzie King wrote, some years afterwards: "I had . . . made up my mind to advocate Canada's immediate participation, but I know I should have had at that time, instead of a unanimous parliament at my back, a House of Commons and a Senate each of which would have been wholly divided." The justification of Munich, he believed in retrospect, was that it provided the time needed to make the issues clear. "But for that extra year there would have been divided councils everywhere."[60]

Mackenzie King, then, was ready to recommend to Parliament a policy of participation in the war, should it have come to war; and it is likely that Parliament would have endorsed the policy, though with many dissenting voices, chiefly from Quebec. Had too many dissented, the policy might have been modified to one of qualified participation; such a course had indeed been urged upon Mackenzie King by Loring Christie, second only to Skelton in the Department of External Affairs.*

But while Mackenzie King had made up his mind to recommend a policy of Canadian participation in the event of Britain's involvement in a war over Czechoslovakia, it was an eventuality that he could only with the greatest difficulty begin to contemplate. His utter relief at learning of the outcome of the Munich conference was, as his own words make clear, at least as much due to his having been spared the ordeal of so grave a test of his powers of leadership as to the world having been spared a war. "The probability of having to meet Parliament with Europe at war," he wrote on 1 October, "was a nightmare. However, we had everything in readiness, and I believe I would have found it possible to keep the Cabinet united though Heaven alone knows to what discussions, in and out of Parliament, the whole business might have led."[61]

*In a paper written on 8 September 1938, Christie posed the problem of Canada's being drawn into war over the Sudetenland and recommended, in that eventuality, the following courses of action:

"To preserve the greatest caution and slowness, realizing there is for Canada no strategic necessity for rapid mobilizations or other action.

"To give no lead to take the people into Europe, but in effect, like the managing minds in Great Britain at present, to take the line which means resisting the war party as far and as long as possible, leaving the thing to develop, if it has to, on the basis of their successive pressures and responsibilities.

"To make it clear, as unequivocally as possible, that Canada does not accept this European preventive war conception in whatever she does.

"To make it clear that Canada is not a participant in the same sense or on the same kind of unlimited scale as the European Allies, but is only what for short may be called an 'associate'—a North American associate.

"To sign no instrument of alliance or commitment to make war or peace all together, and to accept no agreement, declaration or instrument which in any degree limits Canada's freedom of action as regards peace terms or any other aspect of the hostilities.

"To make no statements or declarations in Parliament or otherwise, or be responsible for any propaganda or arguments, that would compromise any aspect of the position and freedom of action as above postulated.

"On such lines," Christie concluded, "there might be some chance—though a slight one—of maintaining something like national unity, of mitigating in some degree the violation done to the French Canadians and the other English speaking elements . . . , and of managing to bring out of the catastrophe a Canadian community with capacity for eventual self-healing and survival as a prosperous and not wholly negligible member of the North American homeland." ("Notes on the Canadian Position in the Event of a German-Czech Conflict involving Great Britain," 8 Sept. 1938, Christie Papers.)

O. D. Skelton, who wanted Canada to stay neutral in September 1939, was not likely to have advocated participation in war in September 1938. Of Munich he was not wholly uncritical: "The settlement," he wrote, "if it can be called a settlement, is not one that can bring pride or satisfaction to anyone in the civilized countries, but I certainly think it the lesser of the evils." (Skelton to Massey, 8 Oct. 1938, Massey Papers.)

AT THE ELEVENTH HOUR

Within six months the Munich settlement lay in ruins. On 14 and 15 March, Hitler sent German troops into Prague. What had been left to Czechoslovakia by the four European powers was seized by force for the Third Reich. There was no question this time of reclaiming Germans for Germany. Of justification there could be none, and there was none. Neville Chamberlain was aghast. The assumptions of appeasement— that there was some justice to the German case, some limit to Hitler's appetite—could no longer be accepted as valid. All this he conceded in a speech at Birmingham on 17 March. "Germany," he declared, "under her present régime has sprung a series of unpleasant surprises upon the world: the Rhineland, the Austrian *Anschluss*, the severence of Sudetenland." In each case, while objection could be taken to the method, there was something to be said for change. "But the events which have taken place this week in complete disregard of the principles laid down by the German Government itself seem to fall into a different category and they must cause us all to be asking ourselves: Is this the end of an old adventure or is it the beginning of a new?"[62]

The events of March 1939 marked a turning point in the attitude of the British Government towards Nazi Germany. Appeasement had failed. Hitler had shown, by his destruction of the rump Czechoslovak Republic, that he could not be trusted. The British guarantees to Poland and Rumania followed.

They marked as well a turning point in the relations between Mackenzie King and Neville Chamberlain. For whereas Chamberlain abandoned appeasement, Mackenzie King remained a true believer. His confidence in Hitler had been shaken less than his confidence in Chamberlain. And whatever confidence in Chamberlain remained, Skelton did his best to shake. "Mr. Chamberlain's personality and convictions," Skelton wrote to the Prime Minister two or three days after the Birmingham speech,

have become a vital factor in the situation. His speeches carry weight because they make clear his simplicity, sincerity, courage and genuine desire for peace. But he has other qualities which make it dangerous to give him a blank cheque. He is self-confident to the point of arrogance, intolerant of criticism, and at the moment sore because he thinks in the eyes of the world Hitler made a fool of him. . . . He is also a Chamberlain, born and bred in a Tory imperialist school, and cannot imagine that any part of the British Empire has any choice but to halt when he says halt and march when he says march. . . .[63]

The tougher approach towards Germany taken by Chamberlain during the spring and summer of 1939 was not welcomed by the Canadian Prime Minister. "He is not in sympathy with recent policies," L. B. Pearson wrote on 16 July, after spending an evening with Mackenzie King at Kingsmere, "and prefers Chamberlain the appeaser to Chamberlain the avenger."[64]

On 20 March 1939 Mackenzie King delivered a brief statement on the European situation in the House of Commons. He began with the frank admission that "the form and place of the latest disturbance was a surprise to me," as it had been to "many governments more nearly concerned and more minutely informed." He characterized the "disturbance" as "a wanton and forcible occupation": unlike "some of the earlier manoeuvres" it could not be defended as "reactions against excessive terms of the treaty of Versailles" or as a legitimate application of the principle of national self-determination. But it was by no means clear what the democracies should do next. Time was required to "sift rumour from fact." Then followed what has been described as Mackenzie King's "most positive declaration since he assumed office in 1935 of willingness to participate in a European war."[65]

If there were a prospect of an aggressor launching an attack on Britain, with bombers raining death on London, I have no doubt what the decision of the Canadian people and Parliament would be. We would regard it as an act of aggression, menacing freedom in all parts of the British Commonwealth.

But, he added, "if it were a case . . . of a dispute over trade, or prestige in some far corner of the world, that would raise quite different considerations."[66] The speech was not particularly well received in the Dominion. The French-language press attacked it as too provocative and interventionist; some newspapers in the rest of Canada attacked it as too flaccid and indecisive. It did not escape attention in Berlin, where the *Berliner Börsenzeitung* for 21 March ran an accurate account under the heading: "Cool Wind from Canada: Mackenzie King and the London Intriguers."

Ten days later, the Prime Minister again spoke to Parliament on external affairs, this time at greater length than in his speech on 20 March. Much of what he said took the form of a review, and a justification, of the events which had led to the Munich settlement. "Mr. Chamberlain," Mackenzie King declared, "made the emphatically right choice in striving to prevent the outbreak of war. It required unusual courage, disregard of risks to his personal prestige, prompt decision and dogged persistence to carry through those last fortnight efforts for peace. Mr. Chamberlain never lost his patience, his temper or his head." Of the

Munich settlement itself, Mackenzie King conceded that the price paid for peace had been high—"it could not have been otherwise after the events of recent years"—but well worth it. "There are some people, both in Canada and abroad, who are continually asserting that war between the democratic and the totalitarian powers is only postponed, and that, when it comes, the forces of democracy will be weaker than they were in 1938." He himself could not share that view. "It must have taken a good deal of confidence in one's powers of guessing the future, to be sufficiently certain of what might happen in 1940 to have been ready to plunge the world into war in 1938. Most inevitable wars have never happened. . . ." Mackenzie King recited, without comment, the events which had led, within the last fortnight, to the process by which "Slovakia was made a protectorate of Germany." He explained why the government of Canada had refused, and would continue to refuse, to "say here and now that Canada is prepared to support whatever may be proposed by the Government at Westminster," should Britain become involved in war. "The international situation changes from year to year, sometimes from week to week; governments change, their personnel changes, policies change. Absolute statements of policy, absolute undertakings to follow other governments, whatever the situation, are out of the question." And even if there was a general will to give such undertakings—which there was not—it would lie beyond Canadian capacities to give them:

. . . what amount of knight errantry abroad do our resources permit? Canada . . . is not a country of unlimited powers; it has not the capacity to stand indefinite strains. We have tremendous tasks to do at home, in housing the people, in caring for the aged and helpless, in relieving drought and unemployment, in building roads, in meeting our heavy burden of debt, in making provision for Canada's defence, and in bringing our standards of living and civilization to the levels our knowledge now makes possible. There is no great margin of realizable wealth for this purpose; we must, to a greater or less extent, choose between keeping our own house in order, and trying to save Europe and Asia. The idea that every twenty years this country should automatically and as a matter of course take part in a war overseas for democracy or self-determination of other small nations, that a country which has all it can do to run itself should feel called upon to save, periodically, a continent that cannot run itself, and to these ends risk the lives of its people, risk bankruptcy and political disunion, seems to many a nightmare and sheer madness.[67]

Mackenzie King's speech of 30 March was intended, in part, to remove any impression conveyed by his speech of 20 March that the Government had drawn any closer than formerly to a policy of automatic participation in British wars. It had that effect. The speech was particularly well received in Quebec, where opinion (as noted above) had been hostile to the earlier statement. The former premier of the province, L. A. Taschereau, wrote to the Prime Minister on 1 April to congratulate him "on your recent great speech. You have no idea of the wonderful effect it had to clarify the situation. There was much uneasiness among our young friends: I believe they are now satisfied."[68]

II

On 1 February, six weeks before the destruction of Czechoslovakia, Mackenzie King had written the following letter to Hitler:

On many occasions, I have thought of sending you a letter to recall our meeting and some of the views expressed in conversation at the time [of their meeting in June 1937]. Oftener, I have wished that other of the public men of our day might have a like opportunity of exchanging views with you on some of the world's most pressing problems, and gain for themselves, as I did, first-hand impressions.

In expressing to you my thanks for the many courtesies extended me in the course of my visit to Berlin, I said, if I recollect aright, in a letter I wrote to you from Brussels [on 1 July 1937], that I believed you could do more than any other man living to help your own and other countries along the path of peace and progress. These words, I believe, are even truer today than they were when I wrote to you a year and a half ago.

I have never wavered in my conviction that to save your people and your country from destruction was the purpose that lay dearest to your heart; also that you believed that war between the great powers of Europe would lead to a condition of anarchy which would mean the ultimate destruction of the nations concerned, regardless of the circumstances which might have occasioned it. On the other hand, I have felt that you believed equally with me that what, in one country, by way of increase in human well-being might be gained through constructive effort would, in the course of time, come to be the portion of other countries as well.

I think I know something of how many and conflicting are the voices that seek to influence your judgment and direct your decisions. I have always, therefore, been comforted in thought when I have read of your being at your mountain retreat at Berchtesgaden, knowing, as I do, how greatly the quiet and companionship of Nature helps to restore to the mind its largest and clearest vision.

The purpose, therefore, of this letter is just to recall to your memory the conversation we had together, and to express anew the hope that regardless of what others may wish, or say, or do, you will, above all else, hold firm to the resolve not to let anything imperil or destroy what you have already accomplished, particularly for those whose lives are lived in humble circumstances. If you would not think it too presumptuous on my part, I should like even more to say how much I hope that you will think not only of the good you can do for those of your own country, but that you will remember, as well, the good that you can do to the entire world.

You will, I know, accept this letter in the spirit in which it is written—an expression of the faith I have in the purpose you have at heart, and of the friendship with yourself which you have been so kind as to permit me to share.[69]

The Führer did not accept this letter in the spirit in which it was written; indeed he did not accept it at all. The German Consul-General in Ottawa, to whom Mackenzie King had given the letter for delivery (the Consul, Erich Windels, was returning to Berlin from Ottawa on leave), was informed by a senior official at the Foreign Ministry that Hitler no longer regarded the Prime Minister of Canada as *persona grata*; the Führer, he was told, had been vexed at not having received a New Year's greeting from Mackenzie King, and had construed this as a diplomatic snub. Windels then left the letter for delivery through routine channels. Back in Canada after some weeks' absence, the Consul-General inquired whether the letter had reached Hitler, and was informed that it had, though it had not been acknowledged. The lack of acknowledgment had been due, so the Foreign Ministry explained, to an oversight.*

Eventually Hitler replied to Mackenzie King's letter, by means of a message transmitted by the Consul-General. It conveyed a personal invitation from the Führer to "a number of Canadian students and officers" to visit Germany for three weeks as guests of the Third Reich. "The guests are to establish contact with similar German circles during their stay in Germany, becoming acquainted at the same time with institutions in the most varied fields, which will convey to them an impressive picture of Greater Germany's newly-won strength and its will to peaceable constructive work."[70]

This message reached Mackenzie King on 21 July. During the previous three weeks, Anglo-German relations had deteriorated still further. There was talk—which filled Mackenzie King with horror—of bringing Winston Churchill and Anthony Eden into the British cabinet. The so-called "Free City" of Danzig, by now completely nazified, was being used by Hitler to provoke the people and Government of Poland. Senator Dandurand, a member of the cabinet, had written to Mackenzie King

---

*This account follows an article by Dr. Paul Schwarz, published in the *Staats-Zeitung und Herold* (a German-language newspaper of New York City), 28 Jan. 1948. From this article, which was written in German, it would appear that the author was a close friend of Erich Windels, the former Consul-General in Ottawa, and that he had obtained his information from him.

on 1 July to say that "We should certainly not be drawn into a conflict arising out of a 'putsch' in that German city," and wondered if the Canadian Government should not advise the British Government to that effect. "I have no faith in Col. Beck," Dandurand declared, "and yet we would be at his mercy or call in a world conflict."[71] Mackenzie King had read Dandurand's letter to his colleagues. "We all concluded," he wrote afterwards, "it would be wiser not to depart from our present policy of not tendering advice until requested to do so, more particularly where the matter referred to has become a *fait accompli*, as I am afraid has been the case in practically all the more important decisions which have been made."[72]

Arriving as it did in the midst of these events, Hitler's invitation appeared to Mackenzie King to be not only (as he wrote to Chamberlain) significant and sincere but as evidence of those "unseen forces," that invisible hand, which the Prime Minister of Canada increasingly believed to be in charge of the world's destiny, and of his own.* He promptly attached the greatest importance to it. Here was an opportunity to practise appeasement at the eleventh hour, and to vindicate it in the eyes of its detractors. He immediately accepted the invitation, telling the Consul-General that he should like to be a member of the visiting party himself. His only concern was the timing of the visit, in relation to the general election which he planned to call that fall. This consideration proved decisive. Mackenzie King determined to arrange the visit in November 1939, by which time he expected a general election to have come and gone and his own mandate to have been renewed. In this decision, the invisible hand does seem to have been at work, and to have worked well; for had Mackenzie King set out with the party as planned, the Prime Minister of Canada, together with a dozen leading Canadians, might have spent the war in an internment camp. It does not seem to have crossed Mackenzie King's mind that precisely this may have been the object of Hitler's invitation in the first instance; although he did write, on 20 November 1939, that "the subtle deceit of the whole Nazi regime surpasses, I believe, anything of the kind in history."[73]

---

*The extent of Mackenzie King's dependence upon spiritualism and other occult practices, and the manner of their influence upon his decisions, is candidly discussed by his biographer. See H. Blair Neatby, *William Lyon Mackenzie King*, vol. II, *The Lonely Heights, 1924–1932* (Toronto, 1963), pp. 403–8. Dr. Neatby puts the matter in a nutshell: "Mackenzie King was influenced by the unseen world to the extent that when he had spiritual confirmation he was less likely to be swayed by mortal colleagues. When the voices did not confirm his own judgment, they were truly immaterial." (*Ibid.*, p. 408).

III

Time, though running out, permitted Mackenzie King a final flurry of pleading with the Axis for reason and restraint. On 25 August, he began to draft a message to Hitler to be added to the frantic communications even then descending upon the Führer from agitated leaders throughout the world, among them Chamberlain, Roosevelt, Daladier, the King of the Belgians (writing on behalf of the Scandinavian powers), and the Pope. That afternoon he read the text of his proposed message to the cabinet, some of whose members were not greatly impressed, and later in the day summoned the German Consul-General. Windels listened as Mackenzie King read the draft, and then commented that it would be well received only if a similar communication were sent to the Government of Poland. Mackenzie King accepted this advice.[74] Two messages, in identical terms, were accordingly transmitted to Hitler and to M. Ignace Moscicki, the President of Poland. They read as follows:

The people of Canada are of one mind in believing that there is no international problem which cannot be settled by conference and negotiation. They equally believe that force is not a substitute for reason, and that the appeal to force as a means of adjusting international differences defeats rather than furthers the end of justice. They are prepared to join what authority and power they may possess to that of the other nations of the British Commonwealth in seeking a just and equitable settlement of the great problems with which nations are faced.

On behalf of the Canadian people, but equally in the interests of humanity itself, I join with those of other countries and powers who have appealed to you, in the firm hope that your great power and authority will be used to prevent impending catastrophe by having recourse to every possible peaceful means to effect a solution of the momentous issues of this period of transition and change in world affairs.[75]

The message to Hitler, though acknowledged, produced no reply. The message to the Polish President produced a justifiably acidulous rejoinder: "The Government of Poland appreciates the efforts of the Prime Minister of Canada for maintaining of the peace and is sure that the Canadian Government has no doubts as to the fact that it is not the Government of Poland who makes the aggressive demands and provokes the international crisis."[76] In passing this message to Mackenzie King, Skelton commented that "reading between the lines, the Poles may possibly seem to be a little nettled by having been sent a message identical with that sent to Hitler." But Mackenzie King rejected this interpretation.

"The reply," he wrote, "seems to me the natural one for the Polish Government to have made. It is a simple statement of fact helping to make clear Poland's position in her own eyes."[77]

Mackenzie King also despatched an appeal for peace to Mussolini. Il Duce replied: "I shall leave untried no effort to safeguard the peace of the world—a lasting peace that is a just peace."[78] This message greatly gratified its recipient.

The last of Mackenzie King's interventions on behalf of peace went unfulfilled. On 26 August, it occurred to him that an appeal by King George VI to Hitler might succeed where the appeals of governments had failed. He at once elaborated this suggestion in a message to Neville Chamberlain, pointing out that the King should speak out "in the interests of humanity as being above all nations." It would be desirable, he suggested, that in the appeal "the King associate with himself Her Majesty the Queen in a special appeal on behalf of women and children who, if war breaks out, will become in many countries the innocent victims." As a final inducement to negotiation at the eleventh hour, Mackenzie King suggested that the King and Queen could themselves become the agents of appeasement. "If thought advisable, it might be added by the King and Queen that there is no service which it is possible for them to render which they would not be prepared to give to help remove from the mind of Herr Hitler and the German people any sense of injustice with respect to matters which they believe to be affecting adversely relations of Germany with other nations."[79] The British Prime Minister had the delicate task of conveying to Mackenzie King that his government did not think well of the suggestion.

IV

Empire and Reich

By 1937, Mackenzie King had so far overcome his distaste for imperial policies made in Downing Street as to lend his, and Canada's, support to Britain's appeasement of the Nazis. But in matters of defence his distrust of centralized control persisted. He opposed attempts to create a deterrent of imperial power against aggression. He rebuffed efforts to work with the United Kingdom militarily and industrially in advance of war.

Canada's influence on Britain's policies could therefore not have been less helpful. In external affairs, what was most needed at this juncture was diversity, not unity; heresy, not orthodoxy—"not a greater consensus of Commonwealth opinion but the more vigorous expression of independent and conflicting opinion."[1] In defence affairs, what was most needed was co-operation, not non-co-operation; compliance in a common cause, not a stubborn reassertion of autonomists' rights. Canada's response to the menace of the Axis was to voice with unaccustomed fervour her approval of appeasement, while resisting improvements in imperial defence. It brought the worst of both worlds.

DOWNING STREET DOMINATED: MACKENZIE KING VINDICATED?

The debate on defence estimates in the House of Commons in February 1937 provided the Prime Minister with an opportunity to still apprehensions, more acute among his own parliamentary following than anywhere, that the impending Imperial Conference would be the scene of a surrender to the centralists. There would be, he said, no such surrender. He conceded that attempts might be made at the Conference to commit the dominions to projects of imperial defence; but he assured the House that any such attempts would be doomed to fail. "Every government," he declared, "is responsible for the attitude that it takes at an Imperial Conference, and I wish to say, here and now, that the attitude which this present administration will take at the forthcoming Imperial Conference is that which it has taken at every other conference, namely, that it is not in a position to bind Canada to anything." He quoted from the defence resolution of the Imperial Conference of 1923, which asserted "the primary responsibility of each portion of the Empire . . . for its own defence"; and from that of the Imperial Conference of 1926, which affirmed that "neither Great Britain nor the Dominions could be committed to the acceptance of active obligations, except with the definite assent of their own governments"—resolutions of which he was principally the author. He then uttered a promise without precedent: "I will guarantee that there shall be no resolution that will go further than either of these with respect to any demand on Canada at the forthcoming Imperial Conference."[2]

The defence debate was not long over before the Canadian government was provided with what it chose to regard as evidence that authorities in the United Kingdom were planning to enlist the support of the dominions in projects of imperial defence. Towards the end of March, there arrived in Ottawa, and in other dominion capitals, a paper of the Chiefs of Staff Sub-Committee of the Committee of Imperial Defence. In this document, the Imperial Chiefs set out a recommended foreign policy for each of the dominions, to be sustained by its respective armed forces; they examined the strategic aspects of several hypothetical wars (against Germany, Italy, and Japan) which, while hypothetical, were deemed so likely to occur as to make speedy preparation for them essential; they summarized the main features of the British rearmament programme; and they advanced a number of suggestions as to how each of the dominions might best co-operate with the United Kingdom in readying the Empire for the coming conflict.

It would be hard to exaggerate the consternation with which this document was received when word of it reached the Department of External Affairs at Ottawa and, through the Department, the Prime Minister. It would be hard to say which of its offensive features—its constitutional impropriety or its strategic conceptions—created the greater consternation. "Is it for the military staff to expound policies?" O. D. Skelton inquired rhetorically as soon as he had perused the paper. "Is it not for the civil arm of government to lay down the scheme of policy and liabilities, and then for the military to submit military plans accordingly?"[3] With this assessment Mackenzie King could not have been in greater agreement. He determined then and there to put a stop to the exchange of military opinion which had passed in the guise of military information. He instructed the Minister of National Defence to examine recent correspondence between the Department of National Defence and the Imperial General Staff to see whether the practice was harmful and should therefore cease.

The correspondence in question consisted of what was known as "the liaison letters." Such letters had been exchanged without interruption (except during the Great War) since 1910 between the General Staff at Ottawa and the Imperial General Staff in London. By 1935 the practice had become known to, and was resented by, the senior officers of the Department of External Affairs, in spite of efforts by the military to convince them that there was nothing sinister about it.* It had also attracted the hostile attention of intellectuals and others outside government circles.† For this reason, if for no other, the Government determined to put a stop to it.

The Minister of National Defence was instructed to go through the files. Ian Mackenzie did so, and reported to the Prime Minister that while they contained much useful information, they exhibited a tendency, "especially in the letters of General McNaughton," to refer to the sending of a Canadian expeditionary force in the event of war. Here was the ultimate indiscretion. "The discussion of possible policies in such liaison letters," Mackenzie concluded, "may be fraught with great danger." He recommended that any future correspondence of the kind be conducted through the Department of External Affairs, where it would be more fully in the civilian view.[4]

The cabinet considered and adopted this recommendation, and on its instructions the Chief of the General Staff, Major-General E. C. Ashton, wrote to the Chief of the Imperial General Staff to advise him that their correspondence in future would have to pass through different channels. General Sir Cyril Deverell replied that while he appreciated the reasons for the change in procedure he hoped that it would not mean

---

*"From a casual remark of Mr. Loring Christie (Ext. Affairs)," the Director of Military Operations and Intelligence wrote to the Chief of the General Staff in January 1936, "I obtained the impression that in certain Ministerial minds there lingers the suspicion that the various Chiefs of Staff in the Empire are inclined to commit themselves to policies which, if known to the Government, would be objected to. . . ." Col. Crerar proposed, as a corrective, to show Christie "a couple of C.G.S.—C.I.G.S. liaison letters, just to get a line on their typical contents." "It is a valued direct link," he wrote to him on 14 January, "and one of great value to us" (Crerar Papers). But Christie's misgivings were only reinforced by what he read.

†See *In Defence of Canada*, vol. I, p. 92.

any curtailment in their free exchange of views. The liaison letters, he wrote, were "merely a demi-official exchange of military information and ideas between different branches of the same staff, and are recognized as such." He proposed to continue addressing his letters to his counterpart in Ottawa, as to those in the other dominion capitals; he did not see how he could properly alter the system without their consent. He would, of course, have no objection if his letters were shown to the Department of External Affairs.[5] This reply General Ashton duly passed on to the Minister of National Defence, with the observation that it appeared eminently satisfactory to him.[6]

But it was not eminently satisfactory to the Canadian Government. Mackenzie King proposed that the question should be discussed by the members of the Government then present in London for the Imperial Conference. A meeting was held, as the result of which Ian Mackenzie was told to inform the Chief of the General Staff that the Canadian ministers did not approve of General Deverell's suggestion, and that the procedure previously endorsed by the Canadian Government would be the one in future adhered to.[7]

The very fact that the British military had taken upon itself the task of advising the Canadian Government what it ought to be doing in matters of imperial defence was thus enough to produce a sense of outrage among its ministers and its civil advisers. But the substance of its recommendations added insult to injury. For Skelton, the substance of the Chiefs of Staff's proposals was even more objectionable than their procedure. He set to work, with the Prime Minister's approval, on a set of counter-proposals, points which might be made in a statement of the Canadian position at the forthcoming Imperial Conference. They emerged as follows:

In a statement of the Canadian position, it might be thought desirable:

(1) To refer to the increased provision being made for Canada's defence.

(2) To reiterate our belief in the League of Nations, on a basis of conciliation, not of coercion.

(3) To show that just as the United Kingdom is influenced by geographical factors in its policy, e.g., making commitments to France but none to Czechoslovakia or Russia or China, so Canada is influenced by its geographical position, its distance from Europe and Asia, and its nearness to the United States.

(4) To emphasize that the task facing Canada in developing and unifying this half continent, with its vast distances, its varied economic interests and racial composition, is analogous to the task of keeping the countries in the similar area called Europe in peace and order, and that we will be lucky if we can do our job without undertaking to do Europe's job also.

(5) To show that our nearness to the United States besides making our

people susceptible to currents of isolationist feeling now sweeping that country, involves serious problems through the interlocking of our industrial systems, and our dependence on the United States for much raw material and semi-finished material essential to our production; and that labour organization relations in peacetime and the possible war-time reactions if we use United States materials to manufacture and ship munitions which the United States itself has embargoed, require the most serious considerations— along with other factors of which neither the Foreign Secretary nor the Chiefs of Staff in the United Kingdom are apparently in the least aware.

(6) That while defence preparations must be recognized as inescapable in the circumstances which have arisen, they cannot be regarded as offering any permanent solution, and will in fact perpetuate unrest and bring in universal bankruptcy, and that accordingly efforts should be made at economic appeasement—fight war hysteria through returning economic prosperity.[8]

On 15 April, Mackenzie King read to the cabinet the paper sent to the Canadian Government by the Committee of Imperial Defence, and read as well the comments Skelton had prepared as rebuttal. Skelton's point of view found general acceptance. The delegation to the Imperial Conference, the Prime Minister warned, would have to fight the same battle "that every Liberal Government had had to fight at every Conference in Great Britain . . . [It] would have a very unpleasant and difficult time in dealing with that aspect of the situation."

II

The attitude of the Canadian Government towards imperial defence, determined before the delegation set sail for London towards the end of April, was faithfully reflected in the statement delivered on its behalf by the Minister of National Defence at the fifth meeting of Principal Delegates held on 24 May.

Ian Mackenzie had been preceded by Sir Thomas Inskip, the holder of the newly created portfolio of Co-ordinator of Defence in the British Government. Inskip told the delegates that his Government had no reason to conceal how gravely it regarded the international scene, nor how much it was counting on the dominions to help pull it through. He would proceed on the assumption that their representatives had come to London to learn how they could help. He then told them very frankly what Britain required, following closely the argument of the Chiefs of Staff Committee to which all the dominion governments had already been exposed. First and foremost were munitions. American neutrality legislation meant that the United Kingdom could not obtain necessary supplies from the United States; the British Government therefore regarded Canada, with its available industrial plant and its comparative isolation from probable theatres of war, as the prime alternative supplier. Next to munitions, foodstuffs. Here again Canada was crucial.

It was an invitation to the dance. But it became clear before Ian Mackenzie had spoken at any length that the Canadians were going to sit it out. Mackenzie began by reviewing Canada's position on defence questions at all the preceding Colonial and Imperial Conferences from 1887 to 1930, so as to show that Canada had consistently opposed imperial policies based on the principle of dominion contributions to the defence of Empire. "The emphatic attitude of Macdonald in the Sudan incident; of Laurier on the Naval issue; of Mackenzie King in relation to the Chanak incident, concluding in the famous Balfour formula of the 1926 Conference, well illustrated the development of the Canadian viewpoint." Then followed a detailed review of what the Liberal Government had accomplished since 1935 to improve the efficiency of the three fighting arms. Next came an analysis of Canadian public opinion. Five schools of thought were distinguished: the imperialists, or "ready, aye ready" Canadians, content to follow Britain in peace or in war; the isolationists "who held that Canada's geographical position and economic interest required that she should dissociate herself from responsibility for troubles in other parts of the world, especially Great Britain's European complications and her Imperial commitments . . ."; League collectivists, avid for collective security under the Covenant; "American or North American collectivists who would have Canada join the Pan American Union . . ."; and, finally, "the moderate or Middle group which believed in no automatic commitments either for military action or for neutrality." This last group, Mackenzie declared, "acted on the formula that 'Parliament will decide.' " It represented the point of view with which the Canadian Government was itself in sympathy. It constituted the largest sector of Canadian public opinion. Mackenzie concluded his statement with the following proposition:

1. Canadian public opinion supported the present defence policy of the Government of Canada.

2. Canadian public opinion would not, under present conditions, support any larger appropriations than those voted this year by Parliament.

3. Canadian public opinion was definitely opposed to extraneous commitments but was prepared to support a national defence policy for the protection of their coasts and the focal areas of their trade routes. The most important contribution they could render at this time, when dark shadows seem to be hovering over the world, was, as far as possible, to preserve *unity* in their councils; to avoid any possibility of dissension, and to respect the heartfelt opinions and profound convictions of those who might differ from the policies which might, to others, be necessary.[9]

In 1937, as in 1923, the main opposition to the Canadian views on imperial defence was provided by the Australians. The Australian Government, well in advance of the Conference, had sent a statement of their position to London and to the various dominion capitals. It had urged the need for a united Empire effort in defence to meet the common peril, and in particular for drawing up plans for unified policies in naval, air, military, munitions, financial, and supply requirements. By the time of the Conference, this document had acquired an addendum, in the form of a draft resolution on imperial defence; this the Australian delegation wished to include in the final report of the Conference, as intact as might prove possible.

The Canadians were not convinced by the Australians' arguments. Their paper, wrote Loring Christie contemptuously on 31 May, "resorts to incantation. . . . The effort is to produce something that looks like meeting the military and totalitarian powers on their own ground—to parade the British Commonwealth as a single military power—a 'manifestation of solidarity,' in the Australian words, as 'a deterrent to aggression.' "[10] That was not the object of appeasement.

The Australian Minister of Defence, Sir Archdale Parkhill, put his case to the Conference. New Zealand supported the Australian position, South Africa opposed. The lines were now drawn. The battle of the communiqué was about to begin. No one was better prepared for it than Mackenzie King of Canada. There was no more experienced campaigner, anywhere, for that kind of campaign.

III

"Never negotiate on the other fellow's draft." This homily from *The Compleat Diplomatist* had come to be taken seriously by British negotiators at successive Imperial Conferences. Accordingly, on the evening of 9 June, there was delivered to the several delegations to the Imperial Conference of 1937 a lengthy draft document on imperial defence. It was the attempt by the British participants to represent the sense of the meeting in a manner satisfactory to all concerned. As such it did not stand a chance. "The proposed Defence statement came late last night," O. D. Skelton wrote to Mackenzie King the following morning. "The first four pages seem not bad, but the rest is in the best manner of the Committee of Imperial Defence who have prepared it."[11] The draft was to come before the Principal Delegates at a meeting later that day; before it was held, Mackenzie King, Skelton, Christie, and one or two of the cabinet members of the delegation went over it paragraph by paragraph. What emerged was no longer recognizable as the original.

The first of the two meetings at which the British draft underwent its metamorphosis was held in the British Prime Minister's room in the House of Commons; it was convened at 5 p.m., and broke up around 8 p.m. Neville Chamberlain opened the discussion by inquiring if the draft prepared by the United Kingdom delegation was generally acceptable. Sir Archdale Parkhill, for Australia, thought it would serve. Mackenzie King said he had some reservations about the wording of some of the paragraphs. The meeting agreed to take these up seriatim.

Mackenzie King's first objection was to a paragraph in the British draft which, as he said, made it appear that "the United Kingdom were undertaking a supervision over the training and equipment of the whole Empire." He proposed an amendment designed to remove that impression. The Australians preferred the original formulation, as did Neville Chamberlain. When Mackenzie King remarked that the original "rather gave the impression of some central Committee which arranged co-ordination," Sir Archdale Parkhill rejoined that "any such impression would give great satisfaction in Australia." The deadlock was broken by a compromise wording, which retained the Canadian coloration rather than the Australian.

Mackenzie King took similar exception to a paragraph in the British draft regarding the importance of safeguarding "the maritime communications of the Empire." As worded, he remarked, "the original draft tended to suggest the impression of Empire forces, and anything connoting that idea would make it impossible for the Canadian Government to obtain the appropriations they desired for defence purposes. The only way in which these appropriations could be got through Parliament was to make clear that the Canadian forces were for Canadian defence, and that their use anywhere else required the approval of Parliament." Again the Australians said that they preferred the original to the amendment; again the substance of the amendment won the day.

The last paragraph but one in the British draft caused more difficulty, for it more than any of the others had been inserted by its authors to accommodate the Australian point of view. It read as follows:

In the course of their discussions, the Conference found general agreement among their members that while it is the sole responsibility of the several Parliaments of the British Commonwealth to decide the nature and scope of their own defence policy, the security of each member of the Commonwealth can be increased by co-operation so far as each Government and Parliament may be prepared to go in such matters as the free interchange of information concerning the state of their naval, military and air forces, the continuance of arrangements already initiated, for concerting the scale of defences of ports, and measures for co-operation, if and when the Governments of the British Commonwealth may so decide, between the forces of the several members of the Commonwealth in defence of communications and other common interests.

It appeared innocent enough. But Mackenzie King saw it as a timebomb which must be delicately defused. He told the meeting that he and his colleagues desired "to get Parliament to go as far as possible in the direction provided for in this paragraph." But its references to "the continuation of arrangements already initiated" in certain defence matters would be bound to make difficulties. He was afraid, he said, that the paragraph as worded "would arouse suspicions in Canada of agreements and commitments." For this reason he proposed a more innocuous statement. Sir Archdale Parkhill, in a final and perhaps despairing plea to save something of the Australian position, asked the meeting to retain the British version in the original. New Zealand supported him. A compromise was reached by inserting after the words "arrangements already initiated" the phrase "by certain members of the Commonwealth." That was Mackenzie King's doing. He could now reply to any charge that he had violated his promise to Parliament by saying that Canada was not among the "certain members" to which the report made reference.

The final paragraph of the British draft had recited four "facts" which, it was asserted, were to be taken by the Conference as noted and approved. These were: that on many occasions dominion representatives had attended meetings of the Committee of Imperial Defence when defence questions affecting their respective countries were under consideration; that the organization of the Committee of Imperial Defence had been improved, notably in the arrangements made for co-ordination among the three services and defence industry; that defence councils or committees had been established in the dominions; and that the dominions had afforded themselves of the facilities of the Imperial Defence College in London "for the education of officers in the broader aspects of strategy." These "facts," Mackenzie King now proposed, should be deleted from the report. It was getting late; the delegates were due at some banquet or other. It was agreed to hold Mackenzie King's final and most far-reaching amendment over for consideration the next morning. It had been an exhausting and, for some, a trying meeting. "I had to battle my way through the report from beginning to end," Mackenzie King wrote afterwards,

taking exception to words, phrases, clauses, sentences and paragraphs, as we went along. I had to be quite outspoken and say that the whole report would be extremely embarrassing to us but that we recognized that some report must be made, and that what I wished to do was to save pitfalls

which would occasion the British Government as well as all of us, considerable embarrassment later on. . . . Sir Thomas Inskip looked very dour
throughout the whole proceedings, and sought to hold on to different parts.
I met him by changed wording here and there but scored the report heavily
at places, taking out references, for example, to armed forces, and any and
every suggestion of either Commonwealth policy or pre-arranged Commonwealth tactics. . . . It was the hardest battle I have had to fight at the
Conference. . . .[12]

It was not quite over yet. The next morning, 11 June, the Principal
Delegates reassembled in the Prime Minister's chambers and resumed
consideration of Mackenzie King's proposal to omit from the final report
the four "facts" which he had thought better left unstated. Mackenzie
King began by disarming his opposition. He was now prepared, he said,
to make a concession on two of the four. He had no objection to it
being stated in the final report that the dominions had created defence
councils, and were sending their officers to the Imperial Defence College
—provided that these statements were made in the body of the report,
and not left until the end where they would be sure to attract undue
attention and excite undesirable speculation. But he did not want the
report to make reference to the activities of the Committee of Imperial
Defence. He recalled that his predecessor, R. B. Bennett, "had protested
in writing against Canada being represented at the Committee of Imperial Defence. He thought Mr. Bennett had been right, as such representation would create great difficulties in Canada. He wanted to see
defence strengthened and co-operation improved, but the idea of a
Committee in London would be open to strong objection in Canada.
Canada definitely was not represented on the Committee of Imperial
Defence, and he did not want a paragraph which rather suggested that
she was." Savage of New Zealand observed that the delegates were
present at an Imperial Conference and were discussing imperial defence:
"Why this objection to a Committee of Imperial Defence?" But Hertzog
of South Africa, knowing Mackenzie King's position and sensitive to his
difficulties, sided with the Canadians. Certain words and phrases, he
recalled, had always created difficulties at Imperial Conferences:
"Empire" and "Defence Committee" were among them. Better not to
mention them at all. Australia and New Zealand demurred. Each of
these dominions, their spokemen pointed out in turn, was represented
on the Committee of Imperial Defence; each wanted its functions to be
enlarged and strengthened; each insisted that the report should take
note of these important facts. But Mackenzie King persevered and, as
always, in the end prevailed. And, as always, he was convinced that,
in prevailing, he had served the Empire well. After several of the British

delegates had offered their congratulations, he wrote: "I think they were sincere and the remarks of the three of them being so much on similar lines, led me to feel they had been discussing my attitude after last night's meeting, and had come to feel that there was more in it than they had previously foreseen. At any rate, by permitting some parts of the last clauses to be inserted elsewhere in the report and keeping out what was objectionable, I met the British Ministers half way and ended in getting the report in first class shape . . . giving the whole emphasis at the close to the Canadian position."[13]

In 1937, as in 1923, Mackenzie King, fighting off "Downing Street domination," had ended by dominating Downing Street. Downing Street was dominated; had Mackenzie King been vindicated?

THE POLITICS OF AIR TRAINING

On 22 May 1935, the Prime Minister of the United Kingdom announced in the House of Commons the decision of his Government to double the front-line strength of the Royal Air Force within two years. It would be hard to produce the aircraft for this unprecedented peacetime expansion; harder still to train the pilots. Many more bases would be required. But more bases in Britain were out of the question: there was just not enough room on the ground or in the air. The place for the new flying schools, it appeared to the Air Ministry planners, was obviously the overseas parts of the Commonwealth. Abu Sueir in Egypt, one of the oldest of R.A.F. training sites, provided a precedent; but the Air Ministry, wisely enough in retrospect, wanted a less exotic, and less exposed, location. Canada seemed the perfect place.[14]

In May 1936, the Superintendent of the R.A.F. Reserve wrote to the Director of Training of the R.C.A.F. He recalled the training plan under which pilots were trained in Canada for the R.A.F. in 1917–18, and wondered if the peculiarly advantageous facilities of the senior dominion might not again be exploited in a common cause. Canada had the wide open spaces; Britain needed airmen. Might not a peacetime training scheme be worked out? If it could be, the Superintendent concluded, it was "infinitely to be preferred to forming a further F.T.S. [Flying Training School] abroad."[15]

In September 1936, the Minister of National Defence, Ian Mackenzie, visited London. While there he was asked by the British Secretary of State for Air whether the Canadian Government would be willing to allow the Royal Air Force to establish training schools in the Dominion.

Mackenzie was non-committal, but undertook to find out. He reported the conversation to the Prime Minister on his return to Canada, and the proposal was discussed by the cabinet. The cabinet decided that "it would be inadvisable to have Canadian territory used by the British Government for training school purposes for airmen. It is the intention of the Canadian Government to establish training schools of its own. The situation might give rise to competition between governments in the matter of fields, pilots, equipment and the like."[16] The British Government was informed of this decision.

As preparations were made for the impending Imperial Conference of 1937, the Air Ministry's proposal was again canvassed by the Canadian authorities. A memorandum of the Joint Staff Committee of 6 May concluded that "from a purely Service point of view" the British scheme was admirable, and recommended "that a training station under the control of the Royal Canadian Air Force, but financed by the U.K., be developed in Canada and manned by the Royal Air Force for the training of R.A.F. pilots on the understanding that it become available to the Canadian Government in the event of Canadian mobilization."[17] Opposite this paragraph Mackenzie King recorded his reaction in a word: "No."

Despite the chilly reception by Canada of all its plans for military co-operation at the Imperial Conference, the British government persisted in its effort to establish R.A.F. training schools in the senior dominion. An opportunity for further negotiation presented itself in May 1938, when an Air Mission from the United Kingdom was visiting North America to investigate the general problem of aircraft supply in the event of war. Between 15 and 20 May the mission was in Eastern Canada. Shortly before its arrival, the British High Commissioner, Sir Francis Floud, called upon the Prime Minister to inquire if the Canadian Government would be willing to assist the mission in its work. Mackenzie King replied that the Government would be ready to provide whatever information it could. He emphasized, however, that it was contrary to government policy to advise the mission where to place its contracts, or to act as an agent or go-between in any negotiations that might be entered into by the mission with Canadian manufacturers.

Three day later, on 16 May, Sir Francis Floud called once again upon Mackenzie King. The latter's record of their discussion follows:

Sir Francis stated that the British Government were much concerned about the air situation in Great Britain. At one stage, he said he thought they had got cold feet in discovering that the Germans had gone ahead so much more rapidly and further than they had anticipated. There was not much opportunity in Great Britain for proper training of pilots for the class of plane which was now being used. The problem was really one of air congestion. England was a small country, thickly populated; the spaces for training pilots comparatively few and close to thickly populated centres. The best spaces were either reserved for park purposes, scenic beauty, etc., or the most fertile farming land in the country. He wanted to know if we would be agreeable to having the British Government construct flying fields in Canada, erect aerodromes, send in necessary machinery, etc., and arrange for the training of numbers of their pilots in Canada. They would like to have those Canadian pilots who were to go to England for training later to receive their preliminary training here.

In reply, I said that the question was not a new one. It had been raised a year or two; was discussed again with Ministers and officials of the Canadian Government when in London, at the time of the [Imperial] Conference. That the position taken was that any step of the kind would be certain to create suspicion, and arouse criticism on the score that an effort was being made to create Imperial forces, and to bring about a condition whereby Canada would be committed to participation in a European conflict. That, as he knew, the policy of the Government was to avoid commitments either with respect to neutrality or participation in wars in which other parts of the Empire might be engaged; that Parliament would decide on the issues at the time, in the light of all existing circumstances. Meanwhile, if a step such as was suggested were taken, it would certainly force an issue in Canada at once which would disclose a wide division of opinion, something that would do the Empire more harm than good by, first of all, creating disunion within Canada, and secondly, prejudicing in advance the position that might be taken at a later time and, secondly, creating a condition which would be helpful to any potential enemies rather than to the United Kingdom.

I explained how careful we had to be to avoid issues of the kind being raised, if we were to keep Canada and the Empire united. I enlarged upon the discussion that would certainly take place in Parliament, also in the Press, etc., and the probable drift more strongly towards complete isolation were it to be thought that pressure was being placed upon the Government by the British Government to make anything in the nature of commitments for war purposes, or to permit courses of action which would be misunderstood. Sir Francis asked if any objection would not be overcome by the knowledge that the British Government are prepared to spend large sums of money, etc.; that Canada's unemployed and industries would profit largely therefrom. I replied that this would only aggravate the situation. Canadians would not wish to have the British Parliament vote moneys to be spent on projects of their own in Canada, for war purposes, any more than they would wish to have American moneys appropriated for military roads in the Dominion as had been suggested in connection with the proposed Alaska Highway. . . .[18]

The presence of the British air mission in the Canadian capital, and the sudden resurrection of the air training scheme by the British High Commissioner, had already been linked in Mackenzie King's mind as more than mere coincidence. Suspicion hardened into certainty when, that afternoon, the head of the mission met with him in the presence of the High Commissioner and spoke approvingly of the air training proposal. "It was clear," Mackenzie King wrote afterwards, "that Sir Francis had been talking with the Mission the night before, and had come to me in the morning presenting a request which had come from Mr. Weir rather than as a result of some despatch received from Great Britain."

It would have been unusual, in these circumstances, had the ensuing negotiations fared well; they did not fare well. Weir began as the High Commissioner had done earlier in the day, and Mackenzie King repeated his reply. Weir thereupon asked the Prime Minister if there would be any objection to his discussing the matter with officials of the Department of National Defence. Mackenzie King said that there would be no objection, provided there were no commitments. To this Weir retorted that there was little point entering into discussions if nothing was to be allowed to come of them. That did not go down at all well. "I confess," Mackenzie King wrote afterwards, "I did not at all like Weir's attitude in speaking. He kept twirling his hat on his knee and talking with a perpetual smile on his face, expressing his feelings with movements of his head and his hands. It seemed to me that his attitude was one of seeking to corner or embarrass me." Many heads of state, let alone heads of mission, had tried that tack before; and, if they were wise, regretted it.

Earlier that day, between his morning and afternoon interviews, Mackenzie King had told his cabinet of the air training plan proposed by Sir Francis Floud. He told Floud and Weir, at the conclusion of their talks, that he had sought the opinion of his Government on the matter, and that there had been "practical unanimity of opinion" against the British proposal. That was stretching things a bit. The majority view, expressed strongly by C. G. Power, Norman Rogers, and others, was (as Mackenzie King wrote) "that it would be insufferable to have a lot of British officers here; that their experience, at the time of the war, had taught them how impossible it was for Canadians and Englishmen to work together in military matters." But James Gardiner and J. L. Ilsley thought otherwise; Gardiner spoke passionately in favour of closer Anglo-Canadian co-operation in defence, and Ilsley wondered how the Government could make a case to the public for refusing to train British airmen in Canada at British expense.

The air mission and the Prime Minister parted company, not altogether amicably, but on the understanding that what had passed between them would be kept deadly secret. Somehow the secret got out. On 14 June, Arthur Meighen rose to question the Government Leader in the

Senate. "I have received information," he said, "to the effect that within recent months the British Government has made a request to the Government of Canada for permission to establish, wholly at the expense of the British Government, a training school in Canada for flyers. . . . The request, I am advised, has been made on two occasions, and refused by the Government of Canada. I would ask whether the information has any truth in it and, if so, why the request is refused."[19] The next day, having consulted with the Prime Minister, Raoul Dandurand delivered the reply he had been instructed to deliver: "No such request has been made to the Canadian Government." Meighen, evidently sure of his ground as he was of his sources, persisted. "It may be," he remarked, "that exactly in the terms in which I have asked there has not been a request, but has there not been one on the same subject-matter and not very far unrelated to the very terms which I used?" Dandurand then declared: "In a word, there has been no request from the British Government to the Canadian Government in any shape or form concerning the matter mentioned in the query of the right honourable gentleman."[20] This reply, on any reasonable reading of the evidence, was a plain mis-statement of what was known to be the fact.

The British High Commissioner must have learned of this interchange with mingled feelings of incredulity and anger. He knew, as a party to the discussions of 16 May, that the United Kingdom Government had asked the Government of Canada for air training facilities in the Dominion; he had indeed been the agent by which its request had been transmitted. He wrote to Mackenzie King to tell him so: "I certainly considered that I was making a definite request to you on behalf of the United Kingdom Government."[21] This interpretation Mackenzie King resisted. "You gave me every reason to believe," he wrote in reply, "that the purpose of the interview was simply exploratory and in the nature of an inquiry."[22] To safeguard his position further, he despatched a message to Neville Chamberlain, seeking to extract from the British Prime Minister an assertion that in instructing Weir and Floud to raise the matter as they had done it was only with the intention of sounding out Canadian reaction, not with putting a formal proposition; a reply from Chamberlain to this effect was duly received. He took the further precaution of asking the Governor General, then visiting England, to see Chamberlain and explain the situation to him. "I hope you may be able to let Mr. Chamberlain know," he wrote to Lord Tweedsmuir on 20 July,

how much we have been embarrassed by representations in the matter which have come to Canada from England. I have been told from more sources than one that Meighen got his information of the Canadian Government's attitude from [Victor] Drury of Montreal, who stated that it was Sir Thomas Inskip who had given him the information. . . . Unless the best of good faith can be kept between Governments dealing with problems of this character, political controversy will develop to a point where anything in the nature of co-operation will be wholly frustrated.

I hope you will let members of the British Government know just how difficult my path has been in seeking to avoid political discussion, in Canada, on lines likely to prove embarrassing to the British Government, and indeed to the very critical situation as we know it. It is perfectly outrageous, for example, that in seeking to find a way to co-operate with the British Government in its wishes with respect to the training of pilots, our Government should, through so much as the mention of conferences which were wholly confidential, have been placed in a position where our whole attitude has been completely misrepresented. . . .[23]

Meanwhile the Conservative Opposition, led by Arthur Meighen (who, it was widely rumoured, was ready to bid for a resumption of the leadership of the party), was criticizing the Government's attitude at every opportunity. Mackenzie King was nettled by the criticism but not dismayed. He was ready, as he told his cabinet, to take the whole issue to the people. There could be no better issue on which to fight a general election, he felt, "than one which would seek to have any branch of the British War Ministry undertake establishments in Canada which would be primarily for the purpose of including Canadians to take part in Imperial wars."

On 1 July, R. B. Bennett asked Mackenzie King in the House of Commons whether he wished, as Prime Minister, to add anything to what the Government Leader in the Senate had stated on 15 June. Mackenzie King replied that he had nothing to add, and then added the following: "Confidential and informal exploratory conversations with respect to training of British air pilots have taken place, but nothing has developed which it was felt warranted a statement of policy." A statement of policy was now forthcoming. Without confirming that the proposal to establish Royal Air Force training schools in Canada had been under discussion, the Prime Minister stated the Government's objection to such a proposal were it to be put forward:

Long ago, Canadian Governments finally settled the constitutional principle that in Canadian territory there could be no military establishments unless they were owned, maintained and controlled by the Canadian Government responsible to the Canadian Parliament and people. In the end the imperial naval stations and army garrisons were withdrawn and Canadian authority took over. A reversal of that principle and that historical process[*] at this

*That "historical process" had become somewhat distorted in Mackenzie King's rendition of it. A modern reader, accustomed to the spectacle of newly indepen-

date is something the Canadian people would not for a moment entertain. Such domestic ownership, maintenance and control of all military stations and personnel is one of the really indispensable hall-marks of national sovereign self-government and an indispensable basis for friendly and effective co-operation between the governments of Canada and those of other parts of the British Commonwealth of Nations, including the government of the United Kingdom.[24]

Having thus ruled out on principle the possibility of the Royal Air Force establishing its own training facilities in the Dominion, Mackenzie King then stated—on the spur of the moment and apparently in response to the agitated comments of his followers in Parliament who were urging him to "sound the loyal note"—the terms on which the Government was ready to co-operate with the United Kingdom in the training of airmen. "We ourselves," he declared, "are prepared to have our own establishments here and to give in those establishments facilities to British pilots to come and train here."[25] Five days later, the British High Commissioner was summoned to a meeting of the cabinet, which formally communicated the offer to him.

II

Here was a basis for further negotiation. But first of all the Canadian Government had to determine the nature of its own offer. The Prime Minister's statement of policy in Parliament had been made without any prior consultation with the R.C.A.F. Indeed, it was only a day before the Canadian offer was formally made to the British High Commissioner that the Air Force had any opportunity to consider it. On 4 July, the Deputy Minister in the Department of National Defence had requested the Senior Air Officer to furnish him immediately with some proposals.

---

dent nations attempting with varying degrees of success to rid themselves of the military presence of their former rulers, might pardonably conclude that the objective of the Canadian Government in the immediate post-Confederation years was to expel the British Army and the Royal Navy from its territory. He would be wrong. It was the British Government, stretched then as now by its far-flung commitments on the continent of Europe and the perimeter of Empire, which wanted to bring its troops back home; the Canadian Government just as determinedly wanted them to stay. "It will be a century," Sir John A. Macdonald wrote in 1869, "before we are strong enough to stand alone." Be that as it might, the British Government had no intention of waiting for a century, or even a twentieth of a century. By the end of 1871 British garrisons remained only at Halifax and Esquimalt; these were withdrawn in 1905.

The doctrine of the incompatibility of national sovereignty and foreign bases was to undergo considerable modification in the years following the Second World War, as the United States and Canada co-operated in the defence of the continent which was their common home.

Air Commodore G. M. Croil responded. The governing consideration, he wrote, was "that the present facilities, insofar as aircraft, flying instructors and mechanics are concerned, are entirely consumed in meeting R.C.A.F. requirements." If R.A.F. pilots were to be trained without affecting R.C.A.F. training, an expansion of the existing plant was unavoidable. Much, of course, would depend upon the extent of the Air Ministry's requirements, as yet undisclosed. If the R.A.F. required pilots to be trained in Canada in very limited numbers—say no more than 50 a year—then, Croil felt, the job could be done by expanding the facilities at the R.C.A.F. station at Trenton, Ont. If larger numbers were to be trained, one or other of two methods might be employed. One was the creation of civilian flying schools under the direction of the Department of National Defence. This method, Croil noted, would be practical for training in elementary flying, but could not turn out fully qualified fighter and bomber pilots. He therefore recommended the alternative method, which was to establish a new training school in Canada. Camp Borden, where a runway, hangars, and barracks already existed, could without difficulty be converted for this purpose. As its facilities were already in use for technical training of R.C.A.F. personnel, room would have to be found elsewhere for the Canadians. In a further memorandum of 19 July, Air Commodore Croil came out still more strongly for the Borden solution. He now furnished an estimate of the costs involved. Assuming that the numbers of R.A.F. personnel to be trained were 300 a year, that elementary and intermediate training only be given, that the new instructors and additional aircraft required would be obtained in Canada, he thought that the scheme would cost roughly $6,700,000 for the first year of operation, roughly $2,188,000 for each subsequent year. The R.A.F., he suggested, should pay much the greater share of these expenses; the cost to the R.C.A.F. should be roughly $75,000 for the first year, and roughly $50,000 a year thereafter.[26]

Reassured by the limited commitments and the modest cost involved in these preliminary calculations, the Government authorized the Senior Air Officer to work out with his colleagues a plan on which they, and the representative shortly to be sent out by the Air Ministry, could all agree. The representative, Group Captain J. M. Robb, commandant of the British Central Flying School, arrived in Canada late in July. Only then were the Air Ministry's ideas disclosed to the Canadian authorities. They differed radically from those contained in Croil's earlier memoranda. The higher number of airmen—300, rather than 50—was specified. The airmen were to complete advanced training in Canada. Most radically, the airmen to be trained for the R.A.F. were to be Canadian, not British. Robb was evidently a persuasive delegate, for by the first week in August he had talked his Canadian counterparts into acceptance of his scheme. On 5 August the Deputy Minister of the Department of National Defence despatched the following urgent message to the Minister, Ian Mackenzie, who was absent from the capital in Vancouver:

Group Captain Robb accompanied by Air Commodore Croil called this afternoon when we discussed air training in Canada. May we prepare detailed plan along following lines which were proposed by Group Captain Robb:

To train as pilots three hundred Canadian candidates per year for at least three years after which yearly number to be governed by then existing conditions.

If sufficient Canadians do not offer then Royal Air Force would send young men from British Isles.

Canadians would be enlisted into Royal Canadian Air Force and after completing training would be transferred to Royal Air Force for five years service after which they would come back to Canadian reserve.

Two elementary training schools the first at Camp Borden the second at Patricia Bay. All intermediate training at Camp Borden. Advanced training at some place to be selected on St. Lawrence River at or below Montreal. Navigational training which is the final portion of the course at or near Moncton N.B.

This scheme is respectfully recommended for approval. Mr. A. H. Self of the Mission now in Canada is empowered to discuss financial arrangements which would follow after detailed scheme as per the above were completed say within ten days or two weeks from now.[27]

Ian Mackenzie, with or without knowing what he was doing, signified his approval of this scheme. But he did not so far forget himself as to do so without seeking the approval of the Prime Minister, and he instructed the Deputy Minister to show a copy of the message of 5 August to Mackenzie King. Colonel LaFlèche accordingly made his way out to Kingsmere, the Prime Minister's home in the Gatineau Hills near Ottawa, and showed him the telegram he had sent to the Minister of National Defence. "I said at once," Mackenzie King wrote that evening, "it was a complete change from what had been agreed to, viz., affording facilities for training Br. pilots in Canada not recruiting Canadians & training in Canada for service in Gr. Br. for 5 yrs. . . , a scheme involving expenditure of 17,000,000, no understanding even as to who was to meet it. . . ." He told LaFlèche he would not approve the scheme until the cabinet had considered it.

The cabinet assembled next day. Mackenzie King recorded that the members saw at once that a most far-reaching change had been worked in what they had previously agreed to. LaFlèche was called into the meeting to explain as best he could what had been done. "It was clear as he talked," Mackenzie King wrote afterwards, "that the plan was *a war plan*—to make sure of *a base for training in Canada* when war comes—with certainty on part of Defence Department Canada wd. be in it—co-operating in defence of Empire." LaFlèche was instructed to tell Group Captain Robb that he had misunderstood the basis on which the Canadian Government was prepared to co-operate, and to draw up new proposals based upon the training by Canada of British, not Canadian, pilots. Mackenzie King was very much annoyed by the episode, and his ill humour was not improved when, before retiring that evening, he read in the Ottawa *Journal* a full account of the Robb proposal.* "It was on the streets while Council was considering the project," he wrote, "like the Chanak incident." He was convinced that the Department of National Defence was in league with the Air Ministry, and that both were engaged in a conspiracy to force the hand of the government. At that he may not have been so very far wrong.

The disclosures in the press caused Mackenzie King to summon a further meeting of the cabinet, at which he requested both LaFlèche

---

*"Tentative plans covering the training of pilots in Canada for the Royal Air Force are believed here to be taking shape in consequence of the survey conducted by Group Captain J. M. Robb. . .

"Already he has made an exhaustive study of the situation at Camp Borden and Trenton. It is understood he will extend his inquiries to Western Canada, and probably the Maritimes.

"The authorities here continue reticent, but the Defence Department is according complete co-operation to the British envoy. While nothing official could be gleaned, it is believed tentative plans are in the making which contemplate the expansion of the Training School at Camp Borden, with others to be established elsewhere throughout the country.

"It was indicated last week there would be one on the Pacific Coast, and two more in Eastern Canada. Moncton was named as the location of a school in the Maritimes, with the other situated on the St. Lawrence, east of Montreal.

"The capacity of the schools will be governed by the character of the training and the length of the courses. Yearly admissions will be limited to the numbers that can most conveniently be handled. At present it takes about a year in which to educate a pilot for the air force, and the likelihood is that this may be the length of the probational training.

"Cadets will be taken on the strength of the Royal Canadian Air Force, probably as provisional units, and transferred to the British Air Service at the end of the training. Their period of engagement in the R.A.F. will likely be the normal five years required at present, at the close of which they may either re-engage or go on the reserve list. Those who return to Canada at the end of their service will probably be transferred to the Canadian reserve.

"Although recruits will be drawn in large numbers from among British youths, young Canadians will also be given opportunities. But in all cases the British Government will reimburse the Canadian Government for all out-of-pocket expenses incurred."

"Plans Take Shape for Training Young Pilots," Ottawa *Journal*, 9 Aug. 1938.

and Group Captain Robb to appear. LaFlèche was the first on the griddle.

I . . . read to him the article which appeared in last night's *Journal* outlining a plan re training that he had submitted to me on Monday, and which I took up with Council yesterday. While we were discussing this matter, the whole thing was reported in the Press as having been settled. LaFlèche had nothing to say other than that this thing had happened before, but he could not say how. I questioned him in considerable detail, and told him quite frankly I thought there were features of the whole matter which he, as Deputy, should have brought to the attention of his Minister, and to the Government's attention, knowing we were considering the problem, for example, the significance of the change from a request for British training schools in Canada to a request to have young Canadians recruited and trained in Canada, for service in the Royal Air Force. . . . I found every member of the Cabinet present shared my view as to what the original proposals had been and were surprised at the complete change now being made. They also were equally surprised at the extent to which the articles in the "Journal" paralleled the secret memorandum given me by LaFlèche. . . .[28]

Next it was Robb's turn. He endured his ordeal in the company of Air Commodore Croil and LaFlèche. "I questioned Robb," Mackenzie King wrote afterwards,

as to who had given him instructions, and what his instructions were. He was quite straightforward saying that his instructions had come from one of the senior [R.A.F.] officers. . . . I outlined what we had understood, namely, that the desire was to give advanced trained people opportunity to fly in Canada, while there were not the same risks of injury to planes or to communities, and that it would be Englishmen coming to Canada, not training Canadians to go to England. However, it is quite apparent that it is the latter that the British Air Ministry have in mind. I pointed out the political considerations that had to be considered, and the dangers there were to the whole project of co-operation if it were launched in the wrong way, and if it carried with it any seeming commitment to participation in war in advance of a decision by Parliament. . . .[29]

Robb's own recollection of the interrogation puts the emphasis elsewhere. It recalls how, after he had set forth the Air Ministry's proposal to the Canadian Government, Mackenzie King testily remarked: "If the war your country wants to prepare for does break out, how do you know that Canada will come into it on your side?" Robb fell silent at this juncture. Soon afterward, he put in a request for permission to return home.[30]

This futile and unpleasant confrontation had two important results. In the first place, it intensified Mackenzie King's suspicion that the British defence authorities, the Department of National Defence in Ottawa, and vested private interests of various kinds were joined in an unholy conspiracy to alter the course that his Government had been following. At the same time it crystallized in his own mind the course to be followed in the future: ". . . the Laurier naval policy in relation to air," as he put it, to create "an efficient service in Canada which, if Parliament so decided, could be made a part of one great service in time of war."

The new plan submitted by the British Government in December 1938 was far from meeting this basic Canadian requirement. The Air Ministry seemed incapable of comprehending the Government's reluctance to countenance any scheme whereby Canadian airmen were to be trained in Canada for service with the R.A.F. It now proposed that 135 Canadians should be so trained, though the final stages of training would take place in the United Kingdom. It advanced detailed financial calculations. The cost to Canada would be £1,450 per pupil. The total annual cost to Canada was estimated at about $1,000,000; to the United Kingdom, at about $2,000,000.

The Canadian Government considered these proposals; and rejected them. On 31 December 1938, Mackenzie King wrote to the British High Commissioner to explain the grounds of his cabinet's decision:

My colleagues and I have noted that the new plan . . . appears to amount to a reversal of the idea as originally broached by the Weir Mission last Spring, which emphasized that what was predominantly in mind was the training of British pilots. . .

Under the proposed arrangement, the Canadian Government would undertake, over a period of years, to recruit and train Canadians for service in the air forces of the United Kingdom, in numbers considerably larger than the total number at present trained for the Canadian service. Such an arrangement does not appear to us consistent with the established policy of autonomy in defence, as in other matters, nor with the primary responsibility of each part of the Commonwealth for developing forces to meet its probable defence requirements. Nor does it appear likely to make for the most effective and responsible co-operation in the event of a conflict in which the Parliaments of both countries have decided it is necessary to participate.

Under the proposed plan of recruiting and training pilots in Canada, a share of the cost would fall on the Canadian Government, and would amount, in effect, to a direct annual financial contribution by Canada to the United Kingdom defence programme.

The letter concluded with a reaffirmation of the willingness of the Canadian Government, as stated by the Prime Minister in the House of Commons on 1 July 1938, to "afford their facilities, as far as practicable, for the training in Canada, under the final direction and control of the Minister of National Defence, of pilots recruited in the United Kingdom for the Royal Air Force."[31]

It was now 1939. Time was running out. The British informed the Canadians in January that they were grateful for the renewed offer of co-operation in the training of British pilots for the R.A.F. and hoped to accept it. After intensive consultations a plan was finally agreed upon, and announced in the House of Commons on 26 April. It was in effect the most modest of the three proposals that Air Commodore Croil had produced on short notice on 5 July 1938. The R.C.A.F. would integrate with its own training plans some 50 British pilots who on completion of their training would enter the R.A.F. The programme was to run for three years.

The first draft of seventeen R.A.F. personnel was scheduled to arrive in Canada in the last week of September. By then the United Kingdom and Canada were at war with Germany. The scheme, barely begun, was cancelled. Now that war had come, the Canadian Government, hitherto concerned at the cost of training pilots by the hundred, would train pilots by the thousands.

III

The luxury of a separate declaration of war by Canada, a week after that by the United Kingdom, was not allowed to interfere with consultation between the two governments about what the Dominion might most usefully do to assist Britain in the earliest stages of the impending conflict. On 3 September 1939, Mackenzie King sent a message to Neville Chamberlain to inquire what the British desired Canada to do. On 7 September Chamberlain's reply was received in Ottawa. It asked for men, money, and matériel. O. D. Skelton, after surveying the list, described it as "a pretty tall order." Still, during the next fortnight, the Canadian Government did what it could to fill it. Only after it had exerted itself did there come to hand the tallest order of them all.

On 26 September, Neville Chamberlain appealed to Mackenzie King for Canada's help in training Commonwealth aircrew for the coming struggle with Germany. It was a modern variant of calling upon the New World to redress the balance of the Old. The redressing to be done, however, was on a scale far exceeding anything Canning had ever dreamed of. As many as 20,000 pilots, and 30,000 aircrew, might be required annually to sustain the war in the air. Chamberlain's message stressed how tremendously important his government thought the plan to be. It could well mean the difference between defeat and victory—not only through the destruction of German power when the strategic bombing offensive got under way, but through the sapping of the enemy's morale. "The knowledge that a vast air potential was being built up in the Dominions where no German air activity could interfere with expansion might well have a psychological effect on the Germans equal to that produced by the intervention of the United States in the last war. . . ." So, at least, it was permissible to hope.

The idea of appealing to Canada for training Commonwealth airmen on so massive a scale had not originated within the British Government, but had been the brain-child of two of the dominion high commissioners. On 13 September, Vincent Massey, representing Canada, and Stanley Bruce, representing Australia, had participated with some Commonwealth air force officers in a dispiriting discussion of the disparity between the power of the Luftwaffe and the meagre aerial resources at the disposal of the Royal Air Force. From this meeting, the two high commissioners went to "a full dress meeting at the Treasury . . . The meeting developed into defensive statements by [the British] in reply to an expression of some apprehension by Bruce and myself [Vincent Massey] particularly in regard to the air position." It was at this juncture that it occurred to the Canadian High Commissioner that his own country might do something to redress the balance by training Commonwealth airmen for the future. Massey consulted with Bruce, who received the idea enthusiastically. A meeting of high commissioners with Anthony Eden, the Secretary of State for Dominion Affairs, on 16 September was the occasion for a formal proposal by Massey and Bruce "that consideration should be given to a scheme whereby Canadian, Australian, and New Zealand air forces should be trained in Canada on 'planes to be specially built in Canada or the United States and should then be sent to the front as distinctive Canadian, Australian, and New Zealand air forces." Chamberlain's despatch ten days later was the outcome of this initiative.[32]

Not only did Vincent Massey originate the proposal, he had an important part in drafting Chamberlain's appeal. Knowing the fate of previous efforts by the United Kingdom to enlist Mackenzie King's support for training R.A.F. personnel in Canada, Massey was apprehensive lest by some infelicity of phrase the new overture would meet with an unsympathetic reception in Ottawa. He turned to advantage the opportunity of offering suggestions as to how the message should be worded. It was at Massey's suggestion that a special paragraph was inserted in the message to Mackenzie King. It read as follows:

I am sure that you will agree that the scheme outlined in the following message is of the first importance. For this reason, and because it invites the co-operation of Canada to a very special degree, I want to make a special personal appeal to you about it. I feel that so far-reaching a project will strike your imagination particularly as it concerns an all-important field of war activity in which Canada has already made so striking and gallant an individual contribution. May I therefore ask that the matter should receive very urgent attention?[33]

This was skilfully put and, in the event, had the intended result. Had Mackenzie King known who was behind the idea, he might not have been so favourably impressed by it: relations between him and his High Commissioner in London had become so strained that he had long since ceased to communicate with him in any serious way, and he regarded his activities with suspicion and with jealousy.

On 28 September, two days after it had been received by the Canadian Prime Minister, Neville Chamberlain's historic despatch was considered by the Emergency Council (a committee of the cabinet formed on 30 August, and the forerunner of the Cabinet War Committee created three months later). Mackenzie King read the message to the gathering,* and then commented that any decision the Government might reach on an air-training programme of such great scope and magnitude would be bound to affect its decision about whether or not to furnish an expeditionary force. This suggestion was not happily received by the Chief of the General Staff, but most of the ministers present were agreeably taken by the thought that Canadian obligations in the war just under way might be fully, or largely, met by training Commonwealth airmen rather than by sending large numbers of soldiers overseas. Their only disappointment, as Mackenzie King noted, was that the British proposal "had not been made at the outset so that our war effort would have been framed on these lines instead of having to head so strongly into expeditionary forces at the start."[34]

As things stood, the Government had already entered into various commitments to what it then believed to be the limit of its capacity. Nevertheless, the Government decided to accept Chamberlain's proposal in principle. It did so, its message of acceptance informed the British Prime Minister, on the assumption that adequate supplies of aircraft and training personnel would be made available by the United Kingdom, and that satisfactory arrangements could be worked out for financing the scheme. (Australia and New Zealand also accepted the proposal; South Africa rejected it; Eire, as a neutral, was not involved.)

---

*Mackenzie King, Raoul Dandurand, Ernest Lapointe, T. A. Crerar, Norman Rogers, C. G. Power, and J. L. Ralston were the participating ministers; the Services were represented by the three Chiefs of Staff, Major-General T. V. Anderson, Rear-Admiral P. W. Nelles, and Air Vice-Marshal G. M. Croil.

The next problem concerned the terms and timing of the announcement of the plan. Complications arose almost at once. On 6 October, Hitler had resorted to his familiar technique of following his latest aggression with a profession of peaceful intent: he was ready, he announced, to call off the war if certain conditions were met. The British Government was anxious to offset any defeatist sentiment which this manoeuvre might arouse. It saw in the impending announcement of the British Commonwealth Air Training Plan an admirable method of answering Hitler's words with deeds. Accordingly, it drafted the text of the announcement more with an eye to its value as an instrument of psychological warfare than as a precise expression of inter-governmental intent.

The British draft did not find favour in Ottawa. Skelton interpreted it as a crude and typical attempt on the part of the Air Ministry to force the hand of the Canadian Government before the all-important details of finance and supply could be attended to, and recommended the postponement of the announcement until these issues had been satisfactorily disposed of. For once Mackenzie King disagreed with his close adviser. "I pointed out to Skelton," he minuted on the latter's memorandum on 8 October, "that for us to delay announcement might be to incur blame of British. . . . I pointed out much of value of announcement lay in its psychological effect (1) in causing Germans to reflect (2) in strengthening position of Britain in effecting basis of settlement. I feel strongly announcement should be made, as soon as possible. . . ."

Timing was one thing, terms another. Mackenzie King no more than Skelton liked the flamboyant language in which the announcement had been drafted. They set to work to have it changed. On 9 October, the British High Commissioner produced a revision which was designed to meet the Canadian objections. Too great a stress on the colossal nature of the undertaking, Mackenzie King had pointed out previously, might instead of over-awing goad the enemy into greater exertions. He had also been concerned that the announcement should emphasize that the plan had been initiated by the United Kingdom, not by the dominions. The British revision went some way to accommodate the draft to the Canadian view, but not far enough. Skelton informed the High Commissioner that

there were two matters on which our suggestions had not in any way been met. The first one was the desirability from our standpoint of including a statement to the effect that this was the most effective form of military co-operation. I reminded him that this had several times been brought to their attention, and that it was the understanding on which the Government had agreed to this scheme in principle. . . .

Next, I pointed out that . . . they had made no alteration whatever in their statement of the scale of the scheme, in spite of our lengthy analysis of the situation in this regard. Sir Gerald [Campbell] said they undoubtedly wished to make the statement as striking as possible. I said we recognised and sympathized with that desire, but that they must give some consideration not only to the enemy but to their allies. We had definitely made it clear from the beginning that while we approved a plan of greatly enlarged air training, we could not reach any conclusion on the scale to which we could commit ourselves until we had some careful and expert report on the technical feasibility of a scheme on the scale they had suggested, and particularly as to the financial commitments which had to be considered as part of the whole financial and credit arrangement on which we had been endeavouring for some time to get a complete picture. . . .

There was also, as Skelton noted, an additional reason why the Canadian Government should refuse to commit itself to any plan it might not be able to carry out successfully: "If we agree to an objective that we can later not attain, that will enable Senator Meighen to say that if the Government had accepted his recommendations last year and had started air training schools on a huge scale, we would now have been able to meet the United Kingdom demands."[35]

Eventually, the United Kingdom met the Canadian demands in every particular: in the assurance that Canada's part in the plan was in the British view the most important contribution the senior dominion might make to the war effort; in the recognition that the main burden for implementing it would fall upon Canada; in the absence of any specific indication of the scale on which the plan was to be mounted; in the admission that the Dominion ran some risk of enemy attack; in the reference to separate dominion air forces. All were specified in the announcement of the plan made public in London and in Ottawa on 10 October. It could hardly have been otherwise: Canadian co-operation was crucial to the very conception of the project.

There was now agreement in principle. To convert it into agreement proper, the British Government despatched an Air Mission to negotiate the details of the plan with the Canadian authorities. The Mission was headed by Lord Riverdale, a prominent Sheffield industrialist, and included Air Chief Marshal Sir Robert Brooke-Popham, Captain Harold Balfour, the Under-Secretary for Air, other R.A.F. officers and Air Ministry officials, and a representative of the de Havilland Aircraft Company. The negotiations lasted the better part of two months; it was a trying experience for both sides.

The shape of things to come was soon disclosed. On 17 October Lord Riverdale conducted his first press conference in Ottawa. "People don't yet realize what an enormous undertaking this [Plan] is," he remarked on this occasion. "It is going to win the war, if we can get everybody to go at it bald-headed. The psychological effect on the Germans has been tremendous. . . . Once we get going, we shall run into very big figures—something like 20,000 to 25,000."[36] These were exactly the sort of statements that the Canadian Government had been trying to avoid, at least until the details of the plan had been settled, and it was displeased by Riverdale's début. It is clear in retrospect that the mission and the Government entertained conflicting notions about the purpose of their impending negotiations. The mission evidently believed that the essentials had already been settled, and that it remained only to clear up relatively unimportant points of detail. The Government considered the points of detail to be all-important. Much acrimony and misunderstanding were to result.

On 31 October, the mission met for the first time with the Emergency Council of the cabinet. Mackenzie King, flanked by Ralston, Rogers, and C. D. Howe, began by stressing that the Canadian Government had as yet made no commitment other than stating its willingness to co-operate in the scheme. Riverdale and Balfour spoke as if all had been settled. Their attitude greatly provoked the Canadian Prime Minister. He replied that "it was unfortunate we had not had this scheme put before us at the outset, before we had worked out what we felt our contribution could be" and that he "hoped the spirit of the Canadian people would not be crushed by seeking to place upon them responsibilities and burdens greater than they could assume." He spoke, he wrote afterwards, "very plainly," though "in a kindly courteous way, and without becoming in the least heated or confused." The deliberate manner of his speech may have only added insult to injury, for in the course of his remarks Mackenzie King used the expression "this is not our war." Matters were not improved when Mackenzie King learned that the mission had quoted this phrase in its report to London as an indication of his attitude. The negotiations thus got off to a start which could hardly have been less promising. "Trouble between King & Lord Riverdale," a correspondent close to the scene wrote privately to his editor. "Lord R. appears to think he was sent out as a kind of colonial administrator & King resents his . . . generally over-bearing manner."[37]

Indeed he did. On 1 November he complained bitterly to the Governor General about the tactics of the mission, in which, he said, it had been abetted by the British High Commissioner. Two days later he took the matter up directly with Neville Chamberlain. The discussions with the Riverdale mission had already revealed "a fundamental misunderstanding as to the basis and responsibility for the project." What had originally been represented by the British Government as a plan for reinforcing the R.A.F. through the training of United Kingdom airmen in Canada had somehow turned into a plan for the training of Canadian airmen at a gigantic cost to Canada. The Canadian economy, already under strain by earlier commitments to the war effort, could not manage to sustain much more. Chamberlain's reply was intended to be mollifying, but it was necessarily evasive.

Meanwhile, on 14 November, a further meeting between the mission and the Government took place, at which the Canadian ministers announced their readiness to sign an agreement on air training subject to two conditions: first, that the British Government would supply a formal assurance, which the Canadian Government could make public at its discretion, that the Air Training Scheme had priority or preference over any portion of the Canadian defence effort other than existing commitments; second, that discussions then in progress in London concerning Canada's economic contribution to the war effort were brought "to mutual and reasonably satisfying agreement." These conditions the British Government would not accept. It proposed, instead, that an Air Training Plan agreement be concluded immediately, and that any difficulties over its operation be adjusted later on. This proposal the Canadian Government rejected in its turn.

On 25 November, Mackenzie King met Sir Gerald Campbell, the British High Commissioner. They traversed in the course of a long discussion the ground which had led to the impasse.

Sir Gerald spoke about the acceptance in principle of an agreement. I told him that we had accepted the principle of a training agreement before the Mission had left for Canada; that the whole purpose of their being here was the working out of the terms. I then asked what he understood by principle of the agreement to be further decided. He said that they would include questions of numbers, financial conditions, etc. I said, precisely, financial conditions—that is the one thing we are trying to get settled so that we can initial an agreement; that I did not see how we could initial any agreement until we had this point settled.

I said to Sir Gerald that he knew very well that I had taken strong exception to the view that the Cabinet's decision depended upon the wish or the view of any one man. That I had always decried the idea of a one-man government. That I had an immediate loyalty to my colleagues, and an equal loyalty to the Canadian people in regard to all the obligations we were placing upon them and that I did not intend to betray that loyalty. I said I might say to him quite frankly that the Cabinet had considered this matter very fully . . . and that it had been agreed that we would use all expedition in getting messages across but that we must have direct understanding between the British Government and ourselves on the two conditions mentioned before we could sign any agreement. . . .

I said it was quite openly stated that the mistake we had made was in not going ahead with our own training scheme ourselves, rather than to have ourselves placed into a false position both as regards delays, contributions, etc., through the way in which matters appeared to be developing at this particular time. I said I doubted very much whether the British Government or the British Mission had appreciated what an extra load had been imposed upon our Ministers, in particular the Ministers of Finance, Defence and Transport, and upon the Public Service immediately concerned by the time and attention we had all been giving to the work of the Mission, which was over and above all the work they had to assume responsibility for in connection with Canada's own war effort at this time. That I thought the Ministers and the officials had been brought almost to the breaking point by the efforts they had put forward to assist the Mission, but, apparently, the only thanks they were now receiving was that pressure was being put on in the way it was to have some agreement initialled before its terms were finally agreed upon. . . .

I said that he, Sir Gerald, had said to me he was sorry the British Government could not get matters settled and understand our position over there. That Lord Riverdale had said the same; that he was being embarrassed. That Balfour had said the same to me . . . That they were all admitting to us here that they could not understand why the British Government should not settle definitely these matters of credit, contract, etc., on which we could base our undertaking. Sir Gerald said that of course they had many problems there and great difficulties. I said that we equally had great problems here and difficulties. He said he thought it was a matter of their several departments. I said I regarded it as a matter of Cabinet policy; that all that was necessary was for the War Cabinet to authorize . . . agreement to these two clauses, and we would then be in a position to set forth the terms of agreement on which we were ready to go ahead. I said a good many of us felt, not only surprised, but hurt; that, in the endeavour to do all we could to help the British Government in this great scheme, matters should be so construed at this stage as to try and throw on us the onus for delays, which we had done everything possible to avoid, and for which we were not responsible. . . .[38]

Some years later, Sir Gerald Campbell wrote in his memoirs that when he first took up his official duties in Ottawa, he "had mighty little idea . . . of what it means to a Dominion to be independent of all control from the country it once called Mother."[39] His disquieting interview with the Prime Minister of Canada was doubtless educational in that respect.

Mackenzie King's advocacy produced action of a kind. On 27 November, presumably after consultation between the Air Mission and London, a message arrived for him from Neville Chamberlain, accepting what the British Prime Minister understood to be the two conditions imposed by the Canadian Government. It promised that the economic discussions then under way would be brought to a satisfactory conclusion; and it offered an assurance "that the Canadian Government's views as to preference of effort are primarily for themselves to decide and that we would accept their decision in that spirit." But this was not at all the assurance for which the Canadians had been pressing. "No," Mackenzie King minuted on the despatch. "That in Br. Govt. view—the scheme will be considered as having priority to anything that may *subsequently* be put forward by Br. Govt."

Chamberlain having in this way misunderstood, or misconstrued, one of the two conditions on which the Canadian Government had been insisting, there was nothing to be done except to postpone the signing of the agreement until the difficulty had been cleared up. Meanwhile, the Australian and New Zealand delegations (which had come to Ottawa after the arrival of the British Mission) had decided to leave for home. Mackenzie King refused to be rushed. His office gave out an announcement to the effect that the discussions had been completed; that a basis of agreement had been worked out; and that the terms of this agreement were being referred to the governments concerned for final decision.

In a message to Chamberlain on 28 November, Mackenzie King sought to explain to him the precise nature of the assurance that the Canadian Government required from the British Government before it felt it could formally commit itself to the Air Training Plan. Chamberlain replied on 1 December. His Government would provide the assurance in the terms desired by the Canadians if, at the same time, the statement made plain "that we also attach very great importance both from a military and a psychological point of view to the presence of Canadian land forces in the theatre of war at the earliest possible moment." At last, from the miasma of messages and memoranda, the real issue had emerged. The Canadians had hoped that their commitment to the British Commonwealth Air Training Plan might relieve them of the obligation of providing the manpower for large land forces. The British did not wish to provide them with this excuse.

A commitment to send an Expeditionary Force to England had, however, already been entered into by the Canadian Government before the proposal for the Air Training plan had been made known to it.*

*See Colonel C. P. Stacey, *Six Years of War: The Army in Canada, Britain and the Pacific* (Ottawa, 1955), pp. 58–64.

There was really no question of substituting the Air Training Plan for the Expeditionary Force, the first drafts of which were already assembling at Halifax for convoy overseas. It was more a question of the priority of effort to be attached to each, and in this connection Mackenzie King noted on 1 December that Chamberlain's telegram constituted the first indication that the Canadian Government had had from London that the presence overseas of a Canadian army was urgently required: "Early despatches indicated that men were seeking to enlist much too rapidly and that the sending of too many men overseas would be an embarrassment." He accordingly proposed some alteration in the wording of the announcement which would make all this clear, and his amendments duly found their way into the final draft made public on 17 December.

The reader of this sorry record of recrimination and delay will hardly find credible the statement that, within a week of the misunderstanding over the nature of the United Kingdom's assurance of the priority of the Air Training Scheme, a further difference of opinion arose between the two governments concerning a matter of principle more cherished by the Canadians than anything else. Yet such is the fact. The matter of principle involved the separate and distinct identity of the Royal Canadian Air Force.

The announcement of 10 October of the intention to proceed with a British Commonwealth Air Training Plan had pointedly referred to the aim of achieving "by co-operative effort Air Forces of overwhelming strength"; that the reference had been to "Air Forces," rather than an "air force" or "air power," was the result of the vigilance of Mackenzie King, as watchful to protect dominion autonomy as he thought others watchful to subvert it. At his first meeting with the Riverdale mission, he had stressed the necessity of "keeping in mind before any final commitments on air training were made, the possibility that public opinion might force us to maintain as an independent Canadian force a considerable proportion of the new pilots." This principle was embodied in Article 15 of the "Memorandum of Agreement" drawn up by the Commonwealth representatives in Ottawa during November but, for reasons already explained, not yet signed by them. Article 15 read as follows:

The United Kingdom Government undertakes that pupils of Canada, Australia and New Zealand shall, after training is completed, be identified with their respective Dominions, either by the method of organizing Dominion units and formations or in some other way, such methods to be agreed upon with the respective Dominion Governments concerned. The United Kingdom will initiate inter-governmental discussions to this end.

So that there would be absolutely no misunderstanding on this point, which to the Canadian Government was crucial, the Minister of National Defence wrote to Lord Riverdale for an assurance that by Article 15, the British Government understood that, upon request from the Canadian Government, Canadian personnel graduating from the proposed training scheme would be organized into R.C.A.F. units and formations in the field. Riverdale's written reply appeared to Norman Rogers and Mackenzie King to be vague and evasive, and they both regarded it as unacceptable. "Mr. Rogers' letter," Mackenzie King minuted upon Riverdale's reply, "is capable of a direct and unequivocal affirmative. If that cannot be given, we should be given the reason why it cannot be given. If Lord Riverdale cannot give the affirmative answer required, British Govt. will have to give it, before agreement can be signed. This matter cannot be left in doubt—or the possibility of any misunderstanding later on." The British Air Ministry, he wrote in his diary, "is trying to keep Canadian squadrons at its disposal, merged into British forces, creating all the trouble in the air field that was created on land with the army in the last war. This must be avoided at all costs and will be by my standing firm on this matter."[40] It was, he added next day, "really shameful the way in which the British Government in these matters seek to evade and undo and to change the meaning of the most definitely understood obligations."

On 14 December, the British Mission proffered a fresh formula. This would have required that before squadrons of Canadian pilots could be identified as Canadian squadrons under R.C.A.F. command they would need to be supported by the necessary number of Canadian ground crews. Mackenzie King detected in this reservation a reluctance on the part of the British to provide Canadian airmen with British ground crews, and he was not beyond interpreting the reluctance as evidence of a master-servant relationship prevalent in London, in which the Canadians were the servants. "What is really in the minds of the British Air Force," he wrote, "is to keep command in their own hands, though they have been obliged to admit, on many occasions, that Canadian pilots have more skill and judgment than their own. . . . I made up my mind we would have to hold out more strongly than ever. . . ."[41]

Negotiations now reached a climax. They were proceeding almost around the clock. On 15 December, having consulted with London, the Air Mission produced yet another proposition. It would have related the number of Canadian graduates of the air training plan who might be eligible to be formed into R.C.A.F. squadrons to the size of the financial contribution of the Canadian Government towards the scheme. Mackenzie King instantly rejected it. He was unable to understand, he told Riverdale, why the organization of the Canadian air force should "be measured by the cold consideration of financial contribution, disregarding entirely Canada's heavy contribution of fighting men in the way of pilots, observers and gunners."[42] He wrote that night that he had been "really astonished" by what the Air Ministry had proposed. It seemed to attach "more importance to money than to human lives." He sat up to 2 a.m. drafting a cable to Chamberlain expressing his indignation; but the British Prime Minister was then in France, and the cable did not reach him until the negotiations had at last been brought to a conclusion.[43]

The course of the last day's negotiations—those of 16 December—has been fully described elsewhere.* It is astonishing that the outcome of the plan should have turned for some hours on whether or not a single word was to be deleted from the draft of a British interpretation of Article 15 of the "Memorandum of Agreement"; and that the word in question was "the." The British wanted their statement to provide that, on request of the Canadian Government, "Canadian pupils, when passing out from the Training Scheme, would be incorporated in or organized as units and formations of the Royal Canadian Air Force in the field." The Canadians wanted the statement to provide that "*the* Canadian pupils. . . ." The Minister of Finance, J. L. Ralston, believed the retention of the "the" to be crucial; he told Mackenzie King that "he would not slaughter his own child; that the objective of the Agreement was to have all the Canadians formed into formations and units under their own command. That was the objective, and we wish to be free to say that, though we realized it might not be possible to reach the objective."[44] When Mackenzie King explained to Ralston that the agreement could be signed providing the "the" were taken out of the British draft, he agreed to let it go, on the understanding that the British were told that their statement meant the same thing to the Canadian Government, with or without the "the." That was done. The agreement was signed in the Prime Minister's office at midnight. The next day—17 December—was Mackenzie King's birthday. The agreement was accordingly dated 17 December. The Prime Minister, as all knew, attached importance to such things.

*J. W. Pickersgill, *The Mackenzie King Record*, vol. I, *1939–1944* (Toronto, 1960), pp. 52–9.

" 'I think I said the right thing . . .' " (p. 39)
Mackenzie King after addressing the Assembly of the League
of Nations, 29 September 1936 (P.A.C.)

". . . Riddell . . . working
side by side with Anthony
Eden . . ."
(p. 26)
(Alfred Pasche, Geneva)

" 'I am certainly going to give him a good spanking' . . ." (p. 26)
Mackenzie King and Walter Riddell (P.A.C.)

" '. . . exceptional opportunities of conversation with the President . . .' " (p. 42)
Mackenzie King and Franklin Roosevelt at Quebec, July 1936 (P.A.C.)

"Never . . . had the Imperial Conference come to so fundamental a dispute . . ."
(p. 59)
London, May 1937. *L* to *R*: Savage, Lyons, Baldwin, George VI, Mackenzie King,
Hertzog (P.A.C.)

" 'Von Neurath impressed me very much . . .' " (p. 46)
Mackenzie King with the German Foreign Minister in Berlin, June 1937 (P.A.C.)

"... the faithful Skelton ..."
(p. 36)
The Under Secretary of State
for External Affairs in 1939
(P.A.C.)

"... second only to Skelton
in the Department of Ex-
ternal Affairs" (p. 72)
Loring Christie in 1939
(Karsh, Ottawa)

"He was not one to underestimate his contribution."
(p. 135)
Ian Mackenzie, Minister of National Defence, October 1935 to September 1939 (P.A.C.)

". . . a brilliant staff officer . . ."
(p. 138)
H. D. G. Crerar, Director of Military Operations and Intelligence, 1935–1938
(Army Records)

ABOVE: " 'The forces of evil have been loosed in the world . . .' " (p. 154)
Mackenzie King broadcasting on 3 September 1939. *L* to *R*: Power, Lapointe, King, Rogers (P.A.C.)

BELOW: ". . . a trying experience for both sides . . ." (p. 107)
Lord Riverdale and Mackenzie King signing the British Commonwealth Air Training Agreement, 17 December 1939 (P.A.C.)

ABOVE: " '. . . the preparations were utterly inadequate . . .' " (p. 153)
1st Division leaving Halifax, December 1939 (P.A.C.)

BELOW: " 'It's so sensible, it's sensational.' " (p. 209)
The Permanent Joint Board on Defence, September 1940 (P.A.C.)
In the front row *L* to *R*: Lt.-Gen. S. D. Embick (U.S. Army); O. M. Biggar (Joint Chairman for Canada); J. P. Moffat (U.S. Minister to Canada); Mackenzie King; Fiorello La Guardia (Joint Chairman for U.S.); J. L. Ralston (Minister of National Defence); Capt. H. W. Hill (U.S. Navy).

MUNITIONS AND SUPPLY

As rearmament began in earnest in Britain, the United Kingdom government gave some thought to encouraging munitions production in the dominions as a supplementary source of supply. A "liaison letter" was sent in April 1936 from the Chief of the Imperial General Staff to his colleagues in Australia and Canada asking them to consider the project.

In Canada, it was favourably regarded by two groups. One was the Canadian military. Creating a munitions industry in Canada would not merely help the British to overcome their own deficiencies in ammunition and equipment; it would help the Canadian forces overcome theirs. "The Canadian Forces today," noted a member of the General Staff on 11 April, "suffer from a surplus of men over material, and if one were to qualify the word 'material' by the adjective 'modern', the surplus is almost infinite."[45] Ordinarily Canada looked to Britain as its source of supply. But now she was likely to look in vain. "It is highly improbable," wrote the Chief of the General Staff, General E. C. Ashton, in July 1936, "that [Britain] will be able to procure her own requirements within the next two or three years. Charity begins at home. The Dominions' orders will, in all probability, be delayed until home interests are met. This means a delay on various lines of possibly four or five years."[46] By creating her own ammunition and equipment plant, Canada could not only help the British rearmament programme, she could help her own. There might even be a mutually profitable division of labour. "If we could promise," a member of the General Staff speculated, "that we would make an important contribution to Imperial munition supply in an emergency—not an impossible promise, in view of what we accomplished during the Great War—we ought to be able to obtain a *quid pro quo* in the way of favoured treatment in re-equipping our forces with guns, machine guns and aircraft."[47]

The other group in Canada looking with favour upon a Canadian munitions industry was composed of industrialists. In 1936, several Canadian businessmen, attracted by the news of the rearmament programme in Britain, offered their facilities to the War Office and the Air Ministry. At this time the British Government was reluctant to place munitions orders overseas; munitions capacity was still not being used to the full at home, and domestic orders were more speedily and economically filled. Even so, one important order—for 50,000 3.7 inch anti-aircraft shells—was placed by the War Office with the National Steel Car Corporation of Hamilton, Ont.[48]

The Government of Canada did not share the enthusiasm of the military and the business community for the stimulus to arms manufacture provided by the British rearmament programme. The Prime Minister especially was unenthusiastic. He was still haunted by the spectre of "the merchants of death." More than once during the next few months was he to express privately his sense of outrage at being victimized by "a lot of men interested in the manufacture of munitions" and who were trying "to force the hand of our Government . . . into playing the Tory game." He was particularly incensed by reports (which could not indeed have been less accurate) that he had returned from his European trip in the fall of 1936 loaded with munitions orders. "I see the need for great caution," he wrote, "in permitting manufacture of munitions, anti-aircraft, etc., in Canada. Already there are many firms seeking contracts from the British Government and trying to use our administration as means to that end."

Publicly his attitude was necessarily more circumspect. He expressed it in a letter to a member of Parliament who had written to request that the Government lend its good offices on behalf of Canadian industrialists seeking to solicit munitions orders in the United Kingdom:

We see no reason why a Canadian firm established for the manufacture of munitions should be precluded from obtaining orders from the British Government. It would be necessary, of course, to see that it was distinctly understood that such orders as were obtained were at the instance of the firm itself, and not either directly or indirectly at the instance of the Government of Canada. Any company doing business will of course be subject to any regulations or control which the Government may decide to exercise at any time.[49]

With this faint blessing, the Canadian merchants of death went forth to sell their wares as best they could.

II

The paper sent to the Canadian government in March 1937 by the Chiefs of Staff Sub-Committee of the Imperial Defence Committee, instead of enlisting its support and co-operation had had the effect of arousing its resentment and alarm.* No feature of the document was more offensive to the Canadian government than its proposal that it should encourage the creation of munitions manufacturing facilities in the Dominion. O. D. Skelton prepared a scathing denunciation of the proposal. "This means," he wrote of it on 29 March, "presumably a

*See above, pp. 82–3.

Canadian 'shadow munitions industry' in peacetime—i.e., factories to be extended or built on the basis of orders for the present U.K. emergency re-armament programme; to be geared also to the purpose of starting a greatly expanded production immediately on the outbreak of war, and to be kept ready for that purpose—i.e., the so-called 'war potential.' " For various reasons Skelton found this undertaking undesirable. There would be complications in regard to the financing and administration of the programme—an aspect, he noted in passing, which the Chiefs' paper had not considered at all. It would not be consistent with the basis of Canadian defence policy, which was to assume responsibility for local defence measures only. There would be undesirable economic side-effects, among them the peril of inflation and a distortion of the structure of the economy. It might constitute a threat to Canadian autonomy: "Once such a Canadian munitions industry were started, would not its progression and consequences pass largely out of Canadian hands, seeing that by hypothesis it would be geared to U.K. requirements?" Last, but by no means least, it would enhance the authority of the military. "The scope of the programme would seem likely to be largely in the hands of soldiers. In view of the munitions history of 1914 and succeeding years, this seems scarcely a reassuring reflection."

Skelton's strictures upon this and other proposals of the British military were, as already noted, placed before a meeting of the cabinet on 15 April by Mackenzie King, where they were endorsed by the Government. Meanwhile, the British Government had made it plain that the question of promoting munitions capacity in the Dominions as a measure of imperial defence would figure prominently on the agenda at the impending Imperial Conference. Among the papers at the disposal of the Canadian delegation in London—papers described by Mackenzie King as required for "combatting demands for centralized policies and programmes on defence and foreign affairs"—was a further memorandum by Skelton, setting out the pros and cons of a policy of Canadian co-operation with the United Kingdom in munitions and supply:

On behalf of this suggestion it may be urged:
1. Such participation would be particularly helpful to the U.K.
2. It would be profitable to Canadian industry, manufactures, mine owners, workmen.
3. It would be more acceptable to some Canadians than sending their own sons.
4. It would be useful for Canada's own defence, in helping to build up available and cheaper sources of supply of munitions we need.
5. We cannot expect preferences in peace trade unless we give aid in war trade.

On the other hand it might be contended:

1. Participation by agreement with the U.K. Government in such a programme in peace time commits us to participation in war, because of claims of honour, creation of vested interests in such trade, and developing staff conversations.

2. Possibility of large war profits would produce a war mentality.

3. No certainty that if the U.S. bans or rations munitions of war material to belligerents, we can count on getting unlimited materials from U.S. to meet our war manufacturing needs; neither the peace nor the profit instincts of the United States people would allow them to see us profit by their self-denial.

4. An alternative policy, without commitment, might be to develop our own moderate munitions industry, in private and/or public plants: in war we can expand this if we then so desire: our peace time requirement would cost us more, but little compared to the cost of a war commitment, or to the cost of making such a public decision *now* before there is any certainty the emergency will arise.

5. Are we to seek this trade just when other countries are realizing its danger and sacrificing profit and old doctrines of prestige to avoid it?

Skelton, it is clear, wanted to have as little to do as possible with any programme for producing munitions in peacetime Canada—particularly a programme designed mainly for United Kingdom requirements. The Prime Minister shared this attitude. The Canadian military, on the other hand, were anxious to accept the suggestion from the imperial Chiefs. They regarded it as "the outstanding issue" in the field of imperial defence co-operation, and had repeatedly pointed out "the very important defence advantages of adopting this course of action." No authorization or instruction on the matter, one way or the other, had reached the Joint Staff Committee even as the Imperial Conference in London got under way; on 5 May they appealed once again to their minister for "approval of this development and of service conversations designed to further it."

On 17 May, the Minister of National Defence asked the Prime Minister for a decision on what he described as the all-important question of munitions and supply. There would soon be a meeting of the Commonwealth Ministers of Defence, and it was imperative that he should know what line to take. He had no doubt in his own mind, he wrote, as to what line he would like to take:

My own opinion is as follows:

We can only carry out our own Defence policy in Canada by co-operation in regard to supply and equipment unless we are immediately prepared to embark upon a policy of Government ownership in regard to our own needs.

If we fail to take every possible step to obtain the supplies voted by Parliament we shall certainly be accused of negligence.

We should establish the principle in regard to private industry that only well-established enterprises be given orders and that no new private industrial undertaking be established for the purpose of providing defence supplies alone.

If such new undertakings must be established they should be government owned.

I see no possibility of harm in co-operating with the British Government in placing orders with well-established private firms. They have already placed an order in Hamilton. The principle was approved in Council. I do not believe it was even mentioned in Parliament.

The British Government can deal with reputable Canadian firms directly, we can deal with the same firms, but not the British Government through us nor the Canadian Government through them. In other words, our only responsibility would be the supplying of information. The principle of limitation of profits, of course, always applies.

I feel very strongly that if we reject the opportunity of co-operation in regard to essential supplies, we shall be subject to very severe criticism. In fact, without such co-operation, I fail to see how the Department of National Defence can successfully function. The only alternative is self-containment through public ownership, as in Australia. That would be quite satisfactory to me personally, but very costly.[50]

Along the lines of this approach, which stopped far short of what the Imperial Chiefs, supported by the Joint Staff Committee, had thought desirable, a Canadian policy was finally decided upon. Ian Mackenzie put it before the Imperial Conference during the first meeting of its Committee on Munitions and Food Supplies on 28 May. In any expansion of Canada's munitions capacity, he stated, the development and extension of government arsenals would be given priority. If, as seemed probable, orders for munitions were to be placed with private industry, the Government was prepared to co-operate with private industry; it was no less prepared to regulate it, with respect to both profit and production. Orders should be taken only by established firms: the Government did not wish new industry to come into being to take advantage of the demand for armaments. Finally, the Government did not wish to enter into negotiations on behalf of either the British Government or of private industry in any orders that might be placed; it would confine its function to that of supplying information to one party or the other.

The last of these principles proved in the event to be more easily enunciated than implemented.

III

Early in 1937, a Canadian firm, the John Inglis Company of Toronto, requested the Government for the benefit of its good offices in negotiating with the British Government a contract for the manufacture of Bren light machine guns. The President of the Company, James Hahn, duly received from the Prime Minister a personal letter of introduction to the High Commissioner in London, requesting Mr. Vincent Massey to facilitate Mr. Hahn's discussions with the British authorities. At the same time, the Canadian Government entrusted Mr. Hahn with a mission to be carried out on its behalf. He was asked to provide it with his confidential assessment of "the possibility of producing the Bren gun in Canada."[51] Mr. Hahn thus acquired a dual status and a dual function. He was a supplicant on behalf of his company. He was also an intelligence agent on behalf of the Canadian Government. It was not easy to reconcile these two roles, or to keep them distinct.

Through the intervention of the High Commission, Mr. Hahn secured an interview, conducted more or less on an official basis, with the British Minister for the Co-ordination of Defence and the Director General of Defence Production. Out of this negotiation, and others which followed, there emerged a proposal for Anglo-Canadian co-operation in the production of Bren guns in Canada. To a projected Canadian order for the guns, the War Office would add an order of its own, thus lengthening the production run and providing economies of scale.

This proposal was considered by the Imperial Conference's Committee on Munitions and Food Supplies. The Committee did not specifically endorse it, but agreed that it was the kind of project which might usefully be followed up. It was followed up. Throughout the remainder of 1937, and during the early part of 1938, a steady stream of communications passed between the Department of National Defence and its liaison officer attached to Canada House, London. It was later frankly conceded by the Minister of National Defence that the object of this exchange was "to press the British authorities for a decision" in favour of the War Office order. It was exactly this sort of pressure that Mackenzie King had wanted his Government to refrain from exerting. He was unaware that it was being exerted.

By March 1937 the terms of a deal had been arranged. The Canadian Government would place an order with the John Inglis Company for 7,000 Bren guns, on a "cost-plus" basis. To this order the War Office would add an order of its own for 5,000 guns. The costs of tooling the plant for production would be borne jointly by the two governments, and the machinery required would become the property of the Canadian Government. The Minister of National Defence placed this proposal before his cabinet colleagues on 21 March, and an order-in-council authorizing the Department of National Defence to sign a contract was passed that day. "Did not like signing this Order," Mackenzie King wrote afterwards, "but the Department of Defence's explanation made it singularly imperative to do so." His premonition that all was not well was to be fully justified by events.

The contract between the Canadian Government and the company was signed on 31 March. It has been described in the official history of the Canadian Army as "the largest and most significant single step towards the re-armament of the Canadian land forces taken before the outbreak of war," and as representing "the only important progress made towards the goal of acquiring the armament of two divisions."[52] The manner by which it had been drawn up was something else again. That became the subject of official enquiry by a Royal Commission. The failure of the officials of the Department of National Defence to place tenders for competitive bids by other companies led critics in the Conservative Opposition to charge that political patronage had played its part in the proceedings. The charge was not sustained by the Royal Commission, but it seemed at least plausible. The Royal Commission recommended that an independent board should assume responsibility for defence contracts between government and private industry. The Government was only too eager to accept the recommendation, and in May 1939 a Defence Purchasing Board was created by Act of Parliament. At least one member of the military thought this a retrograde measure. "The present Government has, in truth, stepped out from under their responsibility," Colonel H. D. G. Crerar wrote privately in August 1939. "You will note a clause which, in effect, says that the Department of National Defence (or its Chiefs of Staff) is required to convince the Board of the necessity of purchasing this type of armament, or that. To my mind this clause is fundamentally improper, dangerous and incompatible with the real responsibilities of the Cabinet, or its chief technical advisers. It means that the Board has power to determine defence policies—whereas its functions, at the most, should be limited to the purchasing of armament."[53] It was fair criticism, though unremarked at the time.

The Report of the Royal Commission investigating the Bren gun contract revealed that throughout the course of the negotiations the Department of National Defence had gone well beyond the limits of what the Prime Minister had intended to be its proper authority. Far from confining itself to supplying the parties concerned with information, the department had brought what the Report described as "a full year of pressure" to bear upon the War Office, in an effort to get it to place its order with the Inglis Company. The end may have justified the means, but the means unquestionably defied the policy.

Policy, so far from being changed, was more stringently than ever asserted following the revelations of the Bren gun inquiry. The desire of the Government not to become involved in the placing of British munitions orders in the Dominion was so intense as to create the impression that it desired to discourage the placing of such orders. Certain Canadian industrialists, on approaching the United Kingdom authorities to solicit purchases of munitions, were told that the British Government was reluctant to buy from the Dominon since it thought the Canadian Government did not want it to. Among those thus rebuffed were representatives of the Ford Motor Company of Canada who were informed by the Secretary of State for Air that owing to the attitude of their Government the Air Ministry could not entertain their proposal to manufacture twenty-five or fifty aircraft engines for the R.A.F.

When word of these affairs reached the Canadian Government, it took steps to try to correct what it regarded as an improper and misleading interpretation of its policy. The High Commissioner in London was instructed to let it be known in the proper quarters that the Canadian Government so far from wishing to discourage the placing of munitions orders in the Dominion would welcome it. At the same time, a meeting was arranged between representatives of the Canadian Manufacturers' Association and members of the Government, at which the former might express their grievances and the latter attempt to clear the air. It took place on 28 June in the East Block. About twenty industrialists attended, led by the past President of the Association, W. D. Black. Mackenzie King opened the proceedings. His account of them follows:

I began by saying the Government had been in advance of public opinion in its beginnings re increasing defence, and showed wherein we were alive to the situation as developing before others were prepared to support us. I saw that Black was in a sort of belligerent and combative mood and ready to have it appear that the Government was indifferent or obstructing. I began then, quite openly before the others, to put them on the defensive, by asking if they could give any instance of the Government's lack of desire to have our manufacturers obtain British contracts. I said if they could not do so, to hold their peace. There was not one of them who could cite any grounds for the rumour. . . . I made it plain we would welcome all contracts that could be obtained in a proper way, and that we would lend our good offices to see that the manufacturers were properly introduced. What they wanted was our Government to have the British Government invite them to come over [to the United Kingdom], and also to have our Government invite the British Government to send munitions to Canada. I made it plain that we had no business to tell the British Government what they were or were not to do, but that we would welcome having placed in Canada any orders which they might care to give to our industrialists. . . . They wanted letters of introduction to the High Commissioner, to have him introduce them to the different departments of the [British] Government. I . . . said that it was for doing this very thing I discovered, to my surprise, when the Bren Gun inquiry opened, that I was the main villain in the piece, because I was the one who had given the letter of introduction to a Canadian manufacturer to the High Commissioner to have him discuss the possibility of obtaining a contract from the British Government. However, I thought that what I had done then was proper, and I would do the same for them. . . .[54]

Arrangements for its reception in Britain having been made, a Canadian Manufacturers' Association delegation set sail in the summer of 1939, arriving in London early in August. It was not exactly an official deputation, but it went with the government's knowledge and approval and it contained, in addition to the supplicant industrialists, Major-General A. G. L. McNaughton (then President of the National Research Council and within weeks to assume command of the 1st Canadian Division), and two representatives of National Defence Headquarters. On 4 August the group was welcomed at Canada House by the High Commissioner. "There is little likelihood," Vincent Massey warned them, "of large contracts or many contracts being placed in Canada just now. As I understand it, however, the enquiries you will be making and the information you will receive will relate to a possible emergency rather than to conditions as they are."[55] But the delegation had arrived too late for any useful long-range or even intermediate-range planning to be done. Before any further peacetime orders could be placed, it was no longer peacetime.

IV

"At the outbreak of war," the British official history of North American supply during the Second World War notes, with perhaps a trace of reproach, "the Canadian munitions industry, outside the Dominion arsenal, still consisted of only one firm in actual production on British orders"—viz., the National Steel Car Corporation, which was by then turning out 3.7-inch shells at the rate of 3000 rounds per week. Who and what were responsible for this desultory showing?

Both the British and Canadian governments must bear a share of the blame. On the British side, a number of factors played their part. One was finance. The British authorities were reluctant to expend dollar reserves in North America, and munitions orders in Canada suffered somewhat as a result. Another was time. At least until the fall of France, British strategy was based on the assumption of a three years' war.* To

*Of the members of the British Government with whom Norman Rogers, as Minister of National Defence, conferred in London in April and May 1940, only

build up in Canada a munitions industry worthy of the name might take as long as three years, by which time (according to the planners) the war would be won—or lost. There may have been some scepticism in Whitehall as to whether the Canadian economy was really up to producing munitions of the kind and on the scale required. There was certainly pressure from British industrialists, who naturally wanted their own unused capacity fully taken up before the British government turned to their competitors in Canada. And the British industrialists were already looking ahead to the situation after the war was over.* Under these circumstances, the Canadian officer representing the Ordnance Service of the Department of National Defence at Canada House had a difficult and frustrating assignment. "Every incoming ship bears its quota of Canadian industrialists all bent on reaping a harvest," Colonel G. P. Loggie reported in July 1938. "It is my job to tote them around when these jobs are sponsored from the Hill [i.e., by Members of Parliament]. Thus far it is an empty dream . . . British capacity is sufficient for present needs . . ."[56]

On the Canadian side, only one factor played its part. It was the pervasive and paralysing policy of "no commitments." The only significant departure from that policy in matters of munitions had been the Bren gun contract: that was entered into with misgiving by Mackenzie King, and the troubles which came in its train only strengthened his resolve not to get embroiled again. Both within his cabinet and without there were those who approved of his attitude, and there were those who did not. One of the latter, the editor of the influential *Financial Post*, wrote a perceptive letter on the subject to the High Commissioner in London on the eve of the manufacturers' mission, and on the eve of war:

It has been difficult to put one's finger upon any single reason why British orders for Canada have been so slow in coming. Exchange may be one, but Britain has been able to find exchange to buy in non-Empire countries. Probably there has been some disappointment around the War Office because Canada's policy has been more isolationist than that of the other Dominions. But the chief obstacle seems to have been Mr. King's indifference (if not his outright opposition) to British munitions orders for Canadian plants— expressed less in a positive way than in many subtle negative ways. . . .

Lord Halifax envisaged a lengthy war. Oliver Stanley thought it would be over in a year; Sir Samuel Hoare (who had formulated the three years' hypothesis) thought it would be over in two. Diary entries for 20 April 1940, 22 April 1940, and 25 April 1940, Rogers Papers.

*"When I was in Europe late last Fall," a member of the Canadian War Cabinet wrote in June 1940, "people were not discussing *how* they were going to *win* the war against Germany but what they were going to do with Germany after the war was won." T. A. Crerar to J. W. Dafoe, 10 June 1940, Dafoe Papers.

The trouble is that for every time Mr. King tells what Canada *will* do in a crisis there are a dozen times when he emphasizes—usually without necessity—what Canada will *not* do. This peculiar habit of his of hedging his support about with limitations of a legalistic nature showed up even in the statement he issued when he announced the Canadian Manufacturers' delegation to the Old Country. Following his policy of the past, he said, the Canadian Government would remain aloof from any direct negotiations for the manufacture of munitions in this country. Negotiations must be carried on between the United Kingdom officials and the Canadian industries.

In the first place, if this is Ottawa's policy, it is best left unsaid. Why publish it to Hitler & Co.? It is little remarks of that kind that infuriate Canadians who have a sense of intense loyalty to the British connection and a keen desire to range Canada in the democratic, anti-aggressor camp.

And, in the second place, is it the right policy? Should the Canadian Government not be co-operating directly and in every way in making Canadian industrial enterprise and equipment available for service to the Empire at this time?

In any event, there are many people in Canada who feel that Mr. King has manoeuvred Canada into an ungenerous attitude towards the Mother Country and their views may be a minor factor at least in the election. . . .

I think that the average Canadian industrialist looks at the problem this way:

Canada would prefer not to become a munitions manufacturing country. The business is not a pleasant one and not a stable one. But a situation has developed in which rearmament has become an unhappy necessity for the democracies.

Rearmament involves the use of industrial capacity. Canadian industry has a job to do and wants to know what that job is.

It is not merely a job for the moment. At any time war may come and Canada will then be an important arm in the British effort. It is the one industrialized British country safe from bombing attack. It is connected with England by the most easily protected sea route. It is adjacent to the world's greatest industrial nation. Through Canada, Britain can tap American technical ability, capital and other resources, even in a war in which the United States remained neutral.

But Canadian industrialists do not want to be suddenly summoned to the colours without preparation. They would like to learn now the job they would have to do if war came. Hence the importance of educational orders, which happily could be added to Canada's small armaments orders to make up economic quantities.

When Canadian industrialists have approached the War Office they have (with few exceptions) found themselves blocked and put off with mysterious evasions: the exchange problem; the fact that British plants could turn out all that was needed; the lack of official credentials from Ottawa. Unofficial but well-informed people in England have told them that England will not favour Canada with orders because our Government does not want them placed here; because Mr. King told the Imperial Conference . . . that Canada might remain neutral and embargo arms shipments; because Canada is lagging in its contribution to Empire defence; and a variety of other similar things.

Perhaps this new mission will get behind some of these smoke screens. But Ottawa, instead of merely loaning them a technical man or two, should be leading this delegation. Surely we have some duty to the Empire and to Democracy.[57]

V

Pre-war co-operation between Canada and the United Kingdom in the production of aircraft was somewhat greater than in the production of munitions. It could hardly have been less.

The Canadian aircraft industry before 1939 was not impressive. It consisted of eight small plants, about 4,000 employees, and an annual average production of around 40 aeroplanes. As late as 1935 no firm existed capable of producing combat aircraft. The first contract for combat aircraft was let in 1936 to the firm of Canadian Vickers Ltd.; it was for Stranraer flying boats, the first of which was delivered to the R.C.A.F. late in 1938.

But already in 1937 the infant Canadian industry was being closely observed by the Air Ministry. Its interest in the wartime potential of aircraft manufacture in Canada was aroused when, late in that year, the Canadian Government embarked upon what one Air Ministry official described as "a very ambitious programme of local construction of airframes of British Service types in quantities confined for the moment to R.C.A.F. requirements."[58] For the British, the operative words were "for the moment."

In May 1938, an Air Ministry mission visited the Dominion. Its main purpose in coming to North America had been to investigate the supply situation in the United States, but it had also been instructed to explore "the possibilities of creating a war potential in Canada." (The same mission, led by Mr. J. G. Weir, had discussed with the Canadian Prime Minister the question of creating R.A.F. training establishments in Canada, with less than positive results.*) During its brief visit to Ottawa, it was informed by Mackenzie King that it should deal directly with Canadian industry and not with the Canadian Government. The venue of negotiations was accordingly shifted from Ottawa to Montreal, where, on 18 May, a meeting was held with representatives of ten Canadian aircraft firms; representatives of the Department of National Defence were kept closely informed of the discussions. The mission informed those present that the United Kingdom aimed at the manufacture of "British types under licence" for the purpose of creating a "genuine war

*See above, pp. 94–5.

potential" and especially "a war potential for the production of heavy long-range bombers which could be delivered by flight across the Atlantic." There was a hint, but no promise, of "small peace-time orders to keep such a potential in existence," and under pressure the Mission mentioned a figure of "5000 airframes a year."[59]

The outcome of these discussions was the incorporation of Canadian aircraft firms in a single company, the Canadian Associated Aircraft Company, with which the United Kingdom authorities would in future negotiate contracts for the production of aircraft in the Dominion. One or two members of the cabinet took a dim view of this scheme. "Every demagogue in the country," wrote C. G. Power to the Prime Minister in some agitation, "will say that the Government is in the hands of . . . the munitions makers."[60] While there was not much the Government could do about that, it did do what it could to check the impression that the arrangement was inter-governmental in character. The Prime Minister took strong exception on this account to the proposed wording of a press announcement prepared by the British High Commissioner:

I pointed out that the communication, which it was proposed to give to the press in England and in Canada, was calculated to create an entirely erroneous impression in that, from the reading of it, it would appear that the whole matter had been carried out under the aegis of the Canadian Government. It also conveyed the impression that we were approving the personnel . . . , and would be assuming the obligation of inspection, etc., for the British Government. In other words, the arrangement was made to look more and more like one between the United Kingdom Government and the Dominion Government, rather than what in fact it was, an arrangement between certain manufacturing interests in Canada. Moreover, as worded, the proposed notice was to enable Canada to supply them with planes, by air, conceivably in a time of emergency, and the Government was committing itself, regardless of the decision Parliament might make with respect to participation in war or a step which might so involve the Dominion.[61]

The text of the announcement was duly revised, and was finally released in a form judged by Mackenzie King to be sufficiently innocuous.

Only one contract was negotiated by the Canadian Associated Aircraft Company and the Air Ministry; it was for the production of airframes for eighty Hampden bombers. As with the Bren gun contract, the cost per unit was higher than if the contract had been placed in the United Kingdom, but the increment of 25 per cent was regarded by the Air Ministry "as a reasonable price for the additional capacity thus created."[62] A further order—for forty Hurricane fighters—was placed with the Canadian Car and Foundry Company. The first Canadian-built Hurricane arrived in Britain on 29 February 1940. It was not a moment too soon.

VI

Just as the British Government sought to place aircraft orders in the Dominion so as to create a wartime potential, so it sought to stimulate the Canadian shipbuilding industry for the same purpose. Once again the Canadian Government's primary concern was not to become involved. A letter by the Prime Minister to the Governor General tells most of the tale:

Yesterday [22 July 1938], Sir Francis Floud [the British High Commissioner] came to speak to me about having the Vickers people begin the manufacture of destroyers for the British Government—and Canadian as well, if desired—at Montreal. I understand that someone representing the Vickers firm has been taking up the matter with the British Government, and the Government has indicated its willingness to place an order for one or two destroyers, if the Canadian Government is agreeable to see them constructed in Montreal.

Frankly, I am a little concerned at a proposal of the kind, particularly following, as it does, so immediately upon the request for the training of British pilots in Canada. When, some years ago [in 1928], we had decided to place orders for a couple of destroyers, the Cabinet went very fully into the question of how far it would be advisable for us to encourage their construction by Vickers, at Montreal. It would have meant an additional cost of about two-thirds than required through having them made in Britain. It was urged, however, that the money would be spent in Canada, and that this was a factor which, at a time of unemployment which we were then experiencing, was not to be overlooked.

However, as I recall the discussion, the Cabinet of the day felt very strongly that there were objections to beginning an industry for the building of warships in Canada, more particularly as once the plant were established, it would mean continual pressure upon the Government for the placing of additional orders. Apart from that, it was felt that a step of the kind might give rise to a controversy which would be unfortunate.

Those factors, of course, present themselves anew, at this moment, in a way, however, many times exaggerated by what has already been discussed with respect to the establishment of British flying schools . . . I realize, that the time is coming, if it is not already here, when we should, perhaps, begin at Montreal or elsewhere construction of an establishment for warships of different kinds. I appreciate too the desire of the British Government to have establishments of the sort in Canada, as also in other Dominions. I am very doubtful, however, as to the wisdom of inaugurating a step of the kind just at this particular time. . . .[63]

The cabinet considered the problem a few days later, and agreed that while the Canadian Government should not stand in the way of Vickers obtaining any Admiralty contract it might come by, it would stand aside from the negotiations and would in no event place a concurrent order for the Royal Canadian Navy. "Our attitude," Mackenzie King wrote to Lord Tweedsmuir in England, "would be the same with respect to the placing of orders for destroyers as it was with respect to the placing of orders for aircraft. It should be a matter of direct negotiation by one Government or another with the industries concerned. . . ."[64] The Admiralty did not proceed with the Vickers order. On the outbreak of war, no ships of any kind were under construction in Canadian shipyards for the Royal Navy.

VII

Pre-war efforts by the United Kingdom authorities to ensure from the senior dominion a wartime supply of food and raw materials were similarly inconclusive.

Of food and raw materials, food, for Britain, presented the greater urgency, in view of the likelihood of blockade. Two methods of dealing with the problem presented themselves. One was to stockpile. The other was to safeguard the sources of future supply by contracting to buy all or most of an exporter's output during any future conflict. The methods were not alternatives but complementary.

The stockpiling solution was canvassed, with no result, as early as 1935. In April 1936, *The Times* suggested that the Canadian Wheat Board might be persuaded to hold some of its surplus stocks in the United Kingdom if the British government would undertake to bear the extra cost involved, but this proposal was not seriously considered.

The method of entering into long-term contracts for future supplies of foods was not as easy as it sounds. Apart from the difficulty of securing the co-operation of the various grain interests in the United Kingdom, there was the difficulty of undertaking so large-scale an operation without disturbing the market: if the Government moved in, or if it was thought to be ready to move in, prices would go up. The wheat market was particularly vulnerable in this respect. It was suggested that prices could be held down if the British Government by-passed the market and instead undertook "to purchase secretly and directly from the Canadian Wheat Board a large block of 'May futures'. . . ; to build silos to hold this purchase on delivery; and in due course to announce to the trade that the wheat had been bought as an emergency reserve, and that no further purchases would be made so long as trade stocks remained normal."[65] But for a year the British authorities held back. Not until early in 1938 did the Government, with the co-operation of the leading millers, put a food storage plan into effect.

The implementation of the plan required government agents to buy wheat in preternatural secrecy, so as to avoid pushing up the price. It thereby by-passed inter-governmental consultations, and it is quite reasonable to suppose that the Canadian Government had no official knowledge, perhaps no knowledge of any kind, of the presence in Winnipeg during the second week of April 1938 of a buyer from the Co-operative Wholesale Society, working under orders from Sir Henry French, Director of the Food (Defence Plans) Department in the United Kingdom Government. But for other commodities, formal contracts, and therefore inter-governmental consultations, could not be avoided.

The question of securing options on food and raw materials supplies in the event of war had figured, along with others, in the paper sent out to the Dominions by the Chiefs of Staff Sub-Committee of the Committee of Imperial Defence in March 1937. O. D. Skelton recorded his views as follows:

It would be urged that this proposal would meet more support than the suggestion of an expeditionary force; that, in any case, these goods would be shipped to Britain in war; that it is only a question of how much; that it is little to ask that steps be taken to ensure adequate supply and that unless this is arranged in advance it will be difficult for the U.K. to make final plans for its requirements.

On the other hand, it might be contended that advance undertakings involve a commitment to active participation in future wars; that aside from this point of principle it would be necessary to consider carefully what the U.K. demand and the Canadian supply might be; and whether and how far curtailment would be possible in supply to neutral countries, particularly to the United States, if we are to continue to be dependent on it for other supplies vital for peace and war; that the difficulty in planning for supplies without commitments in advance applies equally to planning for manpower without commitments in advance, and is inherent in the ambiguous international position of the Dominions; and that in any case a refusal to make such commitments does not mean Britain's foregoing alternative sources of supply, as there are in most cases large alternative sources from which advance commitments could be secured. . . .[66]

The issue came up for discussion in the Committee on Munitions and Food Supplies created by the Imperial Conference of 1937. Only the Australian representative undertook, on behalf of his Government, to make supplies available to the United Kingdom in the event of war. The Canadian representative promised only to provide information. Consequently, the Committee was compelled to come to the conclusion that it was impracticable to make in advance any binding arrangements or even to prepare estimates of the quantity of each product which would likely be required by the United Kingdom in wartime. Such arrangements, it was recognized, would depend on circumstances then impossible to foresee: the character of the conflict; the number and nature of Britain's wartime allies, if any; the availability of shipping.

In the summer of 1938, representatives of the Board of Trade entered into negotiations with the dominion governments for bulk purchases of a number of strategic commodities. The negotiations with Australia and New Zealand were productive, resulting in a contract to purchase the entire wool clip of the two dominions.[67] The negotiations with Canada were inconclusive. The British wanted to sign long-term contracts for the purchase of copper, zinc, lead, and aluminum, much of the output of which was then being sold to Japan. The Canadian Government was unwilling to enter into the necessary commitments. "Until the eve of hostilities," writes the author of the official British history of the control of raw materials, "virtually no preparations had been made for the war-time purchase of raw materials in North America."[68]

VIII

The coming of the Second World War did little at first to accelerate the flow of munitions and supply from Canada to the United Kingdom. Until the great supply crisis of the summer of 1940, no sense of urgency prevailed in the United Kingdom. The same factors which made for inaction before the war—the dollar shortage, the three years' war hypothesis, the reluctance to create post-war competition overseas—continued during the first few months of the war itself to invest the whole supply effort with a deadly lethargy and languor. "Owing to the combination of a long view on finance and a short view on the value of a munitions potential," the official United Kingdom historian has commented, "Canada continued to be treated during the whole period of 'the twilight war' as a purely marginal source of armaments supply. . . . Practically the whole of the munitions programme was still allotted to United Kingdom firms and there was no real attempt to exploit the latent resources of Canadian industry on a coherent plan. . . ."[69]

What was being done? By the end of May 1940 nearly half of the original order of forty Canadian-built Hurricane fighter aircraft had been delivered. Ten corvettes were supplied by June—the result of a barter arrangement whereby Canada built corvettes for the Admiralty in exchange for two Tribal class destroyers built in Britain for the Royal Canadian Navy. The Bren gun contract was starting to produce, but the first deliveries were taken by the Canadian Government for the

Army. "Actual shipments of munitions as such to Britain up to the 15th May 1940 consisted of 25 million rounds of small arms ammunition, 800 tons of toluol and 225 tons of T.N.T.," plus "appreciable . . . quantities of 3.7-inch, 25 pounder and 4.5-inch empty shell for British filling factories. . . . The vast resources of the automobile industry were virtually untapped, and there was a large unused reserve of heavy engineering capacity, especially in the railway workshops."[70] The British Ministry of Supply, by 1 May 1940, had purchased in Canada about £500,000 of boots and socks, and about £40,000 of railway equipment (mainly timber sleepers from British Columbia). These orders did little more, as the British official historian has observed, than to "scrape the surface of the Canadian potential."[71]

What efforts did the Canadian Government make to try to increase the flow of munitions and supply to the United Kingdom? It continued to hold to its pre-war policy of acting as an intermediary between British government purchasing officials and Canadian manufacturers; it was still reluctant to enter directly into inter-governmental negotiations for defence contracts.

The policy of the Canadian Government in this regard had appeared to Canadian manufacturers to have been unduly cautious even before the outbreak of war; now, with Western Europe reeling before the *Wehrmacht*, it seemed really inexcusable. On 5 June 1940 the President of the Canadian Manufacturers' Association presented a memorandum to the Prime Minister to protest the prevailing state of affairs. "Canadian industry," it stated, "is chafing at the bit and yearning to go." It urged that a ministerial delegation be sent to the United Kingdom at once, "clothed with full authority to clear away misunderstandings that presently exist and which would appear to be responsible for Canada having received only minor orders from the British Government up to this time." Canada's manufacturers, it stated, had been "tremendously disappointed" at the failure of large orders from Britain to materialize; they had "a deep-rooted conviction that there do exist some definite causes why substantial orders have not been placed by the British Government."[72] A delegation of ten members of the Canadian Manufacturers' Association waited upon the Prime Minister the following day, and in the course of their interview made it plain to him that they regarded as the source of the trouble the lukewarm attitude of the Canadian Government towards British placement of orders in the Dominion rather than the attitude of the British Government itself. Mackenzie King resisted this suggestion vigorously. "I spoke out from the shoulder," he wrote after the meeting, in telling his visitors what he regarded as the real reason for the failure of British munitions orders to materialise, "which comes down to the British seeking to keep the contracts in their own hands to try and buy the goodwill of other nations whose friendship could not be relied upon. Also their mistaken view of the war in which financial and economic control would settle the day rather than the *blitzkrieg*."[73]

Rearmament

UP FROM THE DEPTHS

During 1933–1934, the armed forces of Canada reached the nadir of their neglect. The money made available for their maintenance—a little over $13 millions—was barely enough to keep them in being, let alone in a condition which by the most lenient standards could be described as one of combat readiness. The slight increases in military expenditure of the next three fiscal years were consumed in repairing the damage caused by excessive austerity, and produced little of new equipment or additional training. So it was that the Mackenzie King Administration, on taking office in October 1935, found that it had inherited armed forces without arms.*

The sea-going Navy consisted of two serviceable destroyers, and two destroyers and a minesweeper something less than serviceable. On shore, barracks were decrepit, the wireless inadequate, the naval magazine at Esquimalt (having been condemned as long ago as 1905) a menace to the surrounding community. The militia had fared no better. Not a single anti-aircraft gun was to be found in the entire Dominion. Ammunition was scarce and, on account of its great age, a gamble to fire. Mechanized transport was a rarity. The Air Force could muster twenty-three aircraft, but not one of them was judged suitable for active service. For all practical purposes, the country lay "defenceless under the night."

The final act of the out-going Chief of the General Staff, Major-General A. G. L. McNaughton, in 1935, had been to set out the deficiencies of the fighting services in a memorandum, "The Defence of Canada,"

*A detailed account of the straits to which the Great Depression had brought the armed forces of Canada will be found in my *In Defence of Canada*, vol. I, pp. 270–319.

and to appear before the cabinet to argue the case for a steady and long-range expansion of defence expenditure. "It is my firm conviction," he wrote, "that the amounts which have been requested in the Supplementary Votes for the current year should be made available, and that provision in subsequent years should be made on a steadily increasing scale to the end that the Land and Air Forces . . . may be developed in the course of the next five years. . . ."[1] The Bennett Government was unconvinced, or, if convinced, wanted to see if it survived the forthcoming general election before committing the country to greater expenditure on defence. It did not survive. On 22 October, a week after it had been swept from power, McNaughton spoke to O. D. Skelton on the telephone. ". . . Inquired whether or not General [E.C.] Ashton [McNaughton's successor as C.G.S.] had sent him a copy of my memorandum of 28 May 1935. He said he had and that this had been read by himself and Mr. [Loring] Christie and others in his office. Ashton asked for the return of the document. I said that I thought that the document should be shown to the incoming Prime Minister at the earliest possible moment after his assuming office and I strongly requested that this should be done, so that he might be under no misapprehension as to the situation. Dr. Skelton agreed and said he would speak to Ashton."[2] In this way an authoritative account of the depletion and depreciation of the armed forces came before the new Government at the outset.

Their rehabilitation was principally the responsibility of the new Minister of National Defence. To this increasingly important portfolio Mackenzie King appointed Ian Mackenzie. Mackenzie had been brought into the Liberal administration early in 1930 as Minister of Immigration and British Columbia's representative in the cabinet, in spite of the fact that his leader had been warned that he "was a convivial fellow who had not 'taken himself or life very seriously'."[3] During the next five years, he served the party well from the Opposition benches, where his formidable powers in debate were felt to good advantage. It must have been with some doubt that Mackenzie King made Mackenzie Minister of National Defence in October 1935. During his first two years in the post, Mackenzie justified his selection. He was not one to under-estimate his contribution. "I have done more in two years," he told a meeting of the Canadian Military Institute in Toronto on 13 December 1937, "than any Minister will ever do in the Dominion of Canada."[4] However that might be, it was not long before his record was being smudged by scandal and becoming a source of glee among his political opponents and of consternation among his political friends. One of the latter wrote privately in March 1939: "We keep hearing increasingly disturbing things about Ian Mackenzie and his administration of the national defence department. It seems to me that he has absolutely lost all public confidence. . . . Certainly in Air Force circles he is both detested and mistrusted. . . . Why Mr. King keeps him on I don't know. . . . He has made a God-awful mess of his department and should be retired."[5] Mackenzie remained Minister of National Defence until 18 September 1939. His resignation was described by O. D. Skelton (in a personal letter to Norman Rogers, his successor) as "a great relief after months of controversy and fumbling."

On assuming responsibilty for the defence of Canada in October 1935, Ian Mackenzie was naturally alarmed at the parlous condition of the military establishment, and anxious to make an early start on improvement. The cabinet decided against this. Two years later, the Prime Minister told the House of Commons why it had determined to go slow:

When the present Government assumed office we had at once to make a survey of all departments of government. The Minister of National Defence reported to his colleagues the condition as he found it in the Department of Defence. . . . Had the Minister of National Defence been able to carry out his wishes and what he believed to be his duty, most of the present estimates would have been submitted last year instead of this year, because even at that time the world was facing a critical situation and the need for precautions was apparent. But there was a special reason why it seemed unwise to present increased estimates for national defence at that time. . . . With the European situation as it stood at the time, as a Government we felt it would be unwise to arouse discussion in this House on matters of defence, especially when there was the possibility that our action would have been entirely misunderstood by other countries as well as our own. We urged the Minister of National Defence not to press for moneys to make good the depletions and deficiencies in defence to the extent he deemed necessary until the European situation, as it related to the war between Italy and Ethiopia, had somewhat cleared. The understanding was that we would come to Parliament with a full statement of the situation at a time when such a statement was not likely to add to the difficulties of those who were dealing with affairs in Europe.[6]

For this reason, Ian Mackenzie had to be content with only a modest increase in his department's estimates for 1936–37, notwithstanding its evident disrepair. Replying to a critic in the Conference of Defence Associations who had commented adversely on the amount of the proposed expenditure, Mackenzie remarked: "If he had known the tremendous engagement that took place before I got the proposed increases sanctioned I think he might possibly be a little more kindly disposed towards me. I have, I think, got over the first hurdle, but I have still

to face the House of Commons, and I am relying on good friends to
see me through. . . ."[7]

II

By the summer of 1936, the Canadian Government at last determined
to come to grips with the problem of rehabilitating the defence establishment, deferred for the better part of a year. For this purpose it decided
to create a Cabinet Defence Committee. Such an institution had been
urged upon the Government by the Conference of Defence Associations
at its fourth meeting in February 1936. "Certainly I am very much in
favour of this suggestion," Ian Mackenzie had told the Conference. "It
does not matter what government is in power, the great difficulty is
to bring the viewpoint of the Department of Defence to the knowledge
of the other Ministers who are tremendously busy men. Today in Canada
every Minister of the Crown is so overwhelmed with details in regard
to his own Department that he has no time to think, and it is very
difficult for any Minister to know the requirements of another Department, and to my mind I think it is very advisable to have a Canadian
Defence Committee, say three men in the Cabinet, one dealing with
Finance and the Prime Minister the Chairman of that Committee. . . .
That I think will come."[8] Mackenzie King supported the proposal, partly
because (as he told the House of Commons) he "thought it important
that members of the cabinet should have the fullest possible information
with respect to the general defence services," partly because he felt its
creation would offset "criticism that officers of the Department of
National Defence were seeking to increase their own importance and
to enlarge unduly the scope of the defence forces." The "Canadian
Defence Committee," as it was called in the minute of cabinet by which
it was authorized, came into being on 20 August 1936. It consisted of
the Prime Minister (chairman), the Minister of National Defence, the
Minister of Finance, and the Minister of Justice. (The presence of
Ernest Lapointe, as the spokesman for and representative of French
Canada, was rightly deemed essential.) But this institution, like many
others of the kind, failed to live up to expectations, if only because
it was never given the chance. Though it got off to a good start, it soon
fell into abeyance and, apart from the flurry of activity after its formation, met only occasionally prior to the outbreak of war.

Though O. D. Skelton had promised General McNaughton that he
would bring the contents of his memorandum of 28 May 1935 before
Mackenzie King as soon as possible, the Prime Minister did not get

round to reading it until 25 August 1936. (It had been sent to him by
Ian Mackenzie early in the year.) What he read disquieted him greatly,
as well it might. The next morning the Cabinet Defence Committee held
its first meeting. Skelton and Christie, representing the Department of
External Affairs, and Colonel L. R. LaFlèche, Deputy Minister of
National Defence, were present in addition to the four Ministers. Before
this group appeared the Chief of the General Staff, the Chief of Naval
Staff, and the Senior Air Officer, each with briefs recounting the deficiencies of his respective service and the urgency of the need to remedy
them. They made a good impression upon the Prime Minister:

General Ashton gave a review of the existing situation, which was
splendidly presented. I formed a quite different conception of his abilities—
a very clear mind. Commodore Nelles read his report of conditions re naval
defence. It was well prepared . . . Commodore Croil of the Air Force
impressed me very favourably . . . The impression left on my mind was
one of the complete inadequacy of everything in the way of defence—the
need in view of changed methods of warfare, of having some coast armament
against raiders, chance attacks by sea and air. It is going to be extremely
difficult to do anything effective without a cost which this country cannot
bear. We have been wise in placing our reliance mainly on policies which
make for peace. . . .[9]

The next step was the preparation by the armed forces, of a common
appreciation of the military threats against which defence preparations
were required, and an assessment of the forces and equipment needed
to meet those threats over the next five years. The Joint Staff Committee (renamed the "Chiefs of Staff Committee in January 1939, after
the Senior Air Officer was given the title of "Chief of the Air Staff"),
consisting of the three senior officers (Ashton, Nelles, and Croil) who
had appeared before the Cabinet Defence Committee on 26 August,
had had their paper ready by 5 September. It was called "An Appreciation of the Defence Problems Confronting Canada, with Recommendations for the Development of the Armed Forces." Its forthright
repudiation of isolationism—the crises in the Far East and in Europe
both concerned Canada, it affirmed, "no matter how reluctant that
concern may be"—and its prescient discernment of their deterioration—
"the cessation of hostilities in 1918 was but an armistice"—place it
among the key documents of Canadian history. It was largely the work
of Colonel H. D. G. Crerar, a brilliant staff officer, then Director of
Military Operations and Intelligence. [The paper is reproduced below,
as Document 1.]

So far as the members of the cabinet were concerned, what was
arresting about the memorandum of the Joint Staff Committee was not

so much its diagnosis as its cure. The five-year plan was to cost nearly $200 millions, and the first year would be the most expensive—$65 millions, or three times the defence estimates for 1936–37. Even the Minister was forced to concede, in the letter to the Prime Minister with which he enclosed the Joint Staff memorandum, that he did "not think we can get that amount approved without difficulty." He believed that an initial outlay of $50 millions might prove feasible, with $40 millions annually thereafter.[10]

On 10 September—three years to the day before Canada's declaration of war against Germany—the cabinet considered the proposed increases in defence expenditure. It was by no means unanimous in its reactions. "All the French members," Mackenzie King wrote after the meeting, "excepting Lapointe, pretty well content to leave matters as they are. Some of the English members rather fearful of doing very much. . . . Excepting Mackenzie, I myself presented, I think, the strongest case for immediate coast defence, taking the ground that as a Canadian citizen, I thought we owed it to our country to protect it in a mad world, at least to the extent of police service, both on sea and in the air, alike on the Atlantic and Pacific Coasts. I stated it was humiliating to accept protection from Britain without sharing on the costs, or to rely on the United States without being willing to at least protect our neutrality. That we had no enemies, but owed it to ourselves and subsequent generations to lay foundations on which they would have to build. I told Mackenzie he might have to extend his five year programme to ten years."[11]

How the Joint Staff Committee's recommended estimates for 1937–38 were cut back to something more like half that amount has been related by the official historian of the Canadian Army.* The relevant documents were circulated to the members of the government by the Minister of National Defence on 16 November. He admitted that the latest estimate from the military of what the proposed five-year plan would cost the country in the first year of its operation—by this time as high as $69 millions or more—was a "staggering figure," and proposed certain reductions which would have brought the estimates down to something less than $57 millions. In the event, this sum proved too much for the Government by about $20 millions: the total amount of defence estimates (including supplementaries) for the year came to $36,194,839.63. Only a ruthless concentration on essentials and a firm regard for priorities enabled the Government to keep within that figure. Coastal

*Col. C. P. Stacey, *Six Years of War: The Army in Canada, Britain and the Pacific* (Ottawa, 1955), pp. 11–13.

defence came first, and the Pacific Coast before the Atlantic; the Air Force before the Navy, and the Navy before the Militia. "It is not what we might wish to do," Mackenzie King wrote to a correspondent who had urged him to "put the fire into Parliament" on defence matters, "but what we can hope to do, without provoking political and social unrest. . . . I recognize the necessity of the utmost circumspection with respect to every step which, in the practical way, it may be advisable and necessary to take."[12]

III

Clearly it was to be no easy matter to "put the fire into Parliament" on behalf of increased expenditures on defence however slight, let alone on behalf of increased expenditures amounting to about one-third as much again over the preceding year. Discussion in the cabinet had revealed how strongly the opposition to any defensive preparations was running in Quebec; C. G. Power, the influential Liberal from Quebec East, had told Mackenzie King late in November that any extensive defence programme would cost the Government the support of the entire province. The Prime Minister took the earliest opportunity to try to win over his own parliamentary following. On 20 January 1937, he addressed a meeting of the party caucus:

> We are not concerned with aggression. We are concerned with the defence of Canada. . . . The possibility of conflict with the United States is eliminated from our mind. There is nothing here [in the proposed Estimates] for an expeditionary force—only for the defence of Canada against those who might wantonly assail us or violate our neutrality. The defence of our shores and the preservation of our neutrality—these are the two cardinal principles of our policy.
>
> You read what Meighen said in the Senate yesterday, that the amount in the estimates was not enough, that we were concerned with the defence of the Empire as a whole; that the first line of defence was the Empire's boundaries. We cannot accept that. But we can put our own house in order so that we shall not be a burden on anyone else—neither a burden on the States nor a burden on England. Meighen would do so much more—at least so he says—and Woodsworth would do nothing at all. The safe policy is the middle course between these two views—the safe policy is a national policy of domestic defence.
>
> Let us therefore not be afraid. Too many are governed by fear in the days in which we live. Let us first of all have a complete understanding of our own policy—and then, fearing neither of the extremists, let us pursue our moderate way. Let us be united on a sane policy of defence—let us explain that policy to our people and let us above all strive at all times to keep Canada *united*.[13]

He spoke again in this vein to the caucus on 3 February. That little opposition was voiced did not mean that little opposition was felt.

Mackenzie King's determination to increase expenditure for defence in spite of objections within his own cabinet and from his own parliamentary supporters placed the official opposition in a quandary. The spokesmen for Conservatism—Arthur Meighen, now Opposition Leader in the Senate, R. B. Bennett, R. J. Manion (Bennett's successor as Leader of the Opposition in the House of Commons), George Drew (soon to become Leader of the Opposition in the Ontario Legislature)—were all patriotic men. They felt intensely the danger threatening the democracies from Nazi Germany. They were convinced that Canada should do everything possible to ward it off. They were convinced that Canada, under Mackenzie King's leadership, was not doing everything possible to ward it off. They were convinced that the country was dragging behind in the effort to improve the defences of the Empire. All this they passionately believed. But while having no desire to sabotage such efforts as were being made, they were no less partisan than patriotic. They conceived, Meighen especially, an intense dislike for the Prime Minister of Canada. None were in any mood for a bipartisan policy on defence, certainly not of the kind that Mackenzie King was prepared, or in a position, to offer them. What then should they do?

Late in December 1936, the private secretary and close political adviser of the Leader of the Opposition, R. K. Finlayson, wrote to George Drew, in evident perplexity, for advice:

> I am trying to arrive at some estimate of Ian Mackenzie's defence policy. You were present in Ottawa, I understand, as a member of a voluntary Defence Committee which has been making representations from time to time to the Government of the day. Would you mind letting me have your views as to what is actually being accomplished?
>
> In so far as it represents something being done, it seems to me we should support it; but my limited information leads me to believe that what they are doing is a little more than nothing, and that little more is being achieved by Defence Minister Mackenzie in the face of opposition in the Cabinet.
>
> Assuming they do something toward reorganizing the land forces and that they have purchased two second-class destroyers, that leaves the whole matter of air defences still untouched.
>
> If we make the further assumption that this is the beginning of a programme which will lead to adequate defences by air, sea and land, there is the further issue of how these defence forces are to be used; and that, of course, brings us into the realm of foreign policy.[14]

George Drew replied:

> Ian Mackenzie does deserve credit for actively carrying out the plan of reorganization [of the Militia] approved by the Conference of Defence

Associations, and my own opinion is that he should be supported in what he has done. . . . I know it has taken courage to carry this reorganization out because units with long records of efficient service have been forced to merge their identity with other units. As a first step it is splendid.[*]

On the other hand it should be recognized that this is merely a reorganization of units for the purpose of making efficient training possible, and that efficient training can only be carried out when these units are equipped with modern armaments. The reorganization does not meet my own criticism that we have a "bow and arrow army."

There has been no attempt whatever to face the situation in terms of reality either in regard to the Naval Service or the Air Force. While a few modern bombers have been purchased, the fighting aircraft with which the R.C.A.F. are equipped are hopelessly out of date and there are many private aircraft in Canada that could fly rings around them. . . .[15]

On 15 February, debate on the proposed defence estimates for 1937–38 was opened in the House of Commons. During the four days of discussion that ensued, no word of criticism of Government policy came from the Conservative side of the House. Criticism came either from the members of the Government's own party, or from the Left.

At the outset of the debate, a C.C.F. amendment to the Government motion that the House go into committee of supply made the motion one of non-confidence; that in itself spared the Government criticism from its own side. The amendment was as follows: "This House views with grave concern the startling increases of expenditure proposed by the government for purposes of national armament in contrast with the inadequate provision for the social security of all sections of the Canadian people." The mover of the amendment was C. G. MacNeil, the member for Vancouver North. MacNeil had better credentials than many for taking a pacifist line: he had fought in France during the Great War, and, on his return, had been an active figure among the veterans in the politics of re-establishment.† His speech was worthy of the occasion.

He began by declaring that the proposed increases in defence expenditure constituted "a declaration on the part of the Government that Canada must now prepare for war. . . . Step by step we are to be placed on a war footing. . . . We are abandoning the policy followed for eighteen years." He did not accuse the Government of planning a

---

*As a result of the reorganization of the militia, for which planning had begun as early as 1932 and which was completed by the end of 1936, the post-war establishment of eleven infantry divisions and four cavalry divisions was reduced to six infantry divisions and one cavalry division; the strength (on paper) of the N.P.A.M. was reduced from 135,000 to 90,000.

†See In Defence of Canada, vol. I, pp. 43–61.

war of aggression. "The real danger is that we may assist in setting the stage; in erecting, as it were, a scenario of fireworks which may be set off at any moment by a madman or a fool." He quoted General Sir Maurice Wilson: " 'I entered the British Army believing that in order to avoid war we must prepare for war. I now know that when we prepare for war we get war.' " He did not value the advice of the military, least of all the Canadian military. "We have placed our military experts on a sort of pedestal without attempting to question their judgment. It has been accepted that the officers and gentlemen who form the little oligarchy actually in control of the military policy of the National Defence department know all there is to be known with regard to national defence. . . . I submit . . . that the whole atmosphere of their work and their approach to this problem has been without a common-sense appreciation of realities as we find them in Canada." The first step in any rational defence policy ought to be to purge the national defence establishment. There was no threat to Canada. No one was planning to seize and occupy Canadian territory. Why then were defensive preparations necessary? "We are not simply planning for defence of Canadian shores. . . . We are planning to intervene on the side of Great Britain in a European struggle." That, he conceded, might be "a magnificent gesture," but it was not sound strategy. A sounder strategy would be to remain neutral, so as to be able to interpret "the peaceful intentions and good will of the British people to our great neighbour to the south. The more warlike our intentions, the more we disqualify ourselves for such an important mission."[16]

It is difficult to believe that MacNeil's speech did not find a favourable response among many of the French-speaking members of the Government party. Several of them rose to say that while they would vote against the MacNeil amendment because of its allegation of inadequate social services, they would continue in future to oppose increases in defence expenditure. The defeat of the amendment by a vote of 191 to 17 was thus not an accurate reflection of the opinion in the House on the issue of increased defence expenditure alone.

On 19 February the Prime Minister spoke on the motion. It was Mackenzie King's first major statement on defence policy since taking over the Government in October 1935. "When a government brings in its estimates," he observed, "it does not bring in just what it pleases or what pleases it the most. It . . . must consider what is necessary." A review of the course of international events since the Armistice led him to the conclusion that the Government's proposed defence estimates were necessary. He did not say that a world war was inevitable; but he could not say that a world war was unlikely. "Facing such a possibility, . . . can a government that has the responsibility of looking after the defence of its own country, ignore altogether what is necessary for the protection of its coasts, its harbours, its great cities, its people wherever they are, in contingencies that might arise?" He regretted that it had been necessary for the Minister of National Defence to disclose the extent of unpreparedness which had prevailed: "It does not strengthen our country to have the weak spots in its armour known all over the world." But had the deficiencies not been laid bare in all their shocking detail, Parliament and public would continue to believe the country to be safe, whereas it was not safe. He was not going to blame his predecessors for that. "I am prepared to write down those economies to the depression. . . . It was perhaps natural that the Department of National Defence might be considered a department in which economies could be practised. Let us not forget, however, that the depression has operated in two ways: it occasioned economies in defence so far as Canada was concerned, but on the other hand it operated abroad to make nations excessively restless."

What were the proposed estimates intended to do? First, the government was asking Parliament to approve the purchase of two destroyers to replace two which had become obsolete, and of four minesweepers and a small training ship. As for the R.C.A.F., "the entire air force appropriation may be considered as replacement," bringing the force back up to the level it had attained before its attrition during the depression. Finally, the militia. Guns and ammunition were needed to protect Canadian territorial waters and Canadian coasts and harbours. There was no question of equipping an expeditionary force for overseas service. All was being done in defence of Canada. "But," he concluded, "I hope it will not be thought that because we have laid emphasis on the fact that what we are doing we are doing for Canada, we are not thereby making some contribution towards the defence of the British Commonwealth of Nations as a whole, or that we are not making some contribution towards the defence of all English-speaking communities, that we are not making some contribution towards the defence of all democracies, that we are not making some contribution towards the defence of all those countries that may some day necessarily associate themselves together for the purpose of preserving their liberties and freedom against an aggressor, come from wherever he may."[17]

Among the many congratulatory messages received by the Prime Minister for this speech was a letter from the High Commissioner in London. "I well understand the difficulties of the situation and the dangers that lay on all sides," Vincent Massey wrote, "but these were all avoided, if I may say so, most brilliantly." Mackenzie King was inclined to agree. "I am glad you thought well of the defence debate," he wrote in reply to his High Commissioner. "I hope members of the British Government will realize that in taking the step we did, our Government ran the risk of splitting the Party in half. I suppose, more than anyone else, I was responsible for going the lengths we did for I had finally to settle differences between members of the Administration which seemed irreconcilable, and to say what must be done. Fortunately, it all turned out almost to the letter as I said it would."[18]

ON THE EVE

"There is really not very much now," the Minister of National Defence wrote to his Prime Minister concerning the problems of his Department in July 1937. Two questions of policy remained to be decided. One was munitions production. "That question," Ian Mackenzie observed, "has dissolved itself into how far we should go in public ownership by way of developing the Lindsay Plant and how far we should go in control of private industry by limitation of profits." The other was the destroyer programme.

In November 1934, the Navy's planners had recommended a minimum peacetime force consisting of six destroyers and four minesweepers. By 1936, the Navy had four destroyers in commission, but of these, two— H.M.C.S. *Vancouver* and H.M.C.S. *Champlain*—were scheduled to be scrapped by the end of the year. They were replaced in 1937 by two Royal Navy vessels, which entered Canadian service as H.M.C.S. *Fraser* and H.M.C.S. *St. Laurent*; the cost of both to the Canadian Government was roughly $2 millions. Since becoming Minister of National Defence, Ian Mackenzie had been strongly pressed by his naval advisers to add two more destroyers from the same source. "We could get two more of the same type and age this year," Mackenzie wrote to the Prime Minister in July 1937, "for one and one-half million dollars. . . . We should then have in Canada, when our programme is complete, six destroyers, four minesweepers and one schooner. I felt that this would be a modest and reasonable programme under present conditions." Some uncertainty existed about the proper timing of the programme. "Should I bring this matter up in Council now," he inquired, "or postpone it until later in the year?" He himself thought it would be best to wait, "so as to remove the slightest impression that it had any connection whatsoever with the Imperial Conference."[19] The cabinet agreed on 20 July to leave over until September the question of the destroyer programme.

On 14 September, the newly formed Defence Committee of the cabinet confronted the senior service officers, who presented to it their case for increased defence estimates for 1938–39. "Personally," the Prime Minister wrote after this meeting, "I am not opposed to the addn[1] destroyers as I think our Pacific coast needs protection [and] I favour doing all possible or reasonable for air defence, but I share Lapointe's feeling against increasing the Army (mechanization, etc.) It seemed to me these officials sought to have us feel they had not been able to get supplies for which appropriations had been voted, and equally that they had no money left & needed a larger vote for next year. I gave Council the outline, & all agreed we should hold the total defence estimates at 35,000,000 & let them work out within that figure."[20] The outcome was that the militia estimates were cut by about $2 millions, which was given to the Navy for the new destroyers. It was not done without a struggle, as Mackenzie King's diary reveals:

11 January 1938: . . . took up the question of considering an additional two destroyers to the Pacific Coast defence. I pointed out that we might be faced with a world situation at any time. . . . I pointed out where Australia, New Zealand and even [South] Africa were all doing something to assist in their defences, and strengthening the Empire as a whole. For us to do nothing was not playing the game, particularly where Canada had one part of the earth's surface that was the most enviable of all. Also that with the United States materially increasing its large war equipment, that for us to do nothing in meeting our own defence was to become increasingly dependent upon the United States with possible serious consequences; also that aggressor nations would be quick to discern we were reluctant to assist whereas a slight gesture might have large meaning in their eyes. I pointed out beside that on the Pacific Coast with the Islands, etc., there, a few destroyers could be of real service. We had to face possibilities of conflict in which we might be neutral, or a conflict in which the Empire was involved. I found that members of the Cabinet generally were wholly favourable to the purchase of two new destroyers; Dandurand quite frankly so. Dunning, Gardiner equally agreeable. No one really opposed this addition, but there was some discussion on the possible service of two destroyers, the main discussion being on not increasing the total of the estimates. . . .

Dandurand was quite emphatic that coast defences could be defended but not an increase in army estimates which might look to expedition overseas. I think that is now wholly out of the question, and not seriously in the minds of anyone. I opposed absolutely allowing amounts for these two ships to come out of supplementary estimates for the present year, which the Defence Department has kept pressing for on the score of time. Really, I think it will help them with another year. I said we must keep faith with what Parliament was given to understand last Session. I also stressed generally the keeping down of the total outlay for Defence, last year's figure at the outset. We must try to go below it. . . .

1 February: . . . We had some consideration of Defence estimates which had been brought down considerably from what they were when presented by Mackenzie. Today I succeeded in getting nearly another one million cut off, and during the afternoon, managed to get the figures reduced still more so that the estimates will be a couple of millions less than last year, notwithstanding that we shall be purchasing two additional destroyers. Mackenzie agreed to his cutting off another million on the score that we let one of the destroyers go. I said I was sorry for that but felt in my mind Mackenzie would want the destroyers at all costs and the Department would work the reduction somehow. It so proved. . . . The estimates are now ready for submission to the House.

The Minister of National Defence presented his departmental estimates for 1938–39 to the House of Commons on 24 March. "There appeared to be a general acceptance of the Government's proposal," Mackenzie King wrote afterwards, "much less opposition in Quebec than last year. . . . It was plain . . . that the House was conscious that we were face to face with an appalling world situation. . . ."[21]

II

The Navy had reason to be satisfied with the 1938–39 estimates: in June 1938, two former Royal Navy destroyers were commissioned in the R.C.N. as H.M.C.S. *Restigouche* and H.M.C.S. *Ottawa*, and so, four years after it had been first advocated, the six-destroyer programme was fulfilled. The fleet was complemented further by the construction, in Canadian shipyards, of four small minesweepers.

The Air Force had also done well, but not, in the opinion of the Senior Air Officer, well enough. "Notwithstanding the fact that Air Force appropriations for the year 1937–38 and 1938–39 were each more than double the appropriation for 1936–37," Air Vice-Marshal G. M. Croil wrote to the Minister of National Defence on 14 April 1938, "the present and future state of the Air Force is a matter of grave concern particularly in view of present disturbed world conditions." His memorandum continued as follows:

In a national emergency, there is a very definite danger of air attack against our cities, ports, shipping and communications. Such attacks would be launched from enemy warships, improvised carriers and by airships operating from an overseas base. To counter these attacks, we must have the necessary aircraft and, in addition, we must furnish aircraft to assist the Navy and Army in their respective roles. . . . In the past, the value of the Air Force as a defence arm was negligible. Its equipment, consisting for the most part of civil type aircraft, was obsolete, and armament and facilities for war training were practically non-existent. This situation is improving slightly with deliveries of some modern service aircraft made possible by 1937–38 estimates, but the funds available in 1937–38 and those included in 1938–39 estimates will allow of little progress in the expansion of the force to the size necessary. . . .

In September 1936, the Joint Staff Committee, in considering the defence problems confronting Canada, recommended a peace organization of 23 squadrons (11 permanent, 12 non-permanent) and necessary ancillary maintenance and supply units and bases. The Committee further recommended that 9 of the Permanent Force squadrons, to be employed on coast defence duties, be equipped with modern first-line aircraft immediately available and ready for service; that the remaining Permanent Force squadrons be equipped with obsolescent or advanced training type aircraft; and that all Non-Permanent Force squadrons be equipped with 6 training aircraft each, suitable for the function of the particular unit.

The expansion of the R.C.A.F. along [these] lines is a considerable undertaking, but until this is accomplished it cannot be said that an Air Force adequate for the defence of the country exists. . . .[22]

The total cost of bringing the R.C.A.F. up to the strength and standards recommended two years earlier was estimated by the Senior Air Officer at approximately $70 millions. The amount the Air Force had been allotted for 1938–39 was approximately $10 millions.

The crisis in Europe caused by Hitler's designs upon Czechoslovakia drew the Government's attention to the inadequacy of the Dominion's defences, especially to the inadequacy of its air power. On 20 September, the Chief of the General Staff wrote privately: "I have had to urge the Government to take some special action towards obtaining more 'planes immediately by purchase, if necessary, from the U.S.A. . . . I may not get action."[23] He did get action, of a kind. A few days later, the Senior Air Officer was informed by the Minister of National Defence that the cabinet had decided to make money available for the purpose, and that he was to send a purchasing mission to Washington immediately.

On 28 September—hours before the surrender at Munich—a small group of R.C.A.F. officers, led by Air Commodore E. W. Stedman, set out surreptitiously for the United States capital, dressed in civilian clothes and having temporarily discarded military rank. Their instructions were prepared by Air Vice-Marshal Croil. They might purchase whatever aircraft and parts were available up to a total of $6,110,000 (of which $5,000,000 was for aircraft), concentrating, if possible, on reconnaissance and bomber aircraft with a range of 1,000 miles, and on two-seater fighters. "If time permits," the instructions concluded, "decision on aircraft purchases should be referred to N.D.H.Q. before purchase completed."[24] The clear implication of these instructions was that if time did not permit, the mission should act on its own. It was an uncharacteristically liberal mandate, as mandates from Ottawa went. But then it was an unusually urgent situation, as urgent situations went.

The mission reported to the Canadian Legation in Washington early on the morning of 29 September. That afternoon, Air Commodore Stedman, together with the Minister, Herbert Marler, interviewed General H. H. Arnold, the Chief of the U.S. Army Air Corps. "The main point clearly determined in conversation with him," the Canadian memorandum on this discussion affirmed, "was that it was impossible to secure aircraft at all for near delivery except through the Army. Those in production were earmarked for the Army itself. He however indicated that the Army would consider and most likely approve of releasing to Canada alone for substantially immediate delivery the machines chosen by the Mission." This information was telephoned to Air Vice-Marshal Croil in Ottawa.[25]

That evening, a telegram was received by the Canadian Legation in Washington. It contained new instructions for the R.C.A.F. mission. "While all speed is desirable in obtaining information," it stated, "it is desired that proposals be reported to Minister [of National Defence] and approved by Council or Treasury Board before any transactions are closed."[26] Air Commodore Stedman discussed these new instructions with Marler the next morning. By then they had been confirmed in yet another message from Ottawa emphasizing the necessity of consultation: "Under no circumstances are purchases to be made without departmental authority. Submit each proposal by wire in sufficient detail to permit drafting of Order-in-Council and await instructions."[27] Because the new instructions appeared to contradict the original instructions, and because the men on the spot feared that their rigidity could compromise the success of the mission, Marler thought he had better take the matter up immediately with the Department of External Affairs. He called the Department on the telephone, and at 10.30 on the morning of 30 September held the following conversation with Loring Christie:

The Minister said that the telegram [of 29 September] in his opinion somewhat detracted from the instructions. . . . Mr. Christie no doubt appreciated that.

Mr. Christie spoke as to the question of policy, and the Minister replied that he was not discussing or questioning any matter of policy—that he (the Minister) was here to obey instructions. He did however wish to convey to Mr. Christie this observation—that the Mission was here on such a delicate matter and that it was so difficult getting any of "the articles" at all . . . he was afraid that the Legation would be placed in a somewhat embarrassing position. Mr. Christie replied that he quite understood that situation.

The Minister continued that he was asking the Army to do something which might certainly be called preferential for Canada. We could not obtain the articles in the open market or by going to the manufacturers for them. There were however a certain number of different kinds ready for short delivery to "the people" here. It was likely—though not positive—that these "people" might forego their right to a considerable extent in respect to each group of "the articles." From this it will be readily seen that we were entering upon a very delicate piece of negotiation—and when we say that we will take five of one class or ten of another class and so on provided "you will release them to us" and they say "It is a somewhat irregular thing you are asking us to do but seeing the circumstances we will do it" that under the original instructions we could have closed subject to the contract being made and the matter being approved of the officers of Finance here as well as by Air Vice-Marshal Croil of the Air Force. Our new instructions are that when we come to our bargain here we must refer that bargain back again to Council and the Treasury Board and of course we in Washington cannot determine the opinion of either nor have we any right to do so. In short yesterday we had a direct authority—this morning we have a qualified authority.

The Minister continued that it was difficult to go ahead with negotiations in such a way as to achieve success unless we are pretty much in a position to close. In his (the Minister's) opinion he thought it would be very much better for the authorities in Ottawa to determine just what they wanted and to instruct us what to do in place of ascertaining information . . . and then submit information with recommendations which might or might not be accepted.

The Minister continued that he desired to emphasize he was in no way complaining or criticizing anything he was asked to do but he did want to emphasize that the position for Canada had now been built up over the period of a whole year with considerable difficulty and with much delicate negotiation and he would be very sorry indeed if that position as so achieved was altered—by reason of saying that we intended to do something now and that later on saying we were merely seeking information. . . .[28]

A message incorporating these views was telephoned from the Legation to Ottawa a few hours later. The next day, 1 October, a reply was received from the Department of External Affairs. It did not retract in any way the order to refer any contemplated deal to the government, but it did promise urgent and speedy consideration of any matter thus referred. "Delay informing Mission [of a decision] should not be longer than one day, except Sundays. Presumably the Mission itself, quite apart from necessity to refer offers here, might reasonably expect at least that much delay to be allowed by those concerned in Washington before closing any transactions."[29]

Meanwhile the mission had been pondering a new problem. By 1 October the results of the confrontation at Munich had become known: "the voice of Reason"—so Mackenzie King had publicly declared—had "found a way out of the conflict. . . ." Had the emergency then passed, and with it the need for the mission to continue its work? Stedman and Marler conferred on this question, and decided "that it should be determined whether a state of emergency still exists. If an emergency still exists it was proposed to proceed as planned and the preferences to be granted in the way of securing the planes and their delivery exercised to the fullest extent possible. If no state of emergency exists then the Minister thought it would be difficult to ask the United States Army authorities to grant the preferences they apparently intended to grant Canada."[30] That evening Stedman talked on the telephone to the Senior Air Officer in Ottawa. Air Vice-Marshal Croil advised his head of mission to carry on with the purchasing. When Stedman pressed him as to the continued existence of the emergency, Croil replied that the Government had not as yet withdrawn the funds made available under Governor General's warrant, and that so long as the funds were available they should be spent on aircraft.

Armed with this authority, the mission continued its work. Between 3 October and 5 October, it entered into "active and continual negotiations" with authorities of the U.S. Army Air Corps. On 5 October, Stedman reported to Croil on the progress made thus far; the Senior Air Officer "approved of all that had been done. . . . As a matter of fact", Marler's report of the incident observed, "he was then pressing Stedman for quotations." On 6 October, Croil telephoned Washington again to inquire of the Legation when the quotations would be coming through: prices for two types of aircraft were sent to Ottawa that night.

There then occurred exactly what Marler had feared might occur, and which he had done all in his power to prevent. Having exploited to the full its special relationship with the United States Army authorities to secure release to Canada of aircraft, the Legation now had to inform the authorities that Canada no longer desired or required aircraft. The head of the Air Mission was instructed by telephone on the afternoon of 7 October "to desist from any further negotiations." The Government had cancelled the Governor General's warrant.

On 8 October, O. D. Skelton telephoned the Legation to explain what had happened. The Government had decided that the emergency had passed and that it would be wise to withdraw the warrant for the expenditure of funds. Otherwise, "explanations before Parliament might be difficult." The Minister was instructed to explain the situation to the Americans. Marler and Stedman went immediately to call on the Assistant Secretary of War. Louis Johnson was very nice about it. He told his Canadian visitors that he understood what had happened, and that he and his colleagues "would be glad to be of assistance in the future." But the moment had passed, and the opportunity had been missed. When, ten months later, Air Commodore Stedman attempted again to purchase planes in the United States, he found he was too late.*

III

Of the three Services, the militia fared worst in the Government's policy of cautious and selective rearmament. A memorandum by the Chief of the General Staff, dated 10 January 1938, surveyed the militia's requirements in these words:

> In the preliminary estimates for 1938–39, after providing for the maintenance of the Militia, including a necessary increase for training, it was possible to set aside for New Services a sum of $4,490,646 of which $1,060,000 was allotted to fortification works and $3,930,646 to new equipment and ammunition. But when these estimates had been duly prepared, instructions were received at very short notice to reduce the total amount of the Militia vote by a sum of $2,326,889. This action was taken and as the bulk of a reduction of this nature can be applied only to the "controllable" portion of the vote, the amounts which can now be allotted to New Services [are] $1,000,000 for fortification and $1,970,646 for new equipment and ammunition.
>
> I understand that this very drastic reduction in the Militia vote for next year has been made necessary by reason of the decision to purchase two additional destroyers for the Navy while maintaining the ruling that the total amount of the defence vote, as a whole, is not to exceed the sum made available this year. As a consequence, the increase in the vote for the Navy could only be achieved by an equivalent decrease in the Militia and Air votes.
>
> I fully appreciate that it is a matter of extreme importance to the defence of Canada that there should be a considerable and prompt increase in the strength of our naval forces. I must point out, however, that owing to the limitations placed on the departmental vote as a whole, the resultant effect will be still further to delay the already leisurely scheme of coastal defence. Responsibility for policy I am well aware rests with the Government. But I should make it clear that, in my position, as their adviser on the defence requirements of the Militia, I consider that the rate of progress which is now apparently contemplated is but little related to the grave situation which we now face. . . .[31]

General Ashton evidently believed that the militia's low priority was a temporary affair, resulting from the decision to complete the Navy's

*See below, pp. 184–5.

destroyer programme. But he was wrong. The last months of peace saw an increase in militia estimates—from some $16 millions in 1938–39 to some $21 millions in 1939–40—but relative to the increased expenditure on the other two services, especially the R.C.A.F., this was far from generous treatment. It was indeed ruthless, arbitrary, and inadequate. In November 1938, the Chief of the General Staff had presented proposals to the Defence Committee of the cabinet for a total expenditure upon the militia of $28.6 millions. A month later, he was instructed to cut nearly $8 millions from this amount. That meant abandoning the intended construction of East Coast defences, and crucial purchases of armament, ammunition, and stores. The army members of the Defence Council protested strongly, but in vain. "When war broke out," the official historian of the Canadian Army has written, "Canada had no troops ready for immediate action, except for local coastal defence against very small raids. The tiny Permanent Force did not constitute a striking force capable either of counter-attack against a major raid or of expeditionary action. The Non-Permanent Force, with its limited strength, obsolescent equipment and rudimentary training, was incapable of immediate effective action of any sort against a formidable enemy. . . . the preparations were utterly inadequate by comparison with the scale of the coming emergency."[32]

VI

War in the West

AIMS OF WAR AND CONDITIONS OF PEACE

"The fate of a single city, the preservation of the independence of a particular nation, are the occasion, not the real cause of the present conflict. The forces of evil have been loosed in the world . . . That is why the present war is for the Allied Forces a crusade."[1] In these words the Prime Minister of Canada described, on 3 September 1939, the reason for his country's impending belligerency against Nazi Germany. They suggested already a policy of unconditional surrender. One does not properly negotiate with the forces of evil; crusaders, armed as they are with the breastplate of righteousness, may not stop short of victory. But for once Mackenzie King had allowed himself the luxury of rhetoric. War would soon be declared, but not total war. It was not long before he was considering more closely the objectives for which Canada had declared herself ready to fight, and was even scrutinizing the conditions on which Canada was ready to make peace.

In the closing stages of the Polish campaign, Hitler, seeking to create among the Allies a disposition to accept his aggression as a *fait accompli*, put forward a number of proposals to negotiate an end to the fighting. The first of these was offered in a speech at Danzig on 19 September. The British Government gave short shrift to it. "Our general purpose in this struggle is well known," Neville Chamberlain declared the following day in the House of Commons. "It is to redeem Europe from the perpetual and recurring fear of German aggression and enable the peoples of Europe to preserve their independence and their liberties."[2] On 28 September Hitler tried again. In a joint declaration with the Soviet Union, he announced that since "a sure foundation for a lasting peace in Eastern Europe" had been laid with the destruction of the Polish state, "it would serve the true interests of all peoples to put an end to the state of war existing at present between Germany on the one side and England and France on the other."[3] British reaction to this manoeuvre was reported to Ottawa by the Canadian High Commissioner. Hitler's proposal, it was felt, should be answered by a careful statement of war aims. But when Chamberlain spoke next in the House of Commons, on 3 October, no such statement was forthcoming.

It was at this juncture that Mackenzie King intervened. "The United Kingdom and France," he suggested in a cabled message to Chamberlain on 6 October, "should put forward their own positive program of the basis upon which the war could be terminated, framed in such broad terms as to win the support of the United States and other neutral countries." On 8 October he furnished the British Prime Minister with a fuller account of what he felt ought to be said:

I realize the difficulty of finding a basis which will take account both of the principles of freedom and self-determination upon which the Allied resistance to Nazi aggression has been founded and of the actual situation which has been brought about by the fact that the effort to prevent war by alliances and guarantees in Eastern Europe has not proved successful and that Russian intervention following upon German attack has resulted not merely in a German control of part of Poland which would be reversed after Allied victory in the West but a Communist domination of East Poland and the Baltic States which might require another war to upset. I have not therefore ventured to make any suggestions as to the content of any alternative proposals, but I should like to outline a procedure which I believe would if accepted make possible peace on a more stable basis and if rejected by Germany would still more definitely place upon her the onus of continuing war and still more clearly expose the fallacy of her pretended desire for peace.[4]

The procedure Mackenzie King had in mind was that a commission of neutral powers, consisting of the President of the United States, the King of the Belgians, and the King of Italy, should be formed to investigate and report upon "methods of adjusting the European situation" as it had existed on 1 September, and that, pending submission of its recommendations to the belligerent powers, an unconditional truce should come into effect.

Chamberlain replied on 10 October. He fully sympathized, he said, with the wish of the Canadian Prime Minister to come to a peaceful settlement before the horrors of war set in. He would seize eagerly any real opportunity to bring about such a settlement. "But we must remember that all evidence before us goes to show that Hitler's present move is merely a tactical one couched in vague and unsatisfactory terms and intended to weaken our position." He had carefully considered the suggestion that a neutral commission of investigation be formed, but doubted whether its formation would be acceptable either to the belligerents or to its proposed members. Finally, he noted, the British Government had composed a rejoinder to the Nazi-Soviet declaration (the text had been relayed in a circular telegram to the dominion governments) "intended to achieve the object which you have in mind of placing upon the German Government the onus of rejecting a peaceful solution."

But the British rejoinder was not well thought of in Ottawa. "It is negative rather than positive," was the reaction of O. D. Skelton, the Under Secretary of State for External Affairs. "It is easy to say what we are 'against'; everybody is against Hitler; the difficulty comes when people try to say what they are 'for'. . . . There will be many who consider that a more positive statement of war aims should be made, and the fact that this is difficult merely indicates that the Government [of the United Kingdom] has not been able to make up its mind what its objectives are."[5] Mackenzie King agreed. "The general feeling of my colleagues and myself," he informed Chamberlain, was that the British rejoinder should be rephrased "in order to give a more positive statement of war aims and of the conditions or procedure upon which the Government of the United Kingdom consider that the war might now be terminated. . . ."[6] He repeated the message to the Prime Minister of Australia, who replied that he had also pressed the British Government for a more definite statement of why they were now at war. Confronted with these criticisms from two dominion governments, Chamberlain amended the draft "in a sense which" (as he cabled to Mackenzie King on 12 October) "I think you will feel is in harmony with some of the ideas which you have in mind." But the British draft still left much to be desired in the view of the Canadian Government.

There was in fact a real difference between London and Ottawa at this stage, which language might conceal but could not dispel. Mackenzie King in spite of the summons to Holy War contained in his statement of 3 September was not yet convinced that the Allies could not come to terms with Hitler and Nazism. He still hoped that mediation could save the day, that some *deus ex machina*, perhaps in the shape of a triumvirate of neutral statesmen, might contrive an acceptable formula of settlement even at that late hour. Many (though by no means all) of his countrymen shared that hope. But in Britain the mood was vastly different. The average Briton was sick of Hitler's offers. Nazism was an evil to be extirpated, not a government to be negotiated with. The opportunity for compromise had passed: time spent in working out possible bases for agreement was time wasted. "Chamberlain's uncompromising declaration," two American authorities properly conclude, "certainly reflected the sentiment of his country."[7] One senses, however, at least a twinge of remorse in Chamberlain's final telegram to Mackenzie King at having paid so little regard to the suggestions of the Canadian Prime Minister on the occasion of his first intervention in the grand strategy of the war. "I have warmly welcomed the opportunity of consultation between us," he assured Mackenzie King on 12 October. "After most careful examination and in the light of all the information in our possession from a variety of sources, we are convinced it would not only be unwise but even dangerous at this stage to go further than we have in defining our position."

Not many days after this interchange, the question of war aims arose again. On 18 October, the French Ambassador called upon the Foreign Office to say that his Government believed it to be none too early to begin an exchange of views among the Allies about the purposes of war and the conditions of peace. He took much the same position that Mackenzie King had taken, namely, that it was not enough to reiterate a determination to fight on unless Germany offered satisfactory guarantees that the work of her aggression would be undone: what was required was a positive statement defining the objects for which the Allies had gone to war. Nor was it too early to begin contemplating the shape of the post-war world. A French memorandum of 23 October, setting forth these views in more detail, was communicated to the governments of the belligerent dominions for their consideration. Skelton described it as "one of the most important and significant we have received for some time." While sharing the French Government's desire for a sharper definition of Allied war aims, Skelton recoiled from the definition evidently desired by that Government. "Those now in authority in France have learned nothing and forgotten everything. They apparently desire to revive the Versailles tactics in the most stringent form." It was all the more urgent, Skelton concluded, to press the British Government to state its own views on the subject, lest those of France gain currency among the Allies. The whole subject would "require very full consideration."[8] Mackenzie King minuted: "I agree."

The task of formulating a declaration of war aims, either by contributing to the drafting of an Allied statement or by preparing a distinctively Canadian account, was by no means uncongenial to Mackenzie King, notwithstanding the many pressures to which, in these early weeks of the war, he had already become exposed. He had for many years been addicted to the sweeping view of world politics, and had developed a certain facility for giving verbal and written expression to it. While inhibited in exercising this facility by the subordinate role which Canadian governments had played in international affairs between the wars, no such inhibition beset him now. Peace-making being hardly yet a matter of practical politics, he could indulge himself in peace-making as much as he liked. His eagerness to press his views on the appropriateness of the British Government's rejoinder to the Nazi peace proposals is in marked contrast to that reluctance of earlier years, amounting almost to a fetish, to admit to any opinions on foreign policy lest by doing so he could be thought to have entered into some commitment. On 16 October, he amended a speech that the Governor General thought well to submit to him before delivery. "Perhaps you would consider," he wrote to Lord Tweedsmuir, "either omitting or re-casting the words . . . 'They cannot be converted. They can only be destroyed—not Germany, not the German people, but the false prophets who have betrayed them'. I can see wherein some persons might feel that this precluded any final termination of the war, short of the death of the principals. Also, that it rules out the possibility of imprisonment or banishment."[9] His preoccupation with the problem is reflected further in the first of a series of radio addresses to the Canadian people delivered on 27 October, and even more clearly in the notes he prepared some days earlier for the guidance of his speech-writer:

Broadcast should make clear why impossible to accept overtures for peace at this stage. . . . A very careful statement might be prepared showing the things on which our present day free way of life is based, e.g., belief in spoken and written word, sanctity of contract, Christian attitude towards fellow man, belief in God, etc., and contrasted with this, social order based upon materialistic interpretation of life, resulting in glorification of matter and force, ridiculing spiritual values, etc. The broadcast might close with a careful statement re forces of Bolshevism and Hitlerism, either singly or combined, and effect upon world of same. Need of seeing that Empire of neither should be permitted to expand, Bolshevism aiming avowedly at world revolution; Hitlerism would appear now to have capitulated to that end.[10]

The speech-writer did what he could, but it was evidently not good enough. "I confess," Mackenzie King wrote in his diary after reading the first draft, ". . . it filled me with dismay. . . . I talked with Brockington later and suggested to him the necessity of having the material so recast as to have it reach the man in the blacksmith's shop, with his friends and neighbours; the woman in the kitchen; the labourers coming in from their work on the farm. Nothing else is any good at this time."[11]

Meanwhile the United Kingdom Government had asked for, and was awaiting, the observations of the governments of Canada and of the other dominions as to what ought to be said in reply to the representations of the French on the subject of war aims. Mackenzie King gave very careful thought to this problem, and by 2 November had prepared a lengthy memorandum embodying the results of his reflections. [It is reproduced below, as Document 4.]

Mackenzie King's memorandum on war aims expressed the convictions of a lifetime. They had been formed during the early part of his career as a conciliator of industrial disputes, and they had been confirmed by his experience as Prime Minister during the years between two world wars. A belief in the sweet reasonableness of mankind left to its own devices; confidence in the power of investigation to expose evil and to right wrong; the conviction that coercion in whatever form and for whatever reasons only exacerbates conflict and makes settlement more difficult. It expressed as well a continued mistrust of collective security. The League of Nations had failed because of the attempt to embody a collective security system within the Covenant: had there been no League of that kind there would have been no war of any kind. The aggressors had been goaded into their aggressions. Not so much innately evil designs as the injustices of the Versailles Treaty had been the main cause of the conflict. These views were tenaciously held, and would not be shaken merely by the outbreak of war. As Mackenzie King came into closer contact with the personality and mind of Winston Churchill (to whom all these views were simply folly), and as he gained greater knowledge of the colossal inequities of the Nazi regime, he would modify them in some respects. He would come to regard totalitarianism as a distinctively twentieth-century phenomenon arising from the tensions and insecurities of twentieth-century man, rather than as an aggravation of nineteenth-century nationalism. He would accept collective security, albeit reluctantly, as a necessary evil in an imperfect world. But much as he might during the remaining decade of his time in power talk in the language of a post-war security system—"the new world order," as he somewhat infelicitously described it—he never underwent the kind of conversion that transformed the outlook of a Vandenberg or a Roosevelt. He remained prisoner of his prejudices to the very end.*

II

To his statement of war aims, Mackenzie King attached the utmost importance. It was, he wrote to O. D. Skelton, "even more important than the declaration of war itself." He wanted to delay sending the despatch to the British Government, which would incorporate its argument, until the cabinet had an opportunity to consider it. He expressed the

*I hope to be able to offer some evidence for this statement in a further volume.

wish that Ernest Lapointe—Minister of Justice and, of all his colleagues (according to one of his official biographers) "undoubtedly closest to him"[12]—should be present when the cabinet discussion took place. "He will himself desire that," Mackenzie King wrote, "and, without him, I might encounter difficulties which I should like to avoid in getting a statement of this kind off at this stage. It must be remembered that in sending forward any statement, we will be held responsible later on by the British Government for having 'forced' the hand of the British Government to issue something of the kind."[13]

Before the Canadian Government replied to the British request, a further occasion for an expression of its views on war aims presented itself. It arose out of the joint appeal from the King of the Belgians and the Queen of the Netherlands to His Majesty the King, the President of the French Republic, and to Hitler, offering their services as mediators in a conference for restoring peace. It was a public appeal, and so called for a public reply, one which according to the constitutional proprieties would be tendered by the dominion governments as well as that of the United Kingdom (since the appeal of the two European monarchs had been addressed simply to "The King, London"). The British Government did not see fit to apply the principle of the divisibility of the Crown, but it did seek the advice of the four dominions concerning the text of the draft it proposed to make public in reply. This was received in Ottawa on 10 November. Mackenzie King found it satisfactory with the exception of one of its paragraphs in which, as he noted in a despatch to London, "the aims indicated appear to be too exclusively confined to Europe and might be held to justify states outside that continent refraining from intervention in the present war." Mackenzie King accordingly added the words "to prevent for the future resort to force instead of to pacific means for the settlement of international disputes" to the United Kingdom draft: his revision was accepted, and duly appeared in the text of the King's reply published the following day.

During the next fortnight, the cabinet dealt with the question of war aims to its satisfaction. On 25 November, after careful preparation in the East Block and the Prime Minister's office, a telegram "making some preliminary comment on [the French Government's] proposals and in addition setting forth some of the objectives which in our opinion should be considered in determining allied war aims" went forward to Neville Chamberlain. It took strong exception to any post-war policy imposing upon Germany measures of a severely punitive character, such as territorial dismemberment, occupation, or unilateral disarmament. "An announcement of Allied war aims in such terms would rally the German people in support of the Nazi regime, and alienate neutral countries or at least the United States by foreshadowing a peace much more rigorous than Versailles." The French draft, moreover, was in the Canadian view "occupied too exclusively with Germany." "The Soviet Union as well as other totalitarian powers" ought to be kept "constantly in mind, alike as potential sources of disturbance and as permanent factors in the European equation." At that stage of the war, assuming that the conflict would be long, it did not seem to the Canadian Government to be feasible or desirable to enter into detailed discussion about post-war boundaries or even post-war international machinery. But certain general observations could usefully be set out, and this the Canadian despatch proceeded to do, echoing, in more formal language, the concepts and assumptions of Mackenzie King's memorandum:

. . . individual freedom and political democracy will not bring security so long as the multiplicity of small states and the intensity of racial and nationalist rivalry create instability, tempt aggressors, and prevent the attainment of the broad basis necessary for adequate economic development. Some growth of federalism or regional collaboration appears as essential for international stability as the growth of freedom is essential for internal stability. Neither development can be imposed from without; it must come by growth from within, and all that other countries can do is to assist in establishing conditions and safeguards that will aid rather than hinder such development. . . .

. . . change should not be made by force nor can it long be prevented by force. All the countries which may suffer the repercussions of an open conflict have an interest in peaceful settlement of [international] differences. In industrial disputes private rights cease when they become public wrongs, and in the wider field national rights must be restrained when they become international wrongs. In this connection it may be suggested that in considering future European organization more weight should be given than in the past to the procedure of investigation and report. I am convinced that in international as in industrial disputes the most effective means of providing for the legitimate third party interest and ensuring peaceful adjustment is the adoption of the flexible procedure of investigation and report, supported by the powerful sanction of public opinion. In the long run this procedure, while less theoretically imposing, may be more practically effective than the processes of compulsory acceptance . . . or the imposition of sanctions. . . .

It may be that in some measure undertakings in advance to impose a solution or prevent recourse to force may be considered necessary. In that case, experience indicates the desirability of placing such obligations upon a regional basis. The attempt made in the working of the League of Nations to give such obligations a world basis failed. It diverted the League from the attainable objectives of conciliation and the shaping of world opinion to the unattainable and inconsistent objective of serving as an international war office. The assumption of the readiness of all League countries to use economic or military force in any dispute that might arise at any place and at any time proved to have little basis in reality, and so far as it had any basis it tended to intensify the scale of preparations by potential aggressors and to convert local wars into world wars. In considering how far a general obligation to use force may be relied upon in any plan of international co-operation, it will be all-important also to keep in mind the strain upon the unity of the British Commonwealth which would attend any scheme of indefinite commitments to intervene in future Europe conflicts. . . .[14]

These reflections were far indeed from the minds of the British leaders to whom they were addressed. Mackenzie King's views on war aims were greatly at variance with those of the United Kingdom Government. They were different, as well, from those of the Australian Government.* Realizing how difficult it would be to combine in a single statement the divergent positions of the Commonwealth leaders, Chamberlain suggested that he send the French Government a provisional reply, leaving to future discussion—in which the views of the dominions could be expressed—more detailed consideration of the subject. This procedure met with the approval of the Canadian Government, with the proviso that "when the discussion of war aims becomes more definite we may desire to refer to some of the special points dealt with in our telegram." A memorandum incorporating the provisional views of the British Government was handed to the French Ambassador on 22 December. It invited a further and more intensive exploration at a later date. But before this canvassing of views could take place, Hitler's assault upon Western Europe diverted the attention of the governments concerned upon more urgent questions. The problem of war aims had, for the moment, become eclipsed by the problem of sheer survival.

ECONOMIC WARFARE

The master idea of British strategy throughout the "twilight war" was that the struggle against Germany might be won by economic means. The formula was victory by strangulation. Germany's insufficiency in

---

*"We should not be skeptical of collective security," the Australian Prime Minister had declared on 17 October, "international agreements, and leagues of nations. What we did with the League was to ask an untrained man to do a record high jump." (*The Times*, 18 October 1939). On 29 October, Menzies had cabled Mackenzie King the draft of a proposed text on war aims: "In my opinion," he had stated, "the immediate object is to win the war and to win it in no uncertain way." On Menzies' message, Mackenzie King minuted: "Or to end the war, if possible to secure effective guarantees of peace without further loss of life." A few days later, Mackenzie King wrote: "I do not think much of Menzies' statement. . . . It strikes one rather as a hurriedly expressed personal point of view than as the product of a mature deliberation by the Government of a country." (Memorandum by King, 2 Nov. 1939, King Papers.)

raw materials made it vulnerable to a prolonged interruption of its sources of supply. "What we ought to do," wrote Neville Chamberlain, "is just to throw back the peace offers and continue the blockade. . . . I do not believe that holocausts are required." "Hold on tightly, keep up the economic pressure, push on with munitions production and military preparations with the utmost energy, take no offensive unless Hitler begins it."[15] Here, until Hitler conjured up the prospect of defeat, was Britain's formula for victory. It was, of course, inadequate. "Too much, it is now agreed," writes the official United Kingdom historian, "was expected of the blockade in the Second World War. The able and patient men who prepare their countries for the titanic and incalculable challenges of modern warfare must be allowed a small irrational quota of mysticism and hope; each country deceives itself as much as its opponents in attributing unproveable potentialities to certain of its least understood weapons. Blockade was a familiar enough thing in European warfare; but, adorned and transmogrified with a new name and an ill-defined promise, it had become in 1939 Britain's secret weapon."[16]

If the secret weapon was to wreak its intended destruction upon the enemy, the co-operation of Allies and friendly neutrals was essential. By herself Britain could work little hardship upon the Axis, at least not by cutting off her own exports, for these were negligible. Even her blockade—the interception at sea of contraband carried in neutral ships —depended upon a world-wide network of contraband-control bases, which Britain lacked in the Pacific and in the Caribbean. Much effort was accordingly devoted during the early months of the war to enlisting the aid of allies and others in an attempt to deny Germany (and Japan and the Soviet Union) the raw materials of war.

The Government of Canada necessarily played a part in this enterprise.

I

The licensing of exports was introduced in Canada on 20 September 1939, and nine days later an order-in-council prohibited the export of certain metals and minerals except under permit from the Minister of National Revenue. In January 1940 the list of metals and minerals was enlarged, at the suggestion of the British Ministry of Economic Warfare. At the same time, an embargo was imposed on all goods destined for export to neutral countries contiguous to territory under enemy occupation or control; on 29 February the embargo was extended to include all European neutrals except Eire, Portugal, and Turkey.

The policy followed with respect to the granting of export permits was set out publicly for the first time on 4 September 1940, in a letter from the Prime Minister to the president of the Canadian Legion. The first consideration was to see that there was an adequate supply of the commodity in question; the second, that there was no danger of re-export to enemy or unfriendly countries; the third, that the deal was not taking place at the instigation of enemy interests. The Government also kept a watchful eye on the volume of exports to the country concerned, and investigated if this rose beyond pre-war levels. It was not easy, the Prime Minister confessed, even when these primary conditions were satisfied, to reach a final decision. "The refusal of an export permit for shipment to a neutral country may mean the complete closing down of a Canadian mine or factory and the loss of employment to people whose labour is presently bringing into the country considerable quantities of foreign exchange which we are able to use in financing our greatly expanding programme of armament purchases from the United States." Again, there was the question of whether the denial of the permit would mean in practice the denial of the supply. "Though the export from Canada of all essential raw materials is subject to close control, no such control exists in Central and South American countries which are often large producers and exporters of similar goods." The Government, the Prime Minister concluded, "must take a good many different factors into consideration, and endeavour to maintain a policy which, in the long run, will best serve the national interest."[17]

The application of these general principles proved especially troublesome in respect of exports to the Soviet Union and to Japan.

In October 1939, the Soviet state trading agency, Amtorg, approached the International Nickel Company of Canada for the sale of 8,000 tons of nickel. The Company's officials consulted the British authorities, who advised against the sale, and the Company turned the offer down. At this point it became known that Amtorg was about to ask the Canadian Government whether it was ready to grant an export permit for the sale of nickel to the Soviet Union. The Government was far from anxious to do so. Yet it wondered whether an outright refusal to sell nickel to the Soviet Union might not afford the Soviets a pretext for access to the nickel deposits at the Petsamo concession in Finland, a concession owned by the International Nickel Company. A refusal was also difficult to justify in the light of a barter deal in timber which had recently been concluded between the Soviet Union and the United Kingdom.

A Canadian representative discussed these considerations with officials of the British Ministry of Economic Warfare. These suggested that while it was undesirable to cut off exports of nickel to the Soviet Union entirely, it was desirable to limit exports. They suggested that a quota of 500 tons a month be allowed for the time being, on receipt of assurances from the Soviet Government that the nickel would be used for domestic consumption, not for re-export to Germany. This policy, on which the Canadians subsequently settled, was abandoned following the outbreak of the war between Finland and the Soviet Union. ("A ghastly bit of ruthless aggression" was how Mackenzie King described the Russian invasion.)

In January 1940 the Canadian Government put an end to the shipment of wheat to the Soviet Union. "Public opinion in Canada," Mackenzie King wrote while the matter was before the War Committee of the cabinet, "will be all for . . . sending wheat to Finland if anywhere. . . . These are tremendous problems to decide and require very careful judgment."[18] The great difficulty was that wheat was in over-supply in the Dominion, while (apart from the United Kingdom) overseas markets had been cut off. Meanwhile the prairie wheat farmer had to be appeased. Some months after the policy of embargo on wheat exports to Soviet Russia had been in effect, the matter was discussed in the Liberal party caucus. Mackenzie King "asked the Ontario and Quebec men whether they thought we ought to send Western wheat to Japan and Russia to pass on to Germany. There was a general shout 'No'. I then told them that in the last fortnight we had refused to sell twenty-five million bushels to Japan. . . ."[19]

Japan indeed was the main problem. Minerals and wheat were the principal commodities involved. Nickel, as always, was crucial, especially since Canada controlled nearly all of the available supply. In September 1939, firm Japanese orders for nickel placed with the International Nickel Company amounted to 2,400 tons for the last quarter of the year; inquiries had been made for a further purchase of 1,800 tons. The British Ministry of Economic Warfare hoped that shipments would be restricted to a total of 1,200 tons. On 14 October the Canadian Government granted an export permit for the shipment of 800 tons, a compromise intended to steer a middle course between outright embargo and unrestricted sale. Early in 1940 it became apparent that Japan was prepared to purchase very large quantities of nickel from Canada, as much (so the Japanese Minister in Ottawa had intimated) as 10,000 tons. The British authorities were anxious to hold up delivery so as to secure a bargaining counter in negotiations with Japan over the creation of contraband-control bases in the Pacific, and requested the Canadian Government to withhold permits for the export of nickel to Japan. With some reluctance, the Canadians complied.

Aluminum was another commodity of which Canada was a prime

producer and which became critically important in economic warfare. At the beginning of the war, the British Ministry of Supply entered into arrangements with the Aluminum Company of Canada for purchase of its entire output available for export. Upon learning of this preemptive purchase, the Japanese Government inquired of the Department of External Affairs whether its pre-war order, represented as amounting to 8,200 tons, would be adversely affected by it. The Japanese were informed that further exports, including the pre-war order, were subject to licensing arrangements, and that no permits for export to Japan would be granted for at least two months, after which the position would be reviewed. The two months passed, the position was reviewed, and in May 1940 the Japanese Government was informed that no export permits for aluminum were likely to be granted for the foreseeable future.

In regard to copper and lead, Japan fared better. British Columbia producers were heavily dependent upon Japanese orders. It was not until October 1940 that the Canadian Government refused to issue any further export permits. But by that date, exports of most strategic metals to Japan had been halted or curtailed by the Canadian Government to an extent greater than prevailed in either the United States or the United Kingdom.

In August 1940, following the signing of the Tripartite Pact, the Japanese Government recalled its overseas representatives, and the Minister to Canada stopped in at the Department of External Affairs to say farewell. During his talk with O. D. Skelton, Baron Tomii raised the question of Canada's policy towards exporting to Japan. He observed that the policy was more restrictive than that followed by the United Kingdom, and wondered whether this might not be due "to some extent to the hostile attitude of certain groups in Canada towards Japan in connection with the present conflict in China." Skelton replied:

I told Baron Tomii that the decisive factor in our policy was of course the present and prospective needs of ourselves and our allies. As regards aluminum, our own and allied demand was already ahead of our actual production, and we would have to erect a new plant if we were to meet the minimum requirements. . . . With regard to nickel, we had a larger margin, but in view of our coming needs, by no means an excessive one. . . . At the same time I would readily agree that there was a vigorous demand for restricting shipments of munitions to Japan from a good many quarters on the ground (1) of sympathy with China as the victim of aggression, and (2) because of the extraordinary open and unrestrained anti-British attitude of the leaders of Japanese army and political opinion in recent months. . . . I said I did not think anyone in Japan could complain that it was Canada which was responsible for any cleavage that had arisen. We had not lifted a finger to help China, partly, it is true, because China did not have the money or the ships to buy and carry munitions. However that might be, as a matter of plain fact we had allowed the shipment to Japan of indispensable supplies for their war effort. . . .[20]

A social critic at the time put it somewhat differently:

> . . . Many a brave Canadian youth
> Will shed his blood on foreign shores,
> And die for Democracy, Freedom, Truth,
> With his body full of Canadian ores.[21]

A little more than a year later, men of the Royal Rifles and the Winnipeg Grenadiers lay wounded and dying about Repulse Bay and Stanley Peninsula.

II

Early in the morning of 9 April 1940, German troops crossed the undefended frontiers of Denmark; within a few hours Danish independence was snuffed out. The Allies at once became concerned lest the Danish possessions in the New World be handed over to the Germans by a harrassed or puppet administration in Copenhagen.

Greenland was of vital importance to the Allied war effort, not only because of its strategic position athwart the North Atlantic convoy and air routes, but on account as well of the cryolite mine at Ivigtut. Deprived of the output of that mine, Allied aluminum production would all but cease.

Canada, both as the bearer of responsibility for the safety of Allied convoys in the North Atlantic and as the primary aluminum producer among the Allies, was vitally concerned about the fate of Greenland. Whatever happened, the cryolite mine could not be allowed to be shut down, or to fall under the control of a German landing party. There seemed to be only one way of forestalling that possibility. It was to make sure that a Canadian landing party arrived first. On 12 April, the Chief of the General Staff and the Chief of the Naval Staff met with the Minister of National Defence to discuss the technical aspects of a small-scale Canadian occupation. Admiral Percy Nelles suggested the despatch of an ice-breaker and a small complement of naval and military personnel. It was noted that if intervention of this kind were attempted, the Canadian landing party would have to assume responsibility for the welfare of the inhabitants. Canada would become a colonial power.

On the day that the possibility of intervention in Greenland was being canvassed in Ottawa, the United States Administration was attempting to secure British acquiescence in a diametrically opposed policy. It was the firm conviction of the Secretary of State that no Allied intervention should take place in Greenland, or in any European colony in the New World, lest it should afford a pretext for Axis intervention elsewhere. Cordell Hull put this point of view strongly to the British Ambassador in Washington. After their meeting, Lord Lothian allowed himself to be quoted to the effect that neither the United Kingdom nor Canada would move into Greenland unless a German occupation appeared to be imminent. But he had no right to speak for Canada, where indeed a very different policy was under consideration, and the Canadians were incensed at what was at best a thoughtless initiative. The cabinet, meeting in the absence of the Prime Minister (then at Virginia Beach), was "upset" by what Lothian had said: "It does seem strange," its secretary wrote to Mackenzie King, reporting on its reaction, "that one who has had such great opportunities to observe the growth of the Commonwealth, of recent years, should be guilty of such an obvious impropriety."[22] O. D. Skelton went somewhat further: he described Lothian's act as "one of the most incredibly stupid and embarrassing interviews ever given by a public representative," and observed that his "apparent assumption of a right to speak for Canada was greatly resented by Colonel Ralston and other members of Council."[23] The Government informed the State Department that the British Ambassador had not been authorized to speak for Canada in the matter, and that a reproachful telegram had been sent to London.

On 13 April, the Canadian Minister in Washington saw Cordell Hull to dispel any misapprehension that Lothian's statement might have created. On 16 April, Loring Christie informed the State Department "that in view of the danger of Greenland being made a base for attack, the necessity of protecting the cryolite mining operations essential for aluminium production, and the necessity of assisting the local administration in obtaining supplies and marketing its products, we [the Canadian Government] had been considering the possibility of local action for these purposes, with no thought of a permanent occupation or political control." Christie thought the State Department's reaction could be interpreted as sympathetic; sympathetic or not, it was decidedly shaken.[24] It viewed the prospect of Canadian intervention as a threat to the Monroe Doctrine, as well as an inducement to Japan to occupy the Dutch East Indies. On 19 April, the State Department informed the Canadian Minister that it "would be glad to learn that Canada felt it unnecessary to take any action. . . ."[25]

At this juncture the Canadian Government sought the opinions of the

United Kingdom. The British authorities saw the problem in very
different terms. They regarded the military protection of the cryolite
mines as absolutely essential. They discounted the American objection
that intervention in Greenland would afford the Japanese a pretext for
intervention in South-East Asia: such pretext already existed in the
British occupation of the Faeroe Islands; in any case, the real deterrent
to a Japanese move in the Far East was fear of United States retaliation.
A Canadian expedition, the British felt, should proceed to Greenland
at once, disguised if necessary as some sort of relief mission but, whatever its disguise, equipped to forestall any German takeover.[26]

The Canadian Government was thus placed in its classic predicament of external affairs: the Americans wanted it to do one thing,
the British another. The problem was how to satisfy both. On 23 April,
Mackenzie King discussed the Greenland situation with President Roosevelt at Warm Springs. According to a memorandum of their discussion
(prepared by O. D. Skelton and approved by the Prime Minister),
"Mr. King made it clear that the Canadian Government had not had
in mind any preventive military occupation or assumption of political
control."[27] Having given the President this assurance, Mackenzie King
was somewhat disconcerted to learn from the Canadian Minister in
Washington, with whom he met on 28 April before returning to Ottawa,
that instructions had been sent to the Legation from the Department
of External Affairs to inform the U.S. State Department "that Canada
would prepare a defence force for Greenland. . . . Apparently Ralston
being concerned about aluminium and Skelton zealous to have Canada
rather than England handle Greenland matters on North American
basis, had between them gone farther than I think was wise. I thought
the position taken by the Americans was wise. . . . Clearly our people
had been a little over-zealous in preparing for a little war on Canada's
own account."[28] However, Mackenzie King left Washington under
the impression that any important divergence between Canadian and
American policy had now been removed.

In this he was mistaken. He returned to Ottawa to find that plans
for a military occupation were in an advanced state of preparedness.
"Found to my amazement," he wrote following a meeting of the cabinet
on 2 May,

that between them Ralston and Power had already a military expedition
fitted out to go to Greenland which included guns for mounting, soldiers,
some naval defence, etc. Power asked if they should be demobilized, and
I said certainly and at once. Ralston seemed a bit tenacious about our having
been asked by England to look after the property and what it might mean

to have bombs destroy the cryolite mines. It seemed impossible to bring home the picture of what the United States was doing to keep the Pacific quiet as against Japan. With no British Fleet and the unwisdom in consequence of giving an excuse to the Japanese for adopting toward the Dutch East Indies the kind of protection that Canada would have been exercising over Greenland. It is just matters of this kind which make me feel the importance of not going abroad if that can be avoided.[29]

During the next fortnight, the members of the War Committee of the cabinet, and the senior officials of the Department of External Affairs, grappled with the problem of what to do about Greenland. It was decided to appoint a Canadian consul, and to despatch him to Julianehaab (not far from the cryolite mine) "where he will be a constant reminder of Canadian interests in Greenland and could keep the Canadian Government informed of developments at the mine and elsewhere."[30] It was decided also to send a supply ship. But whether military personnel should be landed, and, if they were, in what strength, was not easily settled. Mackenzie King's diary entries reveal the extent of disagreement within the War Committee of the Cabinet:

8 May: . . . returned to the office to go over Greenland situation with Skelton. In my absence Power and Ralston had organized a military expedition for Greenland and had advised the British Government they were so doing. The British had come back urging that the expedition be carried out and showing no sympathy with the American point of view. I had to be firm about not antagonizing a great nation who is watching the critical situation on the Pacific, by attempting a violation which would be worse than that of the British landing in Norway. This time it is the Maritime Provinces outlook on an industry which is managed by someone from that Province [sic]. This little circumstance blinding the eyes of men to the larger world situation. We are put into the difficult cleft-stick position. . . .
9 May: Took up the Greenland situation anew. Read later despatch to Washington. Mackenzie joined with Ralston in favouring our going ahead with an expedition to Greenland whether viewed with favour by the United States or not. I pointed out that an expedition of the kind, if there were a German attack, would only receive the fate that the British had in Norway, in which event we would be blamed for sending inadequate forces (though not able to send anything else). On the other hand if an expedition were sent, whether a German raid occurred or not, the United States would be terribly offended, at a moment when there is the utmost need for keeping them as cordial as possible. . . .
14 May: . . . I felt that both Ralston and Power were not seeking to be particularly helpful by bringing up again the question of the military expedition, . . . Power coming back to the desirability of sending representatives of the Army, Navy and Air. . . . I felt a little nettled and made it clear that we had previously settled the policy of the Government, which was that our action was to parallel that of the U.S., and that I would not re-open the question of any expedition. . . .

After days of discussion, a final plan was agreed upon and implemented. There was to be an expedition, but not an expeditionary force: the landing party would be neither military nor civilian, but para-military (or quasi-civilian). It would be landed not by a warship but by a supply vessel of the Hudson's Bay Company, the *Nascopie*. It consisted of one artillery officer (in civilian dress), who was responsible for installing a 4″ gun (supplied by the United States) at a suitable site overlooking Ivigtut Harbour; two uniformed R.C.M.P. constables to act as interpreters; and four other R.C.M.P. personnel such as the *Nascopie* customarily carried on her regular Arctic missions. Such a party, it was hoped, would provide a modicum of protection for the precious cryolite (and satisfy the British Government) without provoking hostile reaction from the United States.

The second of these objectives was not attained. On 3 June, a day or so after the *Nascopie* arrived at Ivigtut, the Canadian chargé d'affaires was summoned to the State Department. Its spokesman, Mr. A. A. Berle, administered a sharp rebuke. Up to now, he said, the United States and Canada had worked in harmony on the Greenland situation. The State Department had been astonished to learn that, in spite of all assurances, the Canadians had landed a military detachment. This was not the time "for this type of 1890 imperialism . . . the days of Cecil Rhodes had passed." It transpired that the immediate occasion of this outburst was faulty intelligence: the State Department evidently believed that the detachment which had been landed contained troops, whereas it contained only an Army major in civilian dress about whose presence it had already been informed. But the real reason for its animus was its suspicion that the Canadian Government was deliberately exaggerating the gravity of the German threat to the cryolite mine in order to carve out a sphere of economic influence in Greenland.[31] The Canadian Government did what it could to dispel these suspicions, trying, as it did so, not to lose its temper. The temper was held in check, but the suspicious were not easily dispelled.

The Canadian landing party was not exactly joyously received. When Mr. Kenneth Kirkwood, the diplomatist designated as Canadian consul, arrived at Ivigtut aboard the Danish supply vessel *Julius Thomsen* a day or so after *Nascopie*'s arrival, he found something like a cold war in progress between the Canadians and the local population. So strained, indeed, were their relations that for several weeks the *Nascopie* personnel were unable to go ashore—a circumstance which did little to endear them to the town of Ivigtut and its inhabitants, or they to them. Eventually, the patient efforts of the Canadian Consul made it possible for the *Nascopie* party to fulfil its mission. Supplies were landed, the gun set up, and cryolite ore loaded for the return voyage. Later in the summer a special effort was made by the Canadian authorities to assure Governor Brun and his associates of the Greenland administration a pleasant visit in Ottawa; the next supply ship from Canada brought a present of Christmas trees for the Ivigtut community.

In 1941, not least as the result of the energetic representations of Mr. A. A. Berle who (in the words of the official U.S. Army historians) "was prodding the War and Navy Departments with the suggestion that further inaction on the part of the United States might result in the Canadians moving into Greenland,"[32] the Americans took over the defence of Ivigtut, first by arming the local inhabitants and, in 1942, by sending in a garrison of troops. The Germans were deterred from attack, and the supply of cryolite continued to reach the Allies without interruption for the remainder of the war.

III

Besides embargo and the pre-emption of supply, the third main weapon in the British arsenal of economic warfare was the naval blockade. Having assumed the strategic role of keeping open the North Atlantic convoy route, Canada inevitably became involved in its problems. These were three-fold: the determination of contraband; the creation of contraband-control bases; the interception of contraband.

It was not until December 1939 that the Canadian Government established a contraband list identical with that declared by the United Kingdom at the outset of the war. There were three reasons for the delay. First, contraband control in the early stages of the war was exercised in European waters by the Royal Navy, and there was no practical necessity of following the British lead. Second, it was desirable to refrain from any hard and fast definition of contraband so as to ensure importation of oil into Canada in neutral—that is, American— tankers. Third, it was felt advisable to await the passage of United States neutrality legislation before taking action.

Once it had been determined what was contraband and what was not, methods of interception had to be devised. Contraband-control bases were created in British waters and in the Mediterranean; to them neutral captains repaired of their own volition for inspection of their cargoes; if they did not, they ran the risk and indignity of interception by naval patrol on the High Seas. How to combine efficient contraband-control procedures with tolerably good relations with the neutrals concerned, particularly with the United States, proved in the Second World War as in the First to be a sizeable problem for British diplomacy. The Foreign Office and the Ministry of Economic Warfare sought by various arrangements (of which the navicert system was perhaps the most important*) to allay friction. But friction was by no means allayed.

The Canadian Government followed with mounting concern the steady deterioration of Anglo-American relations which the zealous prosecution of the economic war had caused, and about which it was probably better informed than the British.† At the same time, it lay within its power to do something to alleviate the situation. If a contraband-control base existed on the Canadian East Coast, it would be easier for American shipping to put in there than to proceed to Kirkwall in Scotland. From the Canadian point of view, the merits of this proposal were mixed. It would be helpful, of course, to appease the Americans. It would not be so helpful if the indignation of the President, the Congress and the public, previously directed at the United Kingdom, were now to be directed against Canada.

The British Government, less sensitive to this aspect, had as early as November 1939 been hatching a plan for the creation in Canadian waters of a contraband control base, and through its Ambassador in Washington had put it to the American authorities who, after some equivocation, had agreed to it in principle. Unfortunately, it did not see fit to inform the Canadian Government that these negotiations were in progress; Ottawa learned of them for the first time from the Montreal *Gazette* (which on 8 January 1940 had carried a full and accurate

*"The object of the navicert system, which came into operation on 1st December, 1939, was to allow the British mission in an exporting country to issue a 'commercial passport', known as a 'navicert', in respect of any consignment which did not appear liable to seizure as contraband. Goods covered by a navicert could count on receiving favourable treatment by the Allied contraband-control services." W. N. Medlicott, *The Economic Blockade*, vol. I (London, 1952), p. 94.

†In February 1940, the Canadian Minister in Washington reported the gist of a searching conversation he had had with a distinguished American (probably Mr. Felix Frankfurter) who, while very much pro-Allied in sentiment, had argued that the blockade as practised was doing more harm than good by reason of its adverse effects upon important sectors of American opinion:

"X puts the matter broadly in the following sense. In the recent technical and legalistic polemics the right may be on one side or the other. But that is beside the point. Practically it is a British need not to lose or impair more than necessary the existing sympathy in this country and the chances of getting indirect assistance or favours in various ways. The principle that war and belligerent operations have their hard necessities must of course be admitted. But every practical operation raises questions of expediency, method, judgment, the weighing of gains against losses. . . . There was no sign that such considerations were taken into account."

Loring Christie to Mackenzie King, 23 Feb. 1940, King Papers.

report). When the British High Commissioner raised the matter officially for the first time, on 25 January, "he found Dr. Skelton . . . hard to pacify. His resentment was all the stronger 'in that we were possibly handing Canada a hot potato to hold.' "[33] Eventually, after careful examination, the Canadian Government agreed to the creation of a contraband-control base at Saint John, New Brunswick (changing the proposed site later on to Shelburne, N.S., on the advice of the Navy), on condition that the operations would be conducted by the United Kingdom and on the assumption that its creation would contribute substantially to the easing of tensions between the United Kingdom and the United States arising out of contraband control measures.

By March 1940, the Canadian Government was having second thoughts about the principle of British control at the proposed base. It had itself proposed that principle so as not to become involved in any situation in which United States shipping might have to be forcibly brought to, or detained in, the base. But further discussion with the British authorities indicated that the British also had no thought of employing actual force in the conduct of contraband-control from that base so far as American shipping was concerned. When this became clear, the Canadian Government changed its mind, and decided to assume control of the base itself. However, it turned out that there was no need for it to do so. On 10 April, the United States Administration declared all Scandinavian ports to be within the combat area, and henceforth United States shipping across the North Atlantic came to an end. There was no longer any need for the base in Eastern Canada, and the proposal dropped from view.

There remained the part that Canada might play in intercepting shipping suspected of carrying contraband. Its right to do so was by no means clearly established in international law. It had been exercised in the First World War by the United Kingdom (and France), but only as a reprisal against submarine warfare. Early in December 1939, the British Government decided to intercept shipping on the High Seas, again using the pretext of retaliating against German submarine and mine-laying activities. It requested the Canadian Government to take similar action. O. D. Skelton considered the request in a memorandum of 7 December. "It seems desirable to do so," he wrote, "first because of the value of the political gesture of solidarity and second, because of the desirability of having a uniform legal basis of prize court action in the event of seizures occuring." But the Canadian Government lacked the naval forces needed to intercept all neutral shipping not previously cleared by contraband-control, and had no intention of intercepting on such a scale. Each case would be decided on its merits.

On 1 March 1940, the British authorities requested the Canadian Government to intercept and examine for contraband a Soviet vessel bound for Vladivostok from the American Pacific Coast, and suspected of carrying war matériel for Germany. "This raises a very serious question indeed," Mackenzie King wrote on hearing the news. "With practically no defence forces of our own on the Pacific Coast, the task, if attempted, might well become the occasion of a declaration of war by Russia upon Canada, or might lead, conceivably, to an endeavour on her part, through a combination with Japan, to land forces in B.C. via Alaska."[84] The vessel proceeded to its destination unmolested. Nor did the Canadian Government comply with a similar British request some months later. "Declined to authorize Canadian ships to stop some Russian vessels," Mackenzie King wrote on 9 February 1941. "I felt the situation in the Far East is much too dangerous to have Canada brought into position where we would be held responsible for creating an incident."[85] Two days later the War Committee of the cabinet decided that the Canadian Navy should play no part in intercepting Soviet or Japanese shipping. By the end of the year, Soviet Russia had become an ally, Japan an enemy, and the policy of non-interception no longer relevant.

VII

The Road to Ogdensburg

STANDING IDLY BY

For a decade after the end of the Great War, the United States figured
in the military planning of Canada not as a potential ally but as a
potential aggressor. Only in 1931 was this assumption finally discarded,
and the official plan in which it found expression—Defence Scheme
No. 1—formally repudiated.*

During the next few years, problems of an unmilitary nature beset
the military establishments of each country. In the Great Depression
which settled upon their common continent, each became involved in
relieving unemployed, in girding against possible revolution, in warding
off assaults upon their budgets at times so ferocious that, had they
succeeded, the armed forces could hardly have survived. But the Canadian military and the American endured their trials in isolation. They
did not tell each other of their troubles, they did not share their experiences, least of all did they pool their resources. So it was between
the governments as well. They were as two solitudes.

It was Franklin Roosevelt who brought an end to isolation between
the two nations of North America. A series of his speeches in 1935 and
1936 developed the notion of "the good neighbor." "Between Canada
and the United States exists a neighborliness," the President declared
at Arlington on Armistice Day 1935, "a genuine friendship which for
over a century has dispelled every passing rift." On 3 January 1936,
in a speech to a joint session of the Congress, the President dedicated
the United States "to the policy of the good neighbor—the neighbor
who resolutely respects himself and, because he does so, respects the
rights of others." Among the nations of the Americas, Franklin Roose-

*In Defence of Canada, vol. I, pp. 71–8.

velt insisted, this policy was "no longer a hope—no longer an objective remaining to be accomplished; it is a fact, active, present, pertinent and effective. . . . There is neither war nor rumor of war nor desire for war. The inhabitants of this vast area, 250,000,000 strong, spreading more than 8,000 miles from the Arctic to the Antarctic, believe in and propose to follow the policy of the good neighbor; and they wish with all their heart that the rest of the world might do likewise." Finally, on 14 August, at Chautauqua, N.Y., the President stated: "Our closest neighbors are good neighbors. If there are remoter nations that wish us not good but ill, they know that we are strong; they know that we can and will defend ourselves and defend our neighborhood." The Chautauqua speech was more specific than its predecessors; and in Ottawa, for the first time, the neighbour picked up his ears. "Roosevelt in a speech has spoken of looking after this continent," Mackenzie King wrote; it was a warning, he thought, not to the European dictators but to Japan. "He senses danger there."

The Good Neighbor policy was for continental defence only a slogan, not yet a policy. Good neighbourhood manifested itself in the signing of a trade treaty, in the opening of an international park, but not, so far, in preparations against attacks on North America. It was partly that, in the eyes of the junior partner, no preparations seemed necessary. "The present danger of attack upon Canada," Mackenzie King declared in 1938, "is minor in degree and second-hand in origin."[1] The senior partner had for some time discerned danger in the Orient; so had the junior but again not as a threat to itself. What was envisaged was the possibility of war between Japan and the United States, Canada remaining neutral; in which event, the Dominion's military planners concluded, it would be necessary to "exercise such vigilance over Canadian territory, waters and air as will make it impossible for either belligerent undetected to commit therein acts the performance of which would constitute a violation of Canadian neutrality."[2]

These differing perspectives produced differing senses of urgency. From the early 1930's, the American military had been anxiously scanning its far-flung defences in Alaska, which lay dangerously exposed to the depredations of Japanese raiders. In 1934 a number of requests to fly military aircraft from the continental United States to Alaska *via* British Columbia were received in Ottawa. The Department of National Defence recommended that these requests be refused, but the Government overruled the recommendation.[3]

Another American defence measure was less favourably received. This was the project to build a highway to Alaska across Canadian territory. First broached in 1929, the Alaska Highway gained the support of the premier of British Columbia. In 1932 the Hoover Administration appointed a board of commissioners to report upon its feasibility; it concluded that the highway could be built at a reasonable cost, about $27 millions, and recommended that both countries contribute to the cost of construction. But the great depression caused the project to be put to one side.

In March 1936 it came once again to the fore. The United States Government sought Canada's views on the desirability of proceeding forthwith with the building of the highway. Before replying, the Canadian Government sought the reaction of its military advisers. This was highly unfavourable. "The building of a north and south highway through British Columbia and the Yukon," a General Staff memorandum declared, "would provide a strong military inducement to the United States to ignore our neutral rights in the event of a war between that country and Japan, a danger which we should do everything in our power to avoid."[4]

The Alaska Highway became a pet project of President Roosevelt, as it had been of President Hoover. When Mackenzie King visited Washington in March 1937, the President sounded him out on the idea. "At the end of the evening," Mackenzie King's memorandum of their discussion records,

the President said there was one other matter he did not know whether anything could be done with it or not; it was the possibility of construction of a highway through British Columbia through Alaska. He said this would be of a great advantage for military purposes, in the event of trouble with Japan. . . . I said that that was a matter which could be looked into but I could say nothing at present as to the possibility of any construction.[5]

When Roosevelt visited Victoria, B.C., on 30 September 1937, he found the premier of British Columbia, P. D. Pattullo, much more enthusiastic about problems of Pacific Coast defence generally and the Alaska Highway in particular, than Mackenzie King had been earlier that year. Pattullo thereafter attempted, in a number of public statements, to encourage the Americans to press the federal government hard to proceed with the highway. His intervention greatly displeased Mackenzie King when he heard about it: "He has acted," he wrote, "like a child." The cabinet was more determined than ever that nothing should be done. "Grounds of public policy," Mackenzie King wrote on 26 April 1938, "would not permit using the funds of a foreign Government to construct public works in Canada. It would be, as Lapointe phrased it, a matter of financial invasion, or, as I termed it, financial penetration." (This view prevailed until March 1942, when the Permanent Joint

Board on Defence recommended to the two Governments the acceptance of a United States proposal to build a highway to Alaska by linking the airports of the Northwest Staging Route. The cost of more than $75 millions was borne entirely by the United States.[6])

Roosevelt's visit to Victoria was what first really roused his interest in Canadian-American co-operation in the defence of the continent. "In his mind" (the Canadian Minister to Washington reported in October 1940 after an interview with the President), "from the point of view of his own interest, he places the real genesis in a trip he made to Victoria, B.C., in a destroyer in September 1937, during the course of a visit to Seattle and the State of Washington. He mentioned having seen the Lieutenant-Governor of the Province and Premier Pattullo. What he gathered then as to the condition of our Pacific naval forces and coast defences disturbed him, as he was thinking of the United States defences, and the British Columbia coast had to be regarded in reality as a link between the United States and Alaska."[7] Soon after this visit, Roosevelt instructed the United States Minister in Ottawa, Norman Armour, to see what might be done to promote the exchange of military intelligence between the General Staffs of the two countries. The Minister's first move was to discuss the matter informally with Colonel H. D. G. Crerar, then Director of Military Operations and Intelligence. Colonel Crerar's record of their conversation follows:

After dinner, Mr. Armour drew me to one side saying that he would like to talk to me, personally and confidentially, about a matter which was much in the President's mind, and, naturally, in his own. This matter was the increasing seriousness of the international situation, the prospects of another great war involving both Canada and the United States, and in that connection the present desirability of somewhat closer contact between the U.S. War Department and the Dept. of National Defence. He emphasized the deep interest he had in these questions by stating that on each of his more recent conferences with the President, Mr. Roosevelt had raised these particular issues. . . .

I agreed that our direct military contacts with the Departments at Washington were non-existent, and that a greater interchange of ideas on military problems of mutual importance would be to joint advantage, but I doubted whether our Government desired to create any formal or continuous liaison. . . .

I said that in my opinion the maximum which might presently be attempted would be to arrange occasional visits by senior Departmental officers of one country to inspect military establishments, experiments or manoeuvres in the other. Such visits need cause no public excitement, they would enable personal liaison to be established, and should the Governments mutually desire, the confidential exchange of certain information concerning their defence policies could at the same time be undertaken. . . .

Mr. Armour appeared to agree that such a policy of "gradualness" would be the better one to pursue in the present circumstances. He concluded, however, by saying that the matter was very much on his mind and that he felt greatly constrained to discuss it personally with the Prime Minister at an early date.[8]

On 7 January 1938, about three weeks after he had raised the matter with Colonel Crerar, the American Minister called upon the Prime Minister and put to him the suggestion that an unpublicized and informal visit of senior Canadian military personnel to Washington in the near future would be opportune. Mackenzie King agreed. Accordingly, the Chief of the General Staff, Major-General E. C. Ashton, and the Chief of Naval Staff, Commodore P. W. Nelles, were instructed some days later to proceed to the American capital for informal discussion with their counterparts in the United States armed forces. "We were to give and to receive all information desired by either party," General Ashton wrote afterwards, "but we were to make no commitments." They were enjoined to take every possible precaution so that their presence in Washington would not be detected; they accordingly travelled to Washington separately, in civilian dress, and remained cloistered in the precincts of the Canadian Legation throughout their visit except for brief strolls along Massachusetts Avenue, undertaken, as General Ashton reported, "for exercise."

On the afternoon of 18 January, the first, and most comprehensive, of the two conversations took place. The participants were Ashton, Nelles, and Major-General Malin Craig, Chief of Staff of the U.S. Army. (The conversation held next day had as an additional participant Admiral William Leahy, Chief of Staff of the U.S. Navy, and covered much the same ground as that held on the previous day.) General Ashton's record of this meeting was as follows:

General Craig . . . asked me what subjects we wished to discuss.

I informed him that we had come at the request of the U.S. Government and were not informed as to what subjects would be covered, but that I was authorized to give and receive information, but to make no commitments.

He stated that he had very limited instructions, but was prepared to talk as "soldier to soldier" on defence questions with particular reference to the Pacific Coast.

He outlined their coastal armaments and their air defence arrangements with particular reference to Juan de Fuca Strait and Puget Sound.

He asked for details of our defence arrangements in that neighbourhood, land, sea and air, and the probable size of the forces, particularly naval and air, which could be assembled.

I gave him this information in general terms and informed him that I could provide him with any details that he required. He stated that the information given was sufficient.

He then stated that the United States Army would be prepared to extend their defensive operations to cover the Pacific Coast from the United States–Canadian border to the Canadian–Alaskan border line, and asked for information as to the landing fields that could be provided on the Canadian coast line for their planes, with which they were well supplied, their bombers being highly efficient.

At this point I informed him that Canada was in a different situation from the United States, in considering a question of this kind, in that the United States had only themselves to think about, but that Canada, while looking after her own defences to the best of her ability and means, was an integral part of the British Empire and also a member of the League of Nations, and these facts must not be lost sight of. He agreed.

I then informed him that we were considering defence questions, particularly on the Pacific Coast, under three conditions—

(a) Canada, with the other Nations of the British Empire, at war with Japan—the United States neutral.

(b) The United States at war with Japan—Canada with the other Nations of the British Empire neutral.

(c) The British Empire and the United States allied against Japan.

He immediately stated that we could "wash out" the first two; that in his opinion it was inconceivable that in a war with Japan both nations would not be engaged at the same time, and, therefore, we need only consider situation (c).

I stated that while we had considered that that situation would be a probable one, we must remember the others, in order to avoid any overt act which might affect Canadian neutrality and thereby react on other portions of the British Empire.

He agreed, but stated again that he did not consider we should give any time to discussing any proposition except (c).

I then stated that with respect to his questions concerning landing fields along the Canadian coast line, there was limited accommodation at Vancouver, a very small field near Victoria, possibly not suited for the heavier types of craft, but that we were taking steps to acquire and develop a larger field near Esquimalt at Patricia Bay; that the whole coastline northwards was mountainous for a considerable distance back, and that no known areas suitable for conversion to flying fields had been located between there and Prince Rupert, and that we were therefore having recourse largely to seaplanes or floatplanes. Further investigations are being carried out.

He stated the U.S. Army was not supplied with seaplanes but that the Navy had a very considerable number. . . . He stated that many of his 'planes had a very wide radius of action and that they would be very useful.

In discussing the question of Coast Defence armament he stated that they had large numbers of 155 mm (6") tractor drawn guns, which could not only be made available to protect the south shore and U.S. territorial waters of Juan de Fuca Strait from the entrance to Puget Sound west, that they would cover their shoreline up to the international boundary, but that they would have guns to spare, with men, to provide additional protection to Canada in the neighborhood of Vancouver or Victoria, up the coast line and at Prince Rupert; that they could also make available, if necessary,

12-inch mortars and guns, together with heavy guns mounted on railway carriages.

He asked where such guns could be used. I stated that the only railway facilities for guns so mounted would be found in the neighbourhood of Vancouver and New Westminster and, to a limited extent, near Prince Rupert.

Scales of Attack. I inquired as to the scales of attack which they were considering, and found them very parallel to our own.

Raids were to be expected. Possibly one or two small cruisers or armed merchant vessels for bombardment purposes, and motor torpedo boats. He stated that the Japanese had some very powerful boats all along the coast. The U.S. authorities were going to force them out; had already taken action at San Diego.

Aeroplane attack in considerable force probably from carriers or improvised carriers protected by destroyers. These might be very heavy. They accepted the principle that they could not intercept or prevent attacks but their 'planes would follow the enemy 'planes to sea, trace them to their parent ship or base and inevitably destroy them—none would escape.

I asked if they had considered the possibility of any raids on a large scale by enemy fleet, or larger-scale landing parties to secure a base. He stated that he did not consider that any such proposition was likely to be attempted at such great distance from Japan, but that if it were attempted, while great damage would be done, the fleet engaged would be intercepted and inevitably destroyed before it could return to Japan.

I told him that we had not considered heavy naval attacks feasible.

At this point I informed him that I had with me a General Staff memorandum on the "Fixed Defences of Juan de Fuca Strait" which covered our own layout and what we presumed to be theirs. This had not been prepared to be given to them, but that if he would like to see it, I should be glad to hand it to him. He would find therein, as far as our armament was concerned, our existing, interim and proposed arrangements. I spoke of the gaps which existed between the areas covered by our coastal defences and theirs. He stated that those gaps would be covered effectively by their air forces and, in places, by mobile guns. I handed the memorandum to him at his request.

He expressed the view of the danger of imminent rupture with Japan and stated that the Philippines would be taken by Japan within 48 hours. . . . He impressed the necessity of immediately interning all Japanese on an emergency arising, and said they had them all listed and located. . . .*

*Memorandum by the Chief of the General Staff, "Conversations on Defence Questions," 23 Jan. 1938, Army Records.

At the conclusion of the discussions, General Craig told the two Canadian officers that for his part he would make no notes or reports on what had transpired; presumably for this reason the staff talks are unrecorded in any of the official United States histories in the series *U.S. Army in World War II*, e.g., Stanley W. Dziuban, *Military Relations between the United States and Canada, 1939–1945* (Washington, D.C., 1959); Stetson Conn and Byron Fairchild, *The Framework of Hemisphere Defence* (Washington, D.C., 1960); and Stetson Conn, Rose C. Engelman, and Byron Fairchild, *Guarding the United States and its Outposts* (Washington, D.C., 1964).

In April 1938, Colonel N. O. Carr, an ordnance specialist of the Department of National Defence, went to Washington for talks with various specialist and technical officers of the U.S. Army. These discussions, which like their predecessors were conducted in the strictest secrecy, "dealt entirely with an examination of the possibility of Canada obtaining military equipment and armament from the U.S. because of probable slow delivery of material ordered from [the] U.K. Discussion for the most part revolved around coast defence and anti-aircraft armament. Decision reached was that orders placed in U.S. could not be filled more rapidly than those placed in U.K."[9]

A third meeting between Canadian and United States officers took place in Washington on 23 November 1938. The Canadian participant on this occasion was the new Chief of the General Staff, Major-General T.V. Anderson, and the object of the visit was not so much to take the earlier staff discussions any further as to bring the Canadian officer into contact with his United States counterparts. The Canadian Government was concerned that no word of what passed between them should be communicated directly to the British military: General Anderson was cautioned to ensure that he "give his information first to the Government here on his return to Ottawa, and then it would be for the Government to convey any information to the British Government through the established channels if, after consideration, that course should appear appropriate."[10]

Mackenzie King was duly informed of the outcome of these various staff conversations. He was not taken by the assumption of the Americans that war with Japan was likely. "The United States view on this," he wrote, "is that of its War Office, and has been a view held for twenty years without much ground."

In August 1938, President Roosevelt journeyed to Kingston, Ont., for a ceremony marking the opening of a nearby international bridge. In his speech he uttered his celebrated declaration (inserted by his own hand in the draft prepared for him by the Department of State) "that the people of the United States will not stand idly by if domination of Canadian soil is threatened by any other empire." Two days later, Mackenzie King responded to the President's assurance by an assurance of his own: "We, too, have our obligations as a good friendly neighbour, and one of these is to see that, at our own instance, our country is made as immune from attack or possible invasion as we can reasonably be expected to make it, and that, should the occasion ever arise, enemy forces should not be able to pursue their way either by land, sea or air, to the United States across Canadian territory." That, he reflected afterwards, was the proper note to sound: it would "please the Americans

above all else, and is right. I think at last we have got our defence programme in good shape. Good neighbour on one side; partners within
the Empire on the other. Obligations to both in return for their assistance. Readiness to meet all joint emergencies."[11]

On two further occasions before the outbreak of war, the problems
of continental defence were in the minds of the leaders of the two
countries of the continent. In November 1938, Mackenzie King spent
a night at the White House, and he and Franklin Roosevelt reviewed
the condition of coastal defences in the course of their informal talks.
And in August 1939, the President took a cruise along the Labrador
coast, ostensibly on holiday, actually (as he later related to the Canadian
Minister in Washington) to spy out the land. "The real origin of that
cruise, he revealed, was that he had found to his surprise that none of
his naval officers seemed to have been in those waters or to know anything about them, so he wanted to get them interested in studying this
area. He had therefore taken a cruiser for a holiday visit and had taken
some of his officers along."[12] "He wanted to see what the naval and air
defence of the Canadian East Coast and of Newfoundland involved. He
was thinking, for example, of the possibility of spotting bays or inlets
where unfriendly submarines might lurk. He was disappointed that the
fog had in fact prevented such a personal reconnaissance."[13]

BELLIGERENT AND NEUTRAL

By the terms of the Neutrality Act of 1935, the United States government was forbidden to sell arms and war matériel to any state at war.
In August 1939, when it appeared that before many more days had
passed Canada would be at war with Germany, an air mission was
sent from Ottawa to Washington. The mission, headed by Air Commodore E. W. Stedman, was instructed to try to purchase military aircraft and accessories for delivery to the R.C.A.F. within three months; an
amount up to $7.5 millions had been authorized for this purpose by a
Governor General's warrant of 26 August. The mission reported to
the Canadian Legation in Washington on 25 August. (It had been preceded, some days earlier, by the Minister of National Defence, Ian
Mackenzie, accompanied by Air Marshal W. A. Bishop, who in informal
conversations with high officials of the United States War Department
had conveyed the urgency of Canadian requirements and expressed the
hope that the American authorities would see their way to meeting
them). During the next week, the members of the mission entered

into negotiations with the representatives of the major United States aircraft manufacturers. They sought to purchase, among other items, thirty-five bomber aircraft (of which fifteen were to be flying boats) and fifteen trainers. The Douglas Aircraft Company undertook to provide twenty Douglas B18A bombers, and North American Aviation fifteen NA-16 trainers; provisional agreements between the mission and the companies were signed on 31 August. The mission returned to Ottawa on 2 September. But it might as well have returned empty-handed. Before delivery of the aircraft and their ancillary equipment could be taken, Canada was at war.[14]

The United Kingdom had declared itself to be at war with Germany on 3 September 1939. The Canadian Government had proclaimed a state of "apprehended war" by order-in-council as of 25 August (so as to permit it to assume powers authorized under the War Measures Act of 1914). But war itself was not formally declared until 10 September.

How Canada's curious condition of "quasi-belligerency"—or was it "quasi-neutrality"?—came to be regarded in Washington now assumed the gravest significance. If Canada's neutrality was recognized, available supplies could be hustled northwards across the border. If not, nothing could be done. The Roosevelt Administration had to make up its mind immediately, and its counsels were divided. Cordell Hull has related that he favoured waiting until a formal Canadian declaration of war before including the Dominion in the list of countries against which the provisions of the Neutrality Act were to go into effect on 5 September, but that he allowed himself to be talked into including it immediately by other members of the State Department. A meeting at the White House was held to secure a final and last-minute decision. One of those present remarked that to leave Canada off the list would upset the British Foreign Office, whereupon the President, observing that he would sooner hurt the Foreign Office then offend his friends in Canada, immediately got the Prime Minister of Canada on the telephone and asked him how he would prefer the matter to be dealt with. Mackenzie King replied that Canada was still neutral, and should be left off the embargo list until a state of war had been formally proclaimed. And that is how it was done. Some months later, when Roosevelt and Mackenzie King met in Warm Springs, Georgia, the President (in Mackenzie King's words) "recalled how he had waited a week and 'phoned me before declaring Canada was at war. Had accepted my word that we were not at war until Parliament had so decided. This to let us get supplies in meanwhile."

No inventory has been kept of what reached Canada from the

United States in the way of war supplies between 3 September 1939 and 10 September 1939, but it did not include aircraft on order for the R.A.F. The British High Commissioner to Canada at the time has recalled in his memoirs the agitation of the United States chargé d'affaires in Ottawa, sitting in the diplomatic gallery in the House of Commons while the Canadian Parliament decided to go to war. "He was getting very restless, repeating quietly to himself, 'I must go, I must go' . . . I guessed . . . the cause of his restlessness. It was due to the fact that, if war was declared, he must telephone Washington immediately so as to enable the President to clamp down on Canada the provisions of the Neutrality Act, and we had a batch of Lockheed planes, which we had ordered and (I think) paid for in California, in the air at that very moment en route to Lethbridge which they would reach not sooner than the Sunday. They did not reach Lethbridge on the Sunday, or any other day just then, for the Act was . . . brought into force before they crossed the border."[15]

The Australian Government, which became affected by the United States embargo proclaimed on 5 September, sought to have Canada take delivery of the aircraft which it had on order until the Canadian state of belligerency came into effect. The Canadian Government, however, refused to become a party to this transaction, pointing out that to do so would be a direct infringement of a provision of the Neutrality Act which forbade delivery of goods destined for trans-shipment to a belligerent, and that to risk a contravention of the Act at that time might have undesirable consequences for the revision of its terms which was then impending, as well as jeopardizing the Dominion's prospective purchases in the United States of munitions and supply.[16]

II

President Roosevelt did not need to be prompted from the wings to realize that the Neutrality Act as written when Britain and the dominions went to war, so far from preserving a fine impartiality between the Allies and the Axis, practically favoured the latter. From the outset of the war Roosevelt deemed it essential to revise the provisions of the Act, particularly in regard to repealing the arms embargo.* As early as 7

*Before the war, however, Roosevelt seems to have thought that the Neutrality Act would not prevent United States assistance to the Allied belligerents. Harold Ickes wrote in his diary on 24 September 1938:

"There could be bought in this country materials, non-military in themselves, such as pipes from which shells could be made, which could easily be turned into shells and bullets and airplanes. The President indicated that even if we had to

September he had caused careful soundings to be taken of congressional opinion: these revealed that some sixty Senators were likely to support a policy of "cash-and-carry neutrality," twenty-five to oppose, the remainder to be in the balance. "I hope and believe," he wrote to Neville Chamberlain on 11 September, "that we shall repeal the embargo within the next month and this is definitely a part of the Administration policy."[17] But the isolationists' reaction proved stronger than the President had anticipated. "I am almost literally walking on eggs," he wrote to Lord Tweedsmuir on 5 October, "and, having delivered my message to the Congress, and having good prospects of the bill going through, I am at the moment saying nothing, seeing nothing and hearing nothing."[18]

On 29 September the text of the proposed new Act was printed. Scrutiny by the Canadian Government disclosed several features which caused it concern. Of these the gravest by far was a provision preventing United States merchant shipping from carrying any goods to any belligerent. Extending "cash" with one hand, the Administration appeared to be withdrawing "carry" with the other. Such a provision would have had disturbing effects upon the Canadian economy: most of the oil then used in British Columbia was shipped from California in tankers of American registry. Another alarming provision was that no credits were to be extended to belligerents. They could buy, but they could not borrow to buy. Some of the opponents of the President's bill declared it would work greater hardship on the Allies than the legislation it was designed to replace; Senator Arthur Vandenberg, a prominent supporter of the arms embargo, expressed himself in this sense to the Canadian Minister in Washington.[19] An American survey of the time described the new bill as "a medly of disharmonies," filled with "manifest contradictions and inconsistencies."[20] These, the Canadian Minister pointed out in an appreciation for his Government, were partly the result of a deliberate strategy—"the arms embargo repealists having tightened up the various other provisions in order to win a number of the arms embargoists to the Bill as a whole"—and partly the result of the Administration's desire simultaneously to pursue two policies which were steadily becoming incompatible, "namely, to stake the cause taken up by the Allies as much as practicable, but at the same time to take every

---

enforce our neutrality laws, there would be a large outlet by such methods for munitions to flow toward England and France by way of Canada and otherwise. In carrying out our neutrality laws we would resolve all doubts in favour of the democratic countries."

The Secret Diary of Harold L. Ickes, vol. II, *The Inside Struggle, 1936–1939* (New York, 1953), p. 474.

practicable precaution against the United States entering the European war."[21]

The Canadian Government saw at once the extent of the threat posed by the new bill to the trade of the Dominion; it was less quick to grasp how drastically it might affect the war effort as a whole. It did not, therefore, consider it necessary to make urgent representations to the United States authorities. On 9 October, however, the Canadian Minister at Washington cabled a full analysis of the adverse effects of a Neutrality Act drawn on the lines of the bill upon the Canadian economy and upon the Allied war effort, and pleaded that he be allowed to take up at least the first of these aspects with the Administration without delay. His authorization duly received, Loring Christie prepared and presented an aide-mémoire to the Secretary of State. It was sympathetically considered. He was later informed that Cordell Hull, who had previously remained aloof from the neutrality battle raging in the Congress, wanted to send the Canadian note to the Chairman of the Senate Foreign Relations Committee; the Canadian Government gave its permission for this to be done. On 19 October, the Chairman introduced a number of amendments, and a week later an official of the Department of External Affairs noted with satisfaction that "all revisions desirable from a Canadian point of view have been made." The legislation as amended allowed United States vessels to trade into Canadian ports on the Pacific coast, thus ensuring the supply of oil from California, and into Atlantic coast ports West of 66° longitude, thus ensuring the trade routes Boston-Yarmouth and Boston-Saint John. The new Neutrality Act became law on 4 November.

III

The repeal of the arms embargo opened the American arsenal to Britain and France to the extent that they were able to pay cash on the barrelhead. For the first few months of the war, the Allies had enough gold and securities to buy all they wanted. It is therefore remarkable, as two American historians observe, that "the repeal of the embargo, on which the democracies professed to count so heavily, resulted in no immediate increase in the orders they placed in the American arsenal now opened to them. . . . During the first five months of war American sales abroad increased only about 30 percent—those to Britain only about 10 percent."[22] The April 1940 issue of *Fortune* magazine recorded that "the Allied purchasing to date, in the words of an army officer charged with keeping an eye on it, 'doesn't amount to a hoot in hell'. The little that has been bought has been bought mostly by the French. . . . The British, beyond an estimated $125,000,000 for aircraft and machine tools, have only dabbled on the U.S. market."[23] The more measured verdict of the official United Kingdom historian of North American supply shows that this contemporary estimate was not far off the mark.*

The reasons why the United Kingdom was slow to exploit the resources of war in North America have already been discussed.† So long as the British drew only sparingly upon the supplies made available by the Neutrality Act of 1939, there was little reason for dissatisfaction with its provisions, and little pressure for their revision. But when in the spring and early summer of 1940 the twilight war deepened into the black night of battle and defeat, the irksome nature of the Neutrality Act, particularly in respect of its "cash-and-carry" provision, became more evident, and voices were raised to the effect that something must be done. Some demanded that the United States should cast neutrality to one side and enter the war on the side of the Allies; others that it should become a belligerent in all but name, modifying, as a first step, its neutrality legislation so that it would bear less onerously upon the Allies.

The Prime Minister of Canada was asked to intervene on behalf of this cause. But he shrank from intervention. No one was more finely tuned to the need to resist the pressures of the moment in order to assure success in the long run than Mackenzie King; and his exceptional sensitivity in this regard gave him a unique insight into President Roosevelt's difficulties in dealing with isolationist opinion in an election year. This

*"The total value of British munitions orders placed in the United States up to the end of April 1940 (including prewar contracts) was $236,049,000. Of this, Air Ministry contracts accounted for nearly eighty-seven per cent.—$204,-835,000—and this figure included only a small fraction of the new Allied programme, under which orders to the value of some $250 million were still to come. Ministry of Supply orders for munitions amounted to $28,691,000, with requisitions outstanding for a further sum of just under $4 million. It is an indication of the extreme narrowness of the margin which American supply was being called on to fill in the matter of Army equipment that one-third of the Ministry's total commitments in the United States consisted of a single order for heavy shells, which did not amount to a fraction of the total gun ammunition programme. Contracts let on behalf of the Admiralty, chiefly for motor-boat engines and degaussing cable, added up to a mere $2½ million. . . . Thus, up to the moment when the shooting war begun in earnest, the British Government had on the whole succeeded in avoiding heavy purchases in the United States. . . ."
H. Duncan Hall, *North American Supply* (London, 1954), pp. 124–5.
†See above, chap. IV, pp. 123–4, 131.

did not mean that he did not place privately before the President his own suggestions as to how the United States could help the Allied cause. But it did mean that he was anxious to avoid a public appeal, or the kind of private appeal which might become public, likely to set back a more far-reaching American intervention in the war effort at some future date.

A speech by the Attorney-General of Ontario, Gordon Conant, on 3 April 1940 provided a perfect example of how not to go about it. The speech urged the Canadian Government to press the Government at Washington to more active participation in support of the Allies. It was widely, and adversely, commented upon in the American press; it drew from the U.S. Secretary of State the extraordinarily sharp rebuke that "no nondescript utterances of minor officials or individuals abroad . . . have anything remotely to do with the policy of this Government at home or in its international relations."[24] Loring Christie, the Canadian Minister at Washington, telephoned to say that the speech had strengthened the hand of the isolationists in Congress; O. D. Skelton described it "as the most stupid and harmful . . . made by any Canadian in years."[25] Mackenzie King was naturally upset by this unhelpful intervention. He tried to rectify matters by issuing a press statement: "The Canadian Government particularly has no thought of attempting to intervene, directly or indirectly, in the affairs or policies of the United States. Any other course would be as harmful as it would be unwarranted, and would show a disregard of the friendly understanding we have for years received from the people and Government of a good neighbour."[26] But the damage had already been done.

Another suggestion, intended to be helpful but judged to be otherwise, came from a former Canadian Minister to the United States, W. D. Herridge.* It was Herridge's notion that Canada might initiate a proposal to send a mission to Washington composed of eminent Allied statesmen, who would inform the Administration, the Congress, and the people of the invincible fighting spirit of the Allies and of their urgent need for immediate aid. The Canadian Minister at Washington was asked by the Government to inquire privately of various officials how such a mission would be received; as expected, he reported that in their judgment nothing could be less helpful.[27] The author of the proposal was so informed. But Herridge was not easily discouraged. On 22 June and again on 22 July he returned to the attack, fortified now with the

*Whose genius for forceful, and unorthodox, diplomacy has been noted earlier. See chap. I, pp. 4–5.

enthusiastic support of Senator Arthur Meighen (and undaunted by the lack of enthusiasm displayed by J. W. Dafoe).[28] On Mackenzie King's behalf, O. D. Skelton sent Herridge the following reply:

Mr. King has given careful consideration to your suggestions. There is no question as to the desirability of obtaining from the United States all possible co-operation in the struggle against Hitlerism. The question is whether the means you suggest—the despatch of an Allied Mission to Washington—would be a feasible and effective means of achieving that end. . . .

My personal opinion is that the specific means you suggest of securing the utmost co-operation by the United States . . . would hinder rather than help that co-operation. It would, I think, give a target and a rallying cry to those forces in the United States which are always ready and eager to allege that foreign countries are trying to tell the people of the United States how to run their country and particularly to force them into the war.[29]

Privately Skelton regarded Herridge's plan as "cockeyed and dangerous."[30] The Prime Minister shared his opinion.

A further proposal for a public appeal to the President could not be so easily deflected, for its author was the Prime Minister of Australia. On 22 May 1940, Robert Menzies sent a telegram to Churchill, with copies to the Prime Ministers of Canada, South Africa and New Zealand, advocating that the Commonwealth leaders join together in an immediate personal appeal to Roosevelt to release at once all available aircraft to the Allies, and to allow as well an Allied campaign for volunteer American airmen. On 24 May Mackenzie King cabled his reaction to Churchill: "I feel strongly that at the present moment any public appeal by outside governments would arrest rather than assist the formation of public and Congressional opinion favourable to action, and consider it would be equally embarrassing if information were to reach the public in any way as to personal approaches or discussions being made." As it happened, Smuts, Fraser, and Churchill himself shared Mackenzie King's appraisal that Menzies' idea was not a good one; nothing further came of it.

While Mackenzie King deplored attempts to bring collective pressure to bear upon the Administration, and resisted attempts at public persuasion, he was not at all reluctant to exploit his own special relationship with the President for the good of the Allied cause.

On 23 and 24 April 1940, Mackenzie King visited Franklin Roosevelt at Warm Springs, Georgia. It was the first meeting of the two leaders since their pre-war encounter at Kingston, Ont., in August 1938. Among Mackenzie King's objectives for this meeting was the securing of further modifications in the practice of American neutrality. He approached this delicate assignment by characteristically quoting Scripture to the President late in the evening—three verses from the Gospel according to St. Matthew:

v. 15: If thy brother shall trespass against thee, go and tell him his fault between thee and him alone: if he hear thee, thou has gained thy brother.

v. 16: But if he will not hear thee, then take with thee one or two more, that in the mouth of two or three witnesses every word may be established.

v. 17: And if he shall neglect to hear them, tell it unto the Church: but if he neglect to hear the Church, let him be unto thee as an heathen man and a publican.

This passage Mackenzie King represented, not uningeniously, "as a Biblical endorsement or sanction of the idea of moral embargo." The President, he thought, "was impressed with the significance of the sequence." Perhaps he was. At any rate, Mackenzie King concluded optimistically, "he has the moral embargo idea very strongly in mind and I believe that is the method by which America can render its greatest assistance to the Allies. . . ." He determined to press the idea upon Cordell Hull when he met him in Washington a few days later.[31]

Mackenzie King called on the Secretary of State on 28 April. He found him "so strongly sympathetic to the Allies and so anxious to do what could be done by the United States that I ventured to recall to his mind his visit to Toronto and what I had said about something in the nature of moral embargo policy."[32] The following day they met again, and Mackenzie King made his proposal more specific; "an amendment to the Neutrality Act regarding its provisions not applying to a country which had been unwarrantedly invaded." To this suggestion the Secretary was non-committal. That afternoon the news of Mussolini's evident intention to enter the war on the side of the Nazis gave to Mackenzie King's notion of a moral embargo more practical significance than it had had a few hours earlier. He seized the opportunity of a brief discussion with the President (who had returned to Washington from Georgia) to suggest that the United States

tell the world that if Italy went to war there would be a moral embargo placed at once on her, that she would get nothing whatever from the U.S.; that the blockade would be launched against her. . . . The President then said that she would know that already. . . . I said it was more important to have it known and declared before any overt act—that this could be made a policy which would apply against any country and not against Italy alone—any country which was an aggressor against neutral countries or countries with which we were not at war. . . .[33]

Mackenzie King returned to Canada well satisfied that these ideas had fallen upon a receptive audience, and that they would, in time, have beneficial results. He was particularly pleased at having suggested that the Neutrality Act should be amended to exempt from its provisions any victim of aggression; that was something, he reflected, that no one else had previously thought of. "I was able to make the suggestion to the President himself, to Mr. Hull, and also to Mr. Norman Davis. . . . It has appealed to all of them. . . . Equally, the proposal regarding the moral embargo as a general policy for the U.S. to follow as a means of helping countries which have been invaded. . . . To have gotten these idea across to headquarters, along with many other suggestions . . . has been worth the present visit a thousand times."[34]

On his return to Ottawa, Mackenzie King took the first opportunity to send to the President a letter setting out in full what he thought the United States could do to "best serve the Allied interests in the light of U.S. present political circumstances which necessitate an isolation point of view." "I feel," he wrote, "the President will not misunderstand this word and will be glad to have it." The "word" ran, in fact, to several hundred words; they included the following:

Having the United States as a neutral nation (1) become the champion of the rights of neutrals, (2) preserve its own neutrality by every means in its power, was, I believe, the policy underlying the Neutrality Act; as the Act has worked in practice this purpose threatens to be defeated by circumstances and conditions unforeseen at the time the Act was passed.

Instead of assisting neutral nations and the United States to preserve not only neutrality; but (in cases of small neutral nations) their existence, it has become an instrument to assist or encourage aggressors in the invasion of neutral countries.

E.g., Norway which prior to aggression could count upon receiving credits, munitions, etc. from the U.S.—no longer possible after a state of war declared.

Everyone must recognize the difficulty, if not impossibility, of the Neutrality Act being *repealed* in the brief time that remains before the Presidential campaign is concluded. But might it not be amended in a manner which would serve to preserve its original purposes, and to remove the injustices which it is or may be inflicting upon neutral nations, by some simple amendment, such as the following:

"The provisions of this Act shall not apply to neutral countries, which have become the victims of ruthless aggression on the part of other countries, or which are seeking to preserve their existence in the face of such aggressions." The party (political or individual) that opposed such an amendment would immediately become an ally of the aggressor nations, and would be recognized as such.

If with this the "moral embargo" policy were given complete and effective application against aggressor nations, the policy of the United States would then be—in its own eyes and in the eyes of the world: (1) to give all possible help to victims of aggression and to those countries that are fighting aggression (Amendment to Neutrality Act); (2) to withhold, in so far as may be possible whatever may be, or become, in the nature of aid to aggressors (Moral Embargo).

Such a policy could be defended on a basis of isolation, neutrality—at the same time it would be a real help to neutral countries seeking to preserve their neutrality, and to countries that are resisting or fighting aggression. It would serve to postpone, if not wholly to forestall the day when the United States itself might become involved in war—something that would appear to be inevitable if aggressor nations are to feel free to further the sweep of their invasion over the surface of the globe.

This policy might justify the United States as a neutral nation seeking to preserve its position of isolation, as well as neutrality, from going the length of taking any or every known practical means of giving effect to (1) and (2) by (3), protecting with its own fleet, in any part of the world, the aid it was seeking to give or to withhold. This may prove in the end the one effective means of avoiding expeditionary forces to the scene of conflict—a scene which all too speedily may become *any* quarter of the globe.

These are just thoughts and reflections based on observations made in the course of my recent visit to the United States, and in the light of the difficulties with which any administration may be faced in the year of a presidential election campaign. I should think all political parties might be willing to agree on (1) and (2) and possibly (3)—and so remove from political controversy altogether these aspects of America's "intervention" or "non-intervention", whichever they may be called.[35]

There is, unfortunately, no record available of Roosevelt's reaction to these suggestions. It is possible, as Mackenzie King believed, that he was glad to receive them; it is certain he felt unable to translate them into policy, at least at this time. On 10 June, when Mussolini finally declared war—a dark day for the Allies, and a black day for Canada, for her Minister of National Defence was killed in an air crash—Mackenzie King seized hopefully upon Roosevelt's radio address that evening. He thought it "surely means that the Neutrality Act will be cancelled, so far as supplying quantities of munitions, etc., to the Allies. I wonder if it is not coming just too late."[36] In fact it was not yet coming. It was still cash on the barrel-head.

IV

While exerting discreet pressure upon the Roosevelt Administration to make American supply available to the Allies and the oppressed neutrals, the Canadian Government did not itself draw to any appreciable extent upon the United States arsenal much before Hitler's onslaught in the West in the spring of 1940. It sought only the continua-

tion of normal imports, such as petroleum, and one or two special items
of military equipment, such as yachts suitable for naval patrol. It was
trying to create a manufacturing potential in the Dominion, both for its
own armed forces and for Britain's, and was therefore loath to buy in
the United States anything that might be made at home. Matériel which
it did not intend to produce in Canada—such as aircraft engines—was
bought in the main from the United Kingdom, partly out of a feeling
that the mother country was entitled to any business that was going,
partly to help improve the United Kingdom's dollar position (and so
enable it to pay for purchases from Canada), partly in deference to the
doctrine, not yet abandoned, of the standardization of equipment of
imperial forces.

During his visit to the United States in April 1940, Mackenzie King
was offered various unspectacular but nevertheless important items of
equipment by President Roosevelt, who was concerned, as he well
might have been, at the extent to which the Canadian East Coast lay
exposed to the depredations of Nazi U-boats. He offered to supply the
Canadians, at nominal cost, with binoculars, radio parts, submarine
nets, sea mines, and the like. All were urgently needed, and all grate-
fully accepted.[37]

On 10 May 1940 the Wehrmacht struck at the Low Countries. The
"hesitation, confusion and false optimism"[38] associated with the first few
months of the war were now dispelled. Henceforward there would be
no reluctance to make use of the American arsenal. What had been
previously treated as a marginal source of supply became essential to
survival.

The first impact of these new circumstances upon the supply situation
in Canada was felt in the most crucial sector of the Dominion's war
effort, the British Commonwealth Air Training Plan. The invasion in
the West, and the threatening invasion of the United Kingdom itself,
caused the British Government to hold up the delivery of Avro Anson
and Fairey Battle aircraft with which it had undertaken to supply the
Royal Canadian Air Force as part of the British contribution to the
plan. The message imparting this information suggested that the
Canadian Government attempt to make up the deficiency by securing
the necessary aircraft from the United States.

The Government had no other choice. Mackenzie King accordingly
sent a special emissary, Hugh Keenleyside of the Department of External
Affairs, to plead with the President in Washington. He met with the
President on 19 May. (Two days earlier, Roosevelt had been confronted

with an urgent request for aircraft by the United Kingdom—200 Curtis P.40 fighters—which he had felt obliged to refuse, although he did make available other types of aircraft also in short supply.) The President listened "carefully and sympathetically" to Keenleyside's presentation of the Canadian case, but stated that the Harvard trainers sought by Canada were urgently needed in the United States and could not be released at that time. He also "hinted that political considerations would make compliance with the Canadian request impracticable." He promised, however, that as soon as the United States aircraft production programme reached the annual output of 50,000 Canada or any of the Allies could "obtain 'plane for plane' with the United States." Meanwhile, he suggested, Canadian needs might be partly met by having recourse to purchasing among the 11,000 or so privately owned aircraft in the United States. It turned out, on investigation, that none of the aircraft available were suited to Canadian requirements.[39]

The reluctance of the Administration to make available to Canada the aircraft needed for the continuation of the British Commonwealth Air Training Plan prompted the consideration of another proposal, that the United States be asked to accept Commonwealth pilots for training with its own military personnel. This idea occurred first to the United Kingdom Government, which, on 25 May, asked the Canadian Government to join it in a request to Washington. Although the Canadians felt that the proposal would put "a pretty big strain" on American neutrality, they none the less instructed their Minister to join with the British Ambassador in Washington, Lord Lothian, in placing the proposal before the Administration. The State Department pondered the plan for a week, and then rejected it, partly because of the strain it would put upon American training facilities, partly because it was felt it would contravene one of the Hague Conventions on the duties of neutrals.[40]

With this avenue also closed, the Canadian Government, together with the British and the French, renewed its assault upon American supply. Churchill cabled Mackenzie King on 5 June that the President had not yet made "any worthy contribution in destroyers or planes," and that the British Government would consider "invaluable" any "pressure" which the Canadian Prime Minister might "apply in this direction."[41] A legal opinion furnished by the United States Attorney-General, to the effect that it was consistent with the Neutrality Act for the Administration to sell military equipment to private concerns, and for these in turn to sell the equipment to belligerent governments, was announced by the President on 7 June. Encouraged by this turn of events, which enabled guns and munitions to a value of $380 millions to be sold to the United Kingdom and France, Mackenzie King instructed the Legation in Washington to make a further appeal to the Administration for aircraft. The line taken was that the Canadians, in their endeavour to help the United Kingdom, had denuded the East Coast of adequate defences. Flying boats and fighters were urgently needed to ward off the threat of U-boat attack. If these could not be furnished out of current United States supplies, it was hoped they could be provided from stocks ordered by a French Government no longer in a position to take delivery. But the British Government had already spoken for the French contracts, and there were not enough aircraft left over to go round.[42]

The Canadians met with more success in securing small arms and ammunition. On 29 June, C. D. Howe, in his capacity as holder of the newly created cabinet portfolio of Munitions and Supply, wrote to O. D. Skelton to say that negotiations had for some time been in progress between the Administration and the British Purchasing Mission in Washington for the sale of arms and ammunition, but that these had not been going well; there was a feeling in the United States (so Howe had reported the day before to Mackenzie King) "that it was almost wasting material to send much to the United Kingdom; that the feeling had greatly increased in the United States since France had dropped out."[43] Now that the Canadian Army had taken on the defence of Britain, it mattered little whether the munitions were sold to London or to Ottawa; and Howe urged Skelton to bring "the entire resources of the Department of External Affairs" to bear upon the Administration to persuade it to sell to one government or the other. In the event it sold to both. The Canadians purchased 80,000 Lee Enfield rifles, and some 4,000,000 rounds of ammunition, at a cost of about $1,850,000; further matériel, including some 250 American tanks of First World War vintage, was released to Canada in October 1940.*

v

On 15 May 1940, in his first message to President Roosevelt as Prime Minister, Winston Churchill put at the head of a list of requests a plea for "the loan of forty or fifty of your older destroyers." It could not

---

*A striking photograph of the first shipment of 56 tanks on flatcars arriving at Camp Borden on 9 October appears in the Canadian Army's official history, *Six Years of War*, facing p. 83.

have come as a complete surprise: since April, when he had discussed the matter with Mackenzie King, Roosevelt had been turning over in his mind the possibility of making various kinds of warships, possibly even cruisers, available to the United Kingdom. But it was one thing for the idea to occur to the President, another for it to become policy.

To Churchill's imploring message, the President returned, the following day, a dusty answer. Destroyers were in any event scarce and urgently needed by the American Navy. They could not be supplied to the British without the express consent of the Congress; and, said Roosevelt, "I am not certain that it would be wise for that suggestion to be made to the Congress at this moment."[44] After Dunkirk, the British position became still more desperate; and on 15 June Churchill renewed his plea, as he did again on 17 June. The President made no reply to these entreaties, nor, at first, to an appeal from King George VI on 26 June. In mid-July he suggested to his Secretary of the Navy that at some later date Congressional authority might be sought for transfer of the destroyers "to Canada on condition that they be used solely in American hemisphere defense."[45] This represented a more constructive attitude, but it would not meet, still less save, the situation: Churchill needed the destroyers not for hemisphere defence but to protect the British Isles from invasion. On the last day of July 1940 he addressed to Roosevelt a final desperate appeal: "Mr. President, with great respect I must tell you that in the long history of the world this is a thing to do *now*."[46]

This message got home. The next fortnight saw an intensive exchange of messages between London and Washington on the method by which destroyers might be made available to the Royal Navy; it saw as well a debate of unprecedented intensity among the American people. On 7 August the Canadian Minister at Washington reported to Ottawa that within the Administration and within Congress a transfer of destroyers was under active study, and that the British Ambassador, Lord Lothian, had twice suggested to him that in these circumstances a Canadian intervention could be helpful. The Minister's own opinion, however, was that it would not be helpful; and Mackenzie King agreed. "I would not think of so doing," he minuted on Loring Christie's memorandum on 8 August. "It would help to *undo* for the future any influence I may have. Such a step would be in the nature of 'coercion'—no wonder some diplomacies fail."[47] But three days later, Christie reported from Washington that he had learned on good authority that the President himself had been somewhat puzzled and disappointed not to hear from Mackenzie King about the destroyers; under these circumstances, he thought, Roosevelt would attach great weight to a private representation from the Prime Minister of Canada indicating the urgent need of the moment for the transfer of destroyers, and the readiness of the Canadian Government to assist in any way possible in the method of their transfer. Mackenzie King then authorized Loring Christie to make such a representation to the President on his behalf. "Make it clear," he enjoined his envoy, "that I understand fully the President must be his own judge of what can be done and of the time when action can be taken, bearing in mind the effects of any decisions on the general problem of United States co-operation against the European danger. Subject to this qualification, I would like to say that in our opinion aid of this kind would be of the highest value and that Canada would be ready to facilitate the action decided upon in any feasible way."[48]

Christie saw the President on the afternoon of 15 August. Roosevelt informed him that he had already told Churchill that it was now found possible to furnish "as immediate assistance" at least fifty destroyers, motor torpedo-boats, and aircraft; in return, the United States desired an assurance that the British Fleet would not be turned over to the Germans in the event of a United Kingdom defeat, and a lease for purposes of hemisphere defence of bases in Newfoundland, Bermuda, British Guiana, and a number of British possessions in the Caribbean. The President read to Christie Churchill's reply which, so far as the bases proposal was concerned, was accommodating. "The President," Christie reported after the interview, "struck me as having made up his mind to proceed with this business. Some observers here think he has lately been showing impatience with those who have been urging upon him internal political considerations in connection with this destroyer problem and with other aspects of defence of the United States. They estimate him as a man who is convinced that the scene is going to be profoundly changed between now and election day and that neither he nor his opponent can successfully guess the real outcome, and who is therefore going to steer his course upon the best judgment he can make as to the real need of the defence of the United States."[49]

This assessment was quickly and dramatically confirmed. On 16 August, the day after Christie's interview, the President called the Prime Minister on the telephone.

The President said: 'Hello, is that you, Mackenzie?' . . . I replied, Yes. He then said: 'I am going tomorrow night in my train to Ogdensburg. If you are free, I would like to have you come and have dinner with me there. I would like to talk with you about the matter of the destroyers. . . . I have told the press that we will be meeting together. Are you free tomorrow night?' I said: "Yes". . . .[50]

The next day Mackenzie King set off by motor car for Ogdensburg, in the company of the United States Minister to Ottawa.* He took with him a National Defence department memorandum on Canadian military equipment needs, and a hastily prepared list of "brief summaries of certain matters which the Prime Minister may wish to cover in his conversations with President Roosevelt." At the head of it was the destroyer problem.

The Prime Minister found the President in an expansive mood. He had come to Ogdensburg determined to meet the requirements of the Allies to the best of his abilities. He told Mackenzie King that the first of fifty destroyers for Britain could set out within a week; they could be taken to Eastern Canadian ports by American crews, the British to take them across the Atlantic. Motor torpedo boats, flying boats, and rifles would also be made available. Mackenzie King reported the glad tidings to Churchill on 18 August.

Before taking leave of the President, Mackenzie King handed to him the list of military equipment needed by the Canadian forces which the Minister of National Defence had prepared for the occasion. "I . . . said to the President," Mackenzie King recorded, "I disliked taking advantage of all he had done and was doing to proffer a further request, but . . . I had promised our own boys that I would, if possible, bring to his attention something further in the way of military equipment and supplies that we, in Canada, were most anxious to have." Roosevelt, and the Secretary of War, Henry Stimson (who was also present), said that they would do what they could but that, as the items needed in Canada were also in acutely short supply among the United States forces, the Canadians had better not count on getting too much too soon.[51]

One or two obstacles had to be cleared before the destroyers-for-bases deal could be brought to a successful consummation. Of these by far the most difficult potentially was the British Prime Minister's initial refusal to regard it as a deal. "I see difficulties, and even risks," Churchill cabled to the President on 22 August, "in . . . admitting in any way that the munitions which you send us are a payment for the [base] facilities. Once this idea is accepted, people will contrast on each side what is given and what is received. The money value of the armaments would be computed and set against the facilities, and some would think one thing about it and some another." He thought it better

*Jay Pierrepont Moffat. It had been at Moffat's urging that the President had decided to invite Mackenzie King to Ogdensburg. See William Langer and S. Everett Gleason, *The Challenge to Isolation* (New York, 1952), p. 704.

that the President extend the destroyers and the rest as "a grand gesture of generosity" and, with respect to the bases, that the British should do the same. Whatever happened, there should be no trading of horses at such a juncture of human history.[52] There was something to this way of looking at it, and eventually a satisfactory formula was devised. The bases were divided into two different categories, one of which was to be regarded as a gift, the other as a *quid pro quo*. The appropriate documents were redrafted along these lines, signed on 2 September, and within a few hours the destroyers were steaming for Halifax.

What might happen to the American crews on arrival in Canada constituted a further, if minor, difficulty. The United States Secretary of the Navy was concerned lest their presence in Halifax be construed as a violation of American neutrality. He mentioned the problem to Admiral W. H. Standley, a former Chief of Naval Staff, when waiting (as the latter recalled the episode) "on the fourth tee at the Burning Tree Golf Club." "That's easy," the Admiral responded. "Send 'em up in pairs [i.e., the destroyers], one to be turned over, the other to come home with both crews on board."[53] This was the procedure employed.

The remaining problem concerned the Canadian Government's responsibilities for manning the destroyers, and the disposition of the ships between the Royal Navy and the Royal Canadian Navy. The British authorities wanted the Canadians to take over as many of the destroyers as possible, while at the same time agreeing to deploy them in United Kingdom waters. A signal was sent from Ottawa to the First Sea Lord stating that the theatre in which the destroyers in question were to be deployed would depend upon whether they were to be regarded as part of the Royal Navy or as part of the Royal Canadian Navy; if the latter, there would be no objection to maintaining four of six ships whose acquisition was under consideration in European waters, thus bringing the total number of Canadian destroyers in that theatre to eight (four others—substantially the whole destroyer fleet—having been sent there in May 1940). The Admiralty agreed that the ships could enter Canadian service, and the Canadian Government agreed to take over seven. All were sent to the Eastern Atlantic in late September. Some months afterwards, the Canadian Government thought it well to inquire of the British what method of payment ought to be made by it for its share of the American destroyer fleet. "The transfer of these seven vessels to Canada," the First Sea Lord replied, "should not be regarded as a commercial transaction, but as an arrangement between the Governments of the United Kingdom and Canada for the disposal of the vessels in the manner best fitted to help the common cause."[54] Not all of the Anglo-Canadian wartime arrangements had as happy an ending.

"ALL THESE TRANSACTIONS WILL BE JUDGED..."

For more than two critical years—between January 1938 and July 1940 —there was no exchange of military information or sharing of defence planning between the military staffs of Canada and the United States. The effort begun before the outbreak of the European war to achieve what the United States Minister in Ottawa euphemistically described as "somewhat closer contact between the U.S. War Department and the Dept. of National Defence" was almost immediately allowed to subside.

In January 1938, it had been the Americans who were anxious, in the face of Canadian apprehension, to initiate staff talks between the two countries. In June 1940, the Canadians were anxious, and the Americans apprehensive.

On 14 June, the Prime Minister of Canada sent word to the American Minister at Washington that he wished urgently to see him. "I told him," Mackenzie King wrote afterwards, "I thought the time had come when Chiefs of Staff, or others, should meet similar officers of the United States defence forces and have a distinct understanding as to what was to be done in the event of attack coming across the ocean."[55] Pierrepont Moffat's account of their meeting relates that the Prime Minister realized that "perhaps such a suggestion might embarrass the President," and that "this was the last thing he wanted. On the other hand as no interests were involved, the President might welcome the suggestion. In the circumstances he asked me to feel out the situation and let him know."[56] But so grave was the situation overseas that Mackenzie King, most uncharacteristically, did not wait for the results of this preliminary and informal inquiry. Instead, he instructed the chargé d'affaires at Washington to suggest that a staff conference be held immediately "with respect to the naval, military and air defense of North America, having particular regard to the defense of the Atlantic Coast."[57]

For the Americans, this was moving too fast. The Canadian request for staff talks came before the Administration on 17 June. Ten days elapsed before a reply was received; and the reply was only to state that it was not yet possible to give a definite reply. But this was the reaction of an exceedingly cautious Secretary of State. The President's was more constructive. He suggested to his Minister at Ottawa that he might usefully consult with the Canadian authorities in order to ascertain, in more detail, exactly what they had in mind.[58]

On 29 June, Pierrepont Moffat, at Mackenzie King's invitation, met with the Minister of National Defence and the Minister of National Defence for Air. "Both Mr. Ralston and Mr. Power," he recorded afterwards,

thought the time had come for high officers of the two armies to exchange impressions with a view to helping the other to complete its appreciation of the situation. It was understood that no commitment would be asked for or given. I pointed out that the words "staff talk" had an unfortunate connotation and should be avoided if possible. The American public remembered only too well that the staff talks between the British and French in 1907 were recalled by the French in 1914 as constituting a moral commitment on the part of Britain to action. Obviously neither one of us had anything of this sort in mind so although the term "staff talk" might be roughly used, what we really meant was "informal discussions on our respective problems of defence."[59]

Having secured from the Canadian Ministers a very full and frank account of the immediate defence requirements of the Dominion, Moffat went straight to Washington and engaged there in an intensive round of consultations with senior military and civilian personnel on 2 July and 3 July, painting what the official U.S. Army history describes as "a very dismal picture of the Canadian defense situation." One of those consulted by Moffat was the Chief of Staff. General Marshall was ready to welcome staff officers from Canada but "feared that if they learned the true state of the U.S. supply situation the effect might be more discouraging than helpful. . . . Apart from the obstacles in the way of furnishing material aid to Canada, Marshall, and to a lesser degree [Admiral Harold R.] Stark [U.S. Chief of Naval Operations], did not see how a meeting with Canadian staff officials could be held to discuss matters of substance, since the basic policy decisions had yet to be taken by the United States with regard to the problems that would have to be examined at such a meeting." Notwithstanding these reservations, President Roosevelt, after conferring with the officials concerned, decided that secret and informal staff talks should be held, and Moffat was told to inform Mackenzie King accordingly.[60]

Moffat saw the Prime Minister in Ottawa on 5 July. "I explained," he wrote afterwards, "that . . . the question . . . of sending high-ranking Canadian officers to Washington for informal discussions had been laid before the President. I was glad to say that he had authorized such informal talks on matters of our respective interests in the field of defence. Obviously no commitment would be asked or given. It might also be that the Canadians would feel that there were certain matters into which we could not go too deeply but I did not think that the Canadians would feel that this would rob the talks of their value. I also explained that we felt the Canadian officers should come secretly. . . . The Prime Minister was delighted. . . ."[61]

II

The Canadian-United States staff talks of July 1940 were far franker and more comprehensive than the hesitant exchanges of January 1938. The Canadian officers taking part were Brigadier Kenneth Stuart (Deputy Chief of the General Staff), Captain L. W. Murray (Deputy Chief of the Naval Staff), and Air Commodore A. A. L. Cuffe (Royal Canadian Air Force). The United States participants included General Marshall, Admiral Stark, Brigadier General G. V. Strong (Assistant Chief of Staff, War Plans Division), and other officers of the War and Navy Departments. The Canadians arrived in Washington on 11 July and, following a dinner at the residence of Admiral Stark ("an excellent dinner," one of the Canadians described it afterwards, "which succeeded admirably in breaking down restraint"), a general and preliminary discussion took place on the two principal questions of the hour: "First, the extent to which the U.S. might be able to assist us in the present phase of the war in the field of matériel supplies and, secondly, the possibilities of common action in the event of an unsuccessful conclusion to the present battle for England." Brigadier Stuart's notes of this conversation follow:

We attempted to impress upon our listeners that we were far from pessimistic about the outcome of the present phase of the war. We pointed out that our visit was in no sense dictated by panic but, on our part, was intended to explore the possibilities of common action in the similar problems of defence that confronted both countries. We stressed the vital importance to both of our countries of the present battle for England. If Great Britain was successful it would mean not only her own survival but a postponement of the possibility of extending the war, other than small raids to our respective eastern shores. We expressed the hope, therefore, that any material assistance which might be offered to us in the present phase of the war would not be taken from stocks ear-marked for Great Britain.

Each member of the Canadian group then explained the basic features of our plan of defence in respect to his own branch of the Service and either replied to or made a note of questions asked. . . .

This approach was received in the spirit we had hoped for and all subsequent discussion was carried out with the utmost frankness.

It became obvious as soon as discussion began that both Admiral Stark and General Marshall were primarily interested in the facilities available in Eastern Canada and Newfoundland for the use of U.S. sea, land and air forces in that area and that neither of these officers, nor those with them, felt that the U.S. could assist us in the present phase of the war with material from service stocks. This latter attitude changed the next morning, particularly in the case of the army.

It was obvious, also, that both of the two senior officers referred to, who incidentally are the senior ranking officers in the U.S. Navy and U.S. Army respectively, were greatly concerned about the need for the maintenance of the strictest secrecy regarding our conversations. Both indicated that any leak at the present time would be disastrous and would have the effect of curbing any further preparatory co-operative efforts. General Marshall, in particular, felt that a leak at the present time, because of its political consequences, might even force the Administration to cut some of his existing and contemplated appropriations. . . .[62]

The following day (12 July) more specialized discussion took place, each of the three Canadian officers having interviews with his United States counterpart. Brigadier Stuart's talks were with General Strong, from whom he was able to secure a list of munitions and supply which the U.S. Army was ready to relinquish to the Canadian armed forces, always assuming that the Administration approved. General Strong evinced great interest in the Canadian defence plans. He wanted to know what were the vital strategic areas for which defence preparations ought immediately to be made; what part Newfoundland played in the Canadian defence schemes; what were the time, scale, probable character, objective, and direction of each attack on Canadian territory considered likely by the defence authorities; what the Canadian High Command regarded as the minimum requirements of ground and air forces necessary to protect each strategic area; what portion of these requirements the Canadian Government was prepared immediately to furnish; what was required of United States forces in the defence of strategic areas in Canada. He asked whether the Canadians were prepared to set up, in the event of attack, sectors within the Dominion in which command of operations could be vested in United States officers; and was told that they were. All these questions were answered by the Canadian officer as fully and as frankly as possible.[63]

Captain Murray explored various aspects of naval defence planning with the Director of Plans in the U.S. Bureau of Naval Operations. He explained to the Americans the existing defences of Halifax and Sydney, and the proposed defences of Gaspé and Shelburne, N.S., and outlined the existing system of anti-submarine patrols and minesweeping operations; these disclosures, Captain Murray's report noted, came "as a revelation" to the American officers. He imparted to them highly secret information (the permission of the Admiralty having been previously secured) concerning techniques for outfitting auxiliary vessels as mine-sweepers and for coping with magnetic mines. Some discussion took place on facilities which the United States might make available to Royal Navy ships should these find it necessary to take shelter on the Western side of the Atlantic: the American officers felt that the State Department would not allow repairs to belligerent ships in United States ports so long as the United States remained neutral, and would do everything possible to keep their policy similar to that of Uruguay in the case of the *Graf Spee*, which had allowed the Germans to make only the repairs necessary to get the vessel out to sea.[64]

A third conversation occurred between Air Commodore Cuffe and an officer of the U.S. Naval Air Arm. The latter displayed a lively interest in possible base facilities for American aircraft in the Maritimes, Newfoundland, Labrador, and Greenland, but beyond this did not appear (so the Canadian officer concluded) much concerned with the defence of North America. The supply question was raised with little useful response: "The U.S. Navy did not feel justified in parting with any of their air equipment in service" for use by the R.C.A.F.[65]

III

The initiative in arranging for the Canada–United States military staff talks in July 1940 had come from the Prime Minister of Canada. The initiative in creating the Canada–United States Permanent Joint Board on Defence came from the President of the United States.

Mackenzie King had no idea, as he was driven in his automobile from Ottawa to Ogdensburg on 17 August, that during their meeting that evening Franklin Roosevelt would propose that the two countries should immediately bring into being permanent machinery for planning the defences of North America. He had been made aware of support for some such proposal among influential Canadians. About a month before the Ogdensburg meeting, a group of twenty Canadians prominent in government, business, and academic life had drafted "A Program of Immediate Canadian Action," of which the central feature had been a recommendation for more far-reaching defence planning and co-operation between Canada and the United States,[66] and a number of news-papers had begun to urge editorially some similar course of action.*

*See, for example, the *Montreal Standard*, 3 Aug. 1940: "A treaty [for North American defence] would give form to fundamental understandings that already exist. It would be something that could be read and grasped on both sides of the

But Mackenzie King, sensitive as he was to movements of opinion within his own country, was even more sensitive to the need to avoid doing anything which might prejudice Roosevelt's presidential campaign. He could not have imagined anything more likely to give aid and comfort to Roosevelt's enemies than a Canadian proposal that the United States, a neutral country, should join with it, a belligerent, in a kind of unwritten military alliance. In that he may have been right. It was certainly preferable to allow the suggestion to come from Roosevelt himself. Mackenzie King never expected it would. And in that he was clearly mistaken. "Mr. King," Pierrepont Moffat wrote at the end of 1940,

never dared allow himself to hope for a public recognition that the defence of the two countries constituted a single problem, and the creation of a Joint Defence Board that would be reciprocal and that would be permanent. The famous meeting with the President at Ogdensburg, which was arranged by the President as a daring improvisation, and the understandings reached and announced there, constituted a fitting fruition for twenty years spent in preparing the ground. Yet no one was more surprised than Mr. King that his dream had suddenly come true. Six weeks before he had been cautiously suggesting staff talks, and Washington with equal caution wanted to know before answering just what Canada wished to discuss. But in those six weeks the world outlook had fundamentally changed, and the President changed with it. To his impulsive nature, Mr. King has always seemed overcautious, and apt to let opportunities slip by through unwillingness to take a risk. It is fair to say, however, that the present association of politics between the two countries could hardly have been achieved without the contribution of both authors, the one who with tireless zeal prepared the material, the other who conceived the brilliant climax.[67]

The immediate origins of the Permanent Board are to be traced to a despatch sent by Pierrepont Moffat to the State Department on 16 August. In the message, Moffat outlined the growing demand in the Dominion for some sort of joint defence agreement with the United States, and noted that pressure was being brought to bear on the Prime Minister even by those formerly hostile to closer Canadian–American relations.[68] This message came before President Roosevelt that day, and seems to have caused him to decide that the time had come for creating appropriate machinery for joint defence planning. He said as much at a press conference at Ogdensburg the next morning, while waiting for the Prime Minister to arrive.[69]

Mackenzie King boarded the President's train shortly before 7 p.m. on the evening of 17 August. Henry L. Stimson, the U.S. Secretary of

---

border. It would provide the basis for arrangements for defence against common danger—arrangements of the kind that are so much better when worked out long before any possible need and not in the heat of an emergency."

War, was the only other person present during dinner and the subsequent conversation. According to Stimson's diary, the President at once broached the project of creating a joint defence board, composed of representatives of Canada and the United States, which would be able to discuss and develop plans for the defence of the northern half of the Western hemisphere. Mackenzie King agreed at once to this being done. He seemed, Stimson wrote, "perfectly delighted" at the President's initiative, and when he spoke to Roosevelt of the aid and comfort the measure would be bound to produce among the embattled peoples of the democracies it was "almost with tears in his eyes."[70]

The three men resumed their discussions next morning. Roosevelt drafted a statement to be given to the press concerning the proposed board, and read the finished version to Stimson and Mackenzie King. "It was clearly and concisely worded," Mackenzie King wrote afterwards.

Spoke of a Joint Commission. When he had finished the reading of the draft, I asked him whether he thought the word "Commission" was as good as "Board" or "Committee". Said the word "Board" had been used the night before in conversation. Mr. Stimson agreed that Board would perhaps be better and the President also did. I pointed out that Commission suggested the necessity of formal appointments by Governments. I then questioned him as to the significance of the word "Permanent". He said at once that he attached much importance to it. I said I was not questioning the wisdom of it but was anxious to get what he had in mind.

The President explained he thought the Board should be designed not "to meet alone this particular situation but to help secure the continent for the future." The Prime Minister agreed.[71] A statement incorporating these views was given to the press, for release at 9 p.m.* Mackenzie King was anxious, as always, to make the date of the historic occasion coincide with an event of importance in his own life. "The Ogdensburg *agreement*," he wrote to the President some days later, "as distinguished from the declaration, should, it seems to me, carry the date of August 17. It was reached on the 17th. What took place on the 18th was merely the statement of its terms. I am sure you will agree. Like you, I have associations with the 17th. My birthday came that date December 1874."[72]

*"The Prime Minister and the President have discussed the mutual problems of defense in relation to the safety of Canada and the United States.

"It has been agreed that a Permanent Joint Board on Defense shall be set up at once by the two countries.

"This Permanent Joint Board on Defense shall commence immediate studies relating to sea, land and air problems including personnel and matériel."

IV

"It is not a treaty," Pierrepont Moffat explained to the members of the Canadian Club of Ottawa on 25 September, "it involves no commitments. It is a mere mechanism to study common problems of North American defence." Though there was some feeling that the Ogdensburg Agreement might well have been less, there was little feeling that it should have been more. In the United States, the New York *Herald Tribune* stood almost alone among newspapers in its complaint that the Agreement did not go far enough. "This is not," it observed of it on 19 August, "the full treaty of mutual defense, formally ratified by the constitutional agencies of both countries, for which the situation already urgently calls. . . . The President is still moving tentatively." From the other wing was heard the argument that the Agreement was in fact a treaty and as such should be submitted for ratification to Congress.[73] It is a measure of the widespread support which the Agreement received in the United States that isolationist criticism was centred on its form, rather than on its substance.

In Canada the Agreement was generally acclaimed. Mackenzie King's mail for once brought nothing but congratulations: one correspondent praised his "master stroke," another wrote of "this happy, almost miraculous event," a third of "a candle in the dark."[74] An examination conducted by the Prime Minister's office of fifty-four editorial articles in thirty-seven Canadian newspapers revealed no outright opposition whatsoever. The only note of reservation was the fear expressed lest, as one correspondent put it, "the political independence of our country . . . be impinged by the permanent garrisoning of American troops within our territory."[75] The verdict of a cartoon in a Toronto newspaper summed up the general reaction: "It's so sensible, it's sensational." Gratification was as widespread in the British press as in the Canadian.

Because of the virtually unanimous enthusiasm for the Agreement throughout the Allied world, the strangely discordant telegram which Mackenzie King received from Churchill on the subject wounded him deeply. Churchill's message, in answer to the telegram Mackenzie King had sent on 18 August, apprising him of the impending creation of the Permanent Board and of the munitions and supply the President was ready to turn over to the Allies, curtly took note of "the arrangements you are making for Canada and America's mutual defence," and went on to observe: "Here again there may be two opinions on some of the points mentioned. Supposing Mr. Hitler cannot invade us and his Air Force begins to blench under the strain all these transactions will be judged in a mood different to that prevailing while the issue still hangs in the balance."[76] Mackenzie King read the text of this message to the War Committee of the Cabinet on 27 August. Ralston, Crerar, and Lapointe, he noted, "were quite outspoken and indignant" and "rather felt an answer should be sent which would let Churchill see that his reply had not been appreciated. . . ." But Mackenzie King, characteristically, thought it better to wait to see the tenor of Churchill's next message before venturing any rebuke, implied or otherwise. It was well that he did. The next message arrived on 13 September. "I am very glad to have this opportunity," Churchill had cabled, "of thanking you personally for all you have done for the common cause and especially in promoting a harmony of sentiment throughout the New World. This deep understanding will be a dominant factor in the rescue of Europe from a relapse into the Dark Ages."[77] So it was to prove, not once but twice.

End of Vol. II

DOCUMENTS

DOCUMENT 1

Extract from Memorandum by the Joint Staff Committee,
Department of National Defence, 5 September 1936 (Army Records)

AN APPRECIATION OF THE DEFENCE PROBLEMS CONFRONTING
CANADA WITH RECOMMENDATIONS FOR THE DEVELOPMENT
OF THE ARMED FORCES

• • •

3. AN OUTLINE OF CANADA'S DEFENCE PROBLEMS

(a) *The Direct Defence of Canada*
The direct defence of the national territory is, in the last analysis, the
major responsibility of the armed forces of Canada. But hitherto, owing to
our fortunate geographical position, this problem has not been given a
high degree of priority. Canada's only neighbour is the United States and
there seems to be little likelihood of a disagreement with that country which
would lead to war. Indeed, it rather appears that Canada's external policy
is largely dictated by a firm determination to avoid such an eventuality.
Further, as the conciliation of American opinion has long been a cardinal
point of British policy, the risk of Canada becoming embroiled in a war
resulting from a conflict of British and United States interests has seemed
remote. Indeed, the rise of Japan to a dominant position in the Western
Pacific is inducing an increasing sympathy in the Far Eastern policies of
these two great Powers which is not without its significance to Canada.
Again, the distance factor, coupled with the imperial and international
complications which would be involved, has ruled out the possibility of
invasion from overseas though in this respect recent legislation in the United
States (Air Defense Bases Bill, 1935) indicates that the United States con-
siders herself exposed to air attacks originating in Europe and Eastern Asia,
and that they are taking defensive measures in consequence. As the Eastern
and Western portions of Canada lie on the Great Circle routes from Europe
and Eastern Asia to the United States, respectively, it is clear that Canada is
still more exposed to air operations from overseas and, consequently, the
question of air defence is becoming one of increasing importance to this
country. While, therefore, no plans or preparations have been made against
the contingency of war between Canada (or the British Empire) and the

United States, the continued supposition that Canada is and will remain free from attack by a trans-oceanic power is becoming open to criticism. Nor can the possibility of war between the British Empire and Japan be held to be unreasonable.

(b) *The Defence of Canadian Neutrality in the event of a United States–Japanese War*

Signs are not wanting of a growing conflict of interest between the United States and Japan in the North Pacific. The influence of the Big Navy party, which is said to include the President, the vast sums which have recently been set aside with the object of building up the United States Navy to treaty limits and the important naval manoeuvres held last year off Pearl Harbor and the Aleutian Islands, the several requests received by the Canadian Government to fly U.S. service aircraft over Canadian territory and territorial waters en route to Alaska, and the manifest interest in the construction of a highway through British Columbia connecting the State of Washington with Alaska, are distinct portents of the trend of events. Should war between these countries materialize, one of the following courses would be open to Canada:—

(i) To throw in her lot with the United States independently of the rest of the British Empire.

(ii) In the event of the United Kingdom and the other Dominions deciding to act jointly with the United States, to co-operate in such action.

(iii) In the event of the United Kingdom and the other Dominions deciding to adopt a position of neutrality, to remain neutral herself.

The first is held to be an unlikely contingency. The second and third, in the view of the Joint Staff Committee, are those which this country must now anticipate and for which preliminary defence measures should now be undertaken, thus enabling Canada to secure its position in some measure, either as a co-belligerent or, alternatively, as an effective neutral.

(c) *The Indirect Defence of Canada by Participation Overseas in a Major War*

The possibility of a major war is becoming more apparent. Indeed, the realization is growing in many minds that the cessation of hostilities in 1918 was but an armistice.

A noteworthy feature of Canadian post-war political history has been a growing disinclination to become embroiled in European quarrels. In this respect, Canadian opinion is in line with that of the United States and for the same reason—that of remoteness—though in this connection, owing to the fact that she is a member of the League of Nations and due also to her close association with the United Kingdom as one of the nations of the British Empire, Canada is more directly concerned. In spite of a sincere desire to hold herself aloof from participation in the war of 1914–1918, the United States was inevitably dragged in. It is suggested that in the event of another world war the same forces would again bear the same compelling influence, possibly with even greater intensity. It seems unlikely, therefore, that in such circumstances Canada can hope to remain at peace. It follows that the despatch overseas of Canadian Forces may again be necessary.

4. SUMMARY OF THE CANADIAN POSITION RESPECTING THE EMPLOYMENT OF
ARMED FORCES

From the above review of Canada's obligations, or prospective liabilities, concerning the mobilization and employment of its armed forces, the following conclusions emerge.

(a) Whereas there may be, and indeed are, divergences of opinion as to the constitutional position of Canada in a war in which a portion, or the balance, of the British Empire may be engaged, past history may be expected to repeat itself on a major threat to the integrity of the Empire arising. Although prior military commitments of an Imperial nature will not be entered into, Canadian public opinion might well call for participation overseas by Canadian armed forces, with those raised by other portions of the Empire, in the event of threatened or actual aggression by some foreign Power.

(b) The gradual weakening of the League of Nations, even as a moral force, further reduces any external military commitments which Canada might feel constrained to accept as a Signatory to the League Covenant.

(c) The deterioration in the political situation in the Far East, and the distinct possibilities of war breaking out in that area in the not distant future have brought Canada, as a Pacific Power, face to face with definite local responsibilities concerning defence. Whether as a participant in a Far Eastern War, in which the British Empire, generally, and/or the United States should be engaged, or as a neutral, the mobilization of Canadian forces on a considerable scale must be contemplated.

5. A REVIEW OF RECENT DEVELOPMENTS IN THE ORGANIZATION AND EQUIP-
MENT OF ARMED FORCES

(a) Defence and Industry

The responsibility for national defence can no longer be held to rest solely on the Department which bears that name for it is but to repeat a truism to state that modern war imposes maximum demands on every sphere of civil activity. More and more as time has gone on during the last generation or so, the community has had recourse to machinery in the conduct of its daily life. The growth of the manufacturing industry has been a feature of the present century. And it was but as natural as it was inevitable that the methods of waging war should have evolved along similar lines. As a result, the military effectiveness of the armed forces of the nation are governed today not so much by the numbers of its population, as by the capacity and power of its industry.

(b) Developments in Naval Armaments

Though the Washington Naval Treaty and subsequent naval treaties have prevented any considerable construction of major naval units, such as battleships, battle cruisers and aircraft carriers, modern technical developments have necessitated vast expenditure in modernisation of these types to meet the increasing power of attacks by aircraft and submarine.

In other classes of naval vessels rapid replacement by modern craft to meet requirements of speed, air and anti-submarine defence is taking place. At first this was controlled by the quantitative limitation agreed to in Naval Treaties; now, although a measure of qualitative limitation has been established, strength of navies is virtually only limited by finance and productive resources of the country.

Great Britain has pursued a policy of reduction in naval armaments since 1921 until recently—now she is embarking on a heavy programme of expansion, but for some time she will be short of requirements, particularly in cruisers and destroyers and the forces necessary for the protection of trade and distant imperial interests.

To the necessity for secure anti-submarine defences for naval bases and shipping centres must now be added adequate air defences both for harbours and in the focal areas for trade.

Every post-war measure of development in naval warfare has tended to increased cost, increased personnel and increased technical training, and rapid rearmament is therefore more difficult and throws a heavy burden on industrial resources.

(c) Modern Requirements in Land Forces

The lessons of the late war emphasized in an all too tragic manner the defensive or "stopping" power of the automatic weapons. There are two principal ways in which this superior power of the bullet can be neutralized, firstly, by reducing the time available for its effective use, in other words, by increasing the speed of the movement of the target, and secondly, by providing the soldier with armoured protection. The development of the armoured fighting vehicle, proof against all but special projectiles, and which by means of a powerful internal combustion engine and specially designed traction is capable of transporting its military crew at high and sustained speed over most natures of country has, in consequence, resulted.

The other outstanding development of the last twenty years has been the practical substitution of the motor for the horse in all forms of road transport and a similar and inevitable dependence by the land forces on the same means of transportation for the field supply of personnel, munitions and equipment.

The technical advances in the design and power of weapons, developed by the experience of the late war, are now showing results in the type and capabilities of the armaments with which armies are now being equipped. The ranges of modern artillery are increased in the nature of 50% over similar types of war, or immediate post-war, design. The automatic small-arm weapon is simpler in design, more rugged, more effective, yet lighter in weight.

It should be noted here that the Canadian Militia possesses neither armoured fighting vehicles, supplies of mechanized transport of approved design, nor modern weapons.

(d) Requirements of a Modern Air Force

Modern Air Forces are no longer merely an auxiliary to a Navy or Army. They have developed now to the point where, in addition to co-operating with other arms, they represent a considerable striking force on their own. The Great Powers each possess thousands of aircraft and all are expanding their air forces as rapidly as conditions permit. The rate of expansion at present taking place in some countries is only limited by the capacity of the aircraft industry. While it is not contended that Canadian requirements are comparable to those of the Great Powers, it is perhaps pertinent to mention here that Canada's air force is entirely inadequate to meet her modest defence requirements; and further, that this country does not possess an aircraft industry worthy of the name. Such factories as exist are almost solely confined to assembly and repair work. Aero engines are all imported.

A modern air force requires factories capable of manufacturing aircraft and aero engines in their entirety with adequate facilities for maintenance and stores to ensure that the necessary stocks are available in an emergency. Bases, aerodromes, seaplane sites must be provided in addition to training centres to meet the demand for pilots and mechanics. Finally an adequate supply of modern aircraft engines, bombs, torpedos and ammunition must be immediately available.

6. CANADA'S MILITARY LIABILITIES

(a) Direct Defence of Canada against Invasion

The contingency of a recourse to military action as a solution to political difficulties which might arise between the United States and Canada has been referred to above and has been dismissed on the basis of its improbability. From a purely technical point of view it is essential now, and in the discernible future, for reasons given below, that this equable relationship between the two countries should continue.

The rise in the naval power of the United States to a position of parity with the British Empire has not been disputed since 1922, and parity of fleets means the definite superiority in war of the United States in the waters adjacent to our coasts, with consequent interruption of vital communications between Canada, Great Britain and the balance of the Empire. The Anglo-Japanese Alliance, the continuation of which had been interpreted in the United States as a menace to Anglo-American relations and, in consequence, had become a threat to the political position of Canada, disappeared at the same time. As a result, the naval situation of Canada, even with full Imperial support, is too weak to merit further discussion. But, in addition to these fundamental changes in the naval position, we are now faced with a completely new and overwhelming factor in the advent of the air arm and its effect on the strategical situation of Canada in respect to a hostile United States. When it is considered that the military air forces of the latter country now possess some 2700 machines and, in addition, some three times that number of civil aircraft, these, so far as Canada is concerned, being capable of some degree of military service, and that Canadian centres of manpower and industry all lie within less than one hundred miles of U.S. territory, the situation needs no further comment.

On the other hand, the liability of direct attack on Canada by Japanese forces has become a matter requiring urgent consideration and action in view of the menacing situation which continues to develop in the Far East. The increasingly aggressive attitude of Japan towards all nations whose interests lie in the Western Pacific has resulted in a marked increase in the military preparations in that area of Great Britain, Australia and New Zealand. The noticeable expansion, in recent years, of the armed forces of the United States and the evident fear possessed by that country of possible war with Japan, are conditions which are well known. The prospect of war breaking out at some not distant date between some, or all, of the Anglo-Saxon communities which have important interests in the Pacific, and Japan, are apparent. Under such circumstances the Western Coast of Canada will be within the area of hostilities and is likely to be attacked not only by Japanese naval and air forces, but, in the case of important shore objectives, by Japanese landing parties operating in some strength.

(b) The Maintenance of Neutrality

There is another aspect of local defence, the maintenance of neutrality, for which it is considered that preparations should now be made.

In a war between the United States and Japan it is obvious that a decisive advantage to either would be to bring the British Empire to its active support. It is also apparent that, compared to any other portion of the British Empire, Canada by its geographical position and political and commercial relations with the United States would be peculiarly susceptible to charges of non-neutrality by either of the combatants, and liable to be manoeuvred into a situation where armed supervision of its frontiers would be the only alternative to active participation on one side or another.

A definitely complicating factor for Canada in a war between the United States and Japan is the American possession of Alaska. By utilizing Alaska and the Aleutians, the United States might hope to bring her superior naval and air power within striking distance of Japan and her immediate sea communications.

A glance at the map will reveal that the indented and sparsely settled coast of British Columbia provides an admirable area from which Japanese submarines, and even surface craft, can develop raids against U.S. sea communications and Pacific Coast ports. The fact that Canada and Canadian territorial waters intervene between the United States and Alaska is, in a military sense, a definite handicap. Under the circumstances visualized, with American national feeling running high and with a large army mobilized and impatient to intervene, it is to be expected that should Canada give the United States real reason to complain of Japanese infringement of Canadian neutrality owing to the lack of adequate armed supervision by Canada of its territorial waters, territory or the air supervening, American public opinion will demand that the requisite protective measures along the Canadian seaboard be secured by what would amount to the military occupation of British Columbia by U.S. forces.

It is the considered opinion of the Joint Staff Committee that Canada's existing naval, military and air forces are incapable of ensuring anything approaching adequate supervision of her Western coast. And before passing to a further contingency, external to Canada, it is desirable to point out that this existing inability on the part of Canada to safeguard her neutrality under these circumstances can hardly be regarded with equanimity by Canadians, nor, owing to the Imperial complications that might ensue, by other members of the British Commonwealth.

(c) Participation in a Major Overseas War

The two danger areas in the world today, which concern Canada no matter how reluctant that concern may be, are the Far East and Europe. Of the two, the European situation contains the most serious implications.

The complexity of the European situation and the rapidity with which changes in the political relations of its Powers are taking place render impractical any long term appreciation of future events on that Continent. All one can definitely say is that the conditions that breed war are to be found in abundance from the Black Sea to the North Sea, from the Mediterranean to the Baltic. Nor is the European theatre capable of being considered in a detached sense. Through Russia the actions of Germany and Japan in the sphere of international politics are intimately and dangerously linked.

If a long term appreciation would appear to be impractical a comparatively short distance view might reasonably be attempted. Such a view would embrace the fact that Germany has reached a dominant position in European politics; that its military preparations, which have been proceeding on a colossal scale and with great intensity during the last few years, are rapidly approaching comparative completion; that its economic and financial situation appears to be such that within a short period, perhaps a year, the only alternative to a serious internal situation will be an external distraction such as that afforded by a war aimed at the expansion of its frontiers.

It is possible that this impending outbreak will be initially confined to Central and Eastern Europe. It is quite impossible to assume that it will remain so restricted, however, for whatever the international entanglements, actual and potential, prior to 1914, it is evident that in the world of today the chances of a major European war developing into a world war are definitely great.

The signs are not lacking that Great Britain is striving to keep clear of becoming involved in a war of this description. What is equally evident, however, is that neither the nations forming the British Empire nor, indeed, the United States, can remain unaffected by any development which holds an obvious threat to the continued existence, as a world power, of Great Britain. Should that danger appear in obvious form, 1914 may be expected to repeat itself.

The military problem of Canada, so far as participation in a war in Europe is concerned, is more air and land than sea. There is no naval power which can dispute the supremacy of the United Kingdom and the United States in the Atlantic Ocean, and it is certain that Canada neither would, nor could, participate with other Empire countries in a future European struggle without a friendly neutral, or allied, United States. There are, however, certain essential factors to bear in mind when considering the organization and composition of the forces which Canada might decide to despatch. The first is that the advent of air power and the increased mobility and protection due to mechanized and armoured vehicles have out-dated the conception of the "nation in arms." In other words, "front line" fighting will tend to absorb a smaller percentage than hitherto of the man-power of any nation. Secondly, the speed by which these highly technical forces can be mobilized will be of the very greatest importance. Thirdly, the national arrangements for maintaining these forces in the field and equipping additional ones, that is to say, plans and means for the organization of industry, are now in the very first category of importance.

7. THE REQUIREMENTS OF THE ARMED FORCES OF CANADA

From the above review the following appreciation emerges:

(a) The direct defence of Canada is the major responsibility of its armed forces. While attack by the United States may be ruled out, and the danger to Canada, as an individual nation, of being invaded by an overseas Power (in particular, Japan) is deemed unlikely in the discernible future, there exist two possible, and even probable, contingencies against which this country is urgently required to prepare. There is, firstly, the situation in which Canada, as a neutral, in a war between the United States and Japan, is required to undertake the armed protection of its rights, and the fulfilment of its responsibilities in that capacity. There is, secondly, the situation wherein the United Kingdom (and certainly the Australasian Dominions) feel compelled to ally themselves with the United States in a final challenge to the hegemony of Japan in the Far East. In this latter contingency circumstances would allow Canada no choice other than participation as an active belligerent. Military operations by Japan, directed against the West Coast of Canada, must then be anticipated.

(b) The indirect defence of Canada by the co-operation with other Empire forces in a war overseas is a secondary responsibility of this country, though possibly one requiring much greater ultimate effort. As indicated previously in this review, the action of Canada must in fact await the development of the crisis and will be governed at the time by the situation obtaining between the U.S.A. and Japan, and between the U.S.A., Canada and the balance of the Empire. The completion of preparations necessary to Canada for the adequate armed supervision of neutral rights and responsibilities in the event of a war in the Far East in which this country refused to participate, or those necessary in the event of circumstances compelling Canada to act as a co-belligerent in this contingency will, however, in considerable measure, render Canada capable of taking an early part, with other Empire forces, in overseas operations.

In accordance, therefore, with the appreciation given in 7(a) above, which concerns the direct threats to the security of Canada, the Joint Staff Committee summarizes below those urgent military requirements for which immediate, or short term, provision should now be made:

Naval Forces (Detailed Estimates annexed)

The immediate naval requirements are to build up a fully manned and equipped naval force consisting of at least:

6 modern torpedo boat destroyers
4 minesweepers

with necessary base defence equipment and auxiliary vessels. This force is the minimum required to provide reasonable security on one coast, only.

It is proposed that this plan shall be carried into effect in a period of five years and the initial steps required are:

(i) Increase personnel by 120 (total of 600 additional required)
(ii) Purchase 2 TBDs from England
(iii) Build 4 minesweepers in Canada
(iv) Complete joint service magazine at Esquimalt
(v) Build up reserves of ammunition for RCN ships

(vi) Purchase equipment necessary for anti-submarine defences of Esquimalt and Halifax

(vii) Augment strength of naval reserve personnel

Land Forces (Detailed Estimates annexed)

(i) The modernization of the coast defences of Esquimalt, including the provision of anti-aircraft armament and equipment for the protection of the Naval base, dry dock, magazine, etc., and to provide some measure of military control over the Canadian water and air approaches to the mainland. The required plan has been under review since 1928 and, subject to final check by a Coast Defence expert on loan from the War Office (expected this month), is ready for execution. The proposed reorganization of the fixed defences, when completed, in addition to safeguarding locally Canada's position as a neutral, in the event of war between the United States and Japan, will provide a reasonable deterrent to attack by Japanese surface vessels and seaborne aircraft in the event of Canada being involved in hostilities.

(ii) The seaward defences of Halifax are, in general, considered adequate in quantity to meet any anticipated threat by a hostile overseas Power against the Canadian Eastern seaboard. The modernization of existing armament, defence electric lights, etc., is however necessary. No anti-aircraft defences worth the term exist at this fortress, or are possible, with the few obsolete equipments in the country. Anti-aircraft guns, lights and equipment sufficient to act as a real deterrent to raids by sea-borne or land-based aircraft most definitely require to be obtained.

(iii) The reorganization of the Canadian Militia, already approved, calls for a smaller organization, but one which comprises modern formations and equipment. The necessary armament, equipment and supplies to enable one-third of this future force to mobilize without delay on a war footing, and concentrate in any part of Canada, is considered essential.

Air Forces (Detailed Estimates annexed)

(i) The immediate requirements are modern aircraft, bases, advanced and intermediate operating stations, repair and supply depots and training centres.

(ii) The aircraft requirements of Air Defence on both the West and East Coasts necessitates provision for: the reconnaissance of vast sea areas and lengthy coast lines, the attack of enemy surface craft, submarines and forces violating our territory, the defence of ports from hostile carrier or cruiser borne aircraft, co-operating with naval and military units. The mobility of air forces coupled with the fact that a main threat on both coasts at the same time is unlikely, permits great flexibility in the disposition of air units and allows ready concentration in any threatened area on either coast. For these duties, approximately 300 aircraft will be required to equip 23 Squadrons and about 70 aircraft will be required for Training Schools. To minimize the cost of maintaining this force, it is proposed that 11 Squadrons should be Permanent Units and that 12 Squadrons be Non-Permanent units.

(iii) The composition of this force is to be as follows:—

Permanent Active Air Force	*Non-Permanent Active Air Force*
2 Flying Boat squadrons	4 Army Co-operation squadrons
2 Coastal Reconnaissance squadrons	4 Fighter squadrons

2 Torpedo Bomber squadrons	4 Bomber squadrons
2 General Purpose squadrons	
1 Fighter squadron	
1 Bomber squadron	
1 Army Co-operation squadron	

The first line of the Permanent Active Air Force squadrons, as listed, are for Coast Defence purposes and require to be equipped with modern first line aircraft immediately available and ready for active service. The balance of the permanent Active Air Force squadrons are to be equipped for the present with less expensive aircraft of an obsolescent or training type. It is proposed that all Non-Permanent Active Air Force units will be provided for the present with 6 training type aircraft suitable for the functions of the particular unit.

(iv) The manning of the Permanent Active Air Force squadrons will require an increase of 185 officers and 2400 airmen bringing the present strength of the Permanent Active Air Force of 153 officers and 969 airmen to an ultimate strength of 338 officers and 3369 airmen.

(v) The Estimates submitted include all funds necessary to furnish additional accommodation, aerodromes, etc., together with all stores, armaments, munitions, and other necessary supplies. The placing of orders for the manufacture of aircraft and aero engines with Canadian firms, where possible, will establish an aircraft industry in Canada, which is considered most essential.

DOCUMENT 2

Memorandum Prepared by Mackenzie King for Franklin Roosevelt,
6 March 1937 (King Papers)

PERMANENT CONFERENCE ON ECONOMIC AND SOCIAL PROBLEMS

AIM

Social justice secured through co-operative effort of the nations of the world to remove *the evils* (economic and social) *which lie at the root* of national discontent, world unrest, and international strife—and which are *the fundamental cause of war.*

"Justice is the common concern of mankind." Edmund Burke.

Social Justice is equally a matter of concern to all nations.

Efforts to further social justice at home are likely to be of little or no avail in the long run if the world is kept in a state of fear, and there is danger of another European or world war.

METHOD

Universality of co-operative effort is an essential condition to success.

The United States prepared to meet with countries of the world to consider social and economic problems which lie at root of world unrest and to investigate alleged injustices with a view to ascertaining facts, and permitting world opinion to be intelligently found and brought to bear.

PLACE OF MEETING—ARRANGEMENTS, ETC.

To hold such a conference in the United States would involve setting up new machinery, and an organization for purposes of world conference —conference to be of value would have to be continuous—more or less permanent.

The necessary machinery and organization for purposes of world conference already exists at Geneva—the International Labour Office, etc., etc. League machinery etc. present difficulty—U.S. and other great powers not members of League.

President of United States prepared—if League of Nations agreeable to lending its good offices towards facilitating such a Conference—to approach heads of States—Germany, Italy, Japan and Brazil—nations not at present members of League, or not present at last Assembly—to send their representatives to join with representatives of the President—and representatives of other nations (members of the League) in a conference for purposes described—the cost of the Conference, etc. to be on a basis similar to that of the League—each country contributing its share, so all would be on equal footing—none under obligation to the other.

This would avoid placing any special onus on the United States for program—or specific proposals—or obligations for success of conference, etc. It would mean a "getting together" of all nations interested in preserving the world's peace, by peaceful means—a sure method—by going at once after root causes of unrest.

A NATURAL EXPANSION OF STEPS ALREADY TAKEN

A beginning has already been made by representation of United States on "The Committee on Raw Materials".

Scope of inquiries could be expanded to include outstanding economic and social problems not already being adequately discussed, or discussed at all. It ought, for example, be left to such countries as Germany, Italy, etc., to say what they would like to have probed or investigated—what they regard as underlying injustices.

THE ALTERNATIVE IN SOLUTION OF WORLD PROBLEMS

1. Reliance upon Force—armaments, etc.
2. Reliance upon Reason—public opinion.

Collective Security should not be identified with reliance upon Force.

Collective Security of nations lies in the sense of Social Justice being secured through investigation and exposure of social wrongs, and the power of an organized public opinion founded upon same. Most social evils are more effectively prevented and cured by public opinion than by penalty— World Opinion, a powerful factor.

Nations that feel the necessity of relying upon Force—may make their own Locarnos—agreements of mutual assistance, etc.

No agreement of Conference proposed (if such arrived at) would be binding upon the United States unless approved by President and Senate of the United States.

PROBABLE RESULT

As the method of investigation, etc. discloses its powers, nations will see the folly of placing their reliance on Force—Disarmament would follow in the natural course of things—armaments are proceeding as they are today because *the other method is not being employed.*

The question of disarmament and other *political* issues need not arise, or be drawn into the proceedings of the Conference.

A *World Court* is already in existence—concerned with *Legal Justice.*

A *Conference* on Social and Economic Problems—developed into a permanent organization, would be concerned with *Social Justice.*

PROBABLE EFFECT OF SUCH A CONFERENCE UPON THE LEAGUE OF NATIONS

The character of the League would change—it would gradually—probably, quickly—possibly, immediately—revert to the original intention and idea—of reliance upon Public Opinion—not upon Force—economic or military sanctions.

Nations which are no longer willing to risk being involved in war, because of collective security based on Force—would, in all probability, withdraw from the League unless the application of some of its principles changed— but they would find their opportunity for continuance of co-operative effort for World Peace secured by peaceful means (collective security based on removal of root causes of social injustice) to the World Conference which would continue to meet at Geneva.

With the present character of the League (peace secured by reliance upon Force) undergoing change in this manner,—and a new world organization for Social Justice (Peace secured by peaceful means) coming to the fore— the two would almost inevitably be merged in a world organization—under some other name perhaps—with universal membership—the great objective of the League as proposed by President Wilson.

The time is most opportune—At present, a Committee of the League is considering the revision of the Covenant—The last Assembly seemed to favour its complete separation from the Treaty of Versailles.

THE WORLD SITUATION DEMANDS ACTION OF THE KIND

War would seem to be inevitable unless the nations can be brought into round table conference.

If Nations that have left the League, and Nations still Members can be brought together into Conference, by and with the United States, the one sure path to peace will at last open out before all.

DOCUMENT 3

Memorandum by Mackenzie King on his interview with Hitler,
Berlin, 29 June 1937 (King Papers)

I was received by the Reich-Chancellor at 12.45. I had been given to understand the interview would last for half an hour with the possibility of some
extension of time, if circumstances permitted. The interview lasted till
nearly a quarter past two, Herr Hitler indicating, during its course, that he
wished to continue the conversation and that other engagements would have
to be postponed.

I was received in a friendly manner by Herr Hitler who said he was
pleased that I had visited Germany, and hoped I would carry away pleasant
recollections of my visit. I thanked him for the arrangements which had
been made through Herr von Ribbentrop to enable me to see much of
interest in a short time, and particularly for the opportunity of meeting
himself and other members of the Government. I spoke of my residence
of a few months in Berlin, Germany, in 1900, and of having been born in
Berlin, Canada, and, for a time, representing in Parliament the constituency
of North Waterloo in which there were a number of small communities
named after important German cities. I found that my knowledge of German
was sufficient to enable me to follow pretty closely what Herr Hitler was
saying, and that his knowledge of English seemed to be sufficient to enable
him to understand some of the things I was saying. Herr Schmidt acted
as interpreter, and did so in an exceedingly effective manner.

I opened the conversation by making clear to Herr Hitler that my visit
was purely a personal one, that I was anxious to get a first-hand knowledge
of questions, and, that having been recently in England at the Imperial
Conference, I had had exceedingly good opportunities of learning about
European conditions and was anxious to supplement that information by
such opportunities as a brief visit on the Continent might afford before my
return to Canada.

I spoke of what I had seen and learned of the Chancellor's effort to
improve the conditions of the working classes and those in humble circumstances; told him of my own interest in these questions as one who had
organized the Department of Labour in Canada, and had been Minister of
Labour some years ago. I said all that constructive side of his work had
appealed very strongly to me, and that I hoped nothing would be permitted
to destroy the good that it was sure to effect in the end. Herr Hitler was
very modest in what he said about the Government's efforts along the lines

of social legislation. He said the Government did not claim any special proprietorship in the measures to which they had given or were giving effect. Where they had obtained an idea from some other country which they thought was a right one, that would be helpful, they had seized upon it and sought to apply it.

After touching on social questions, I said to Herr Hitler that another of the reasons which had brought me to Germany was the concern which, in common with all men having responsibility, I felt in the European situation; that I had meant to pay the visit in the Autumn of last year, and would have done so but for the fact that I gathered it might not have been possible to see him at that time. I mentioned that I had made known my desire and intention to Mr Eden who had expressed to me the hope that I might find it possible to carry it out, and mentioned what Mr Eden had said about it being unfortunate that so many visiting Geneva and London, came so often to and fro only via Paris, thereby altogether omitting Germany. He thought we should see as much as possible of all countries.

Herr Hitler said that there were no matters outstanding which he did not think could be satisfactorily settled. Time, however, was an important factor, many questions were more easily adjusted if dealt with promptly; if allowed to drag on too long, they became increasingly difficult of settlement; the sooner understandings could be reached, the better. At this point, I said to him that no person disliked everything that had to do with expenditures for defence purposes more than I did, that the members of my Party in Canada all felt alike in this particular; that the Parliament was strongly Liberal; that I had a large majority at my back. Such, however, had become the fear of the possibility of another war, that our Government had felt obliged at the last Session, in order to keep our Party united and in accord with the sentiment of the country, to bring in increased estimates for expenditure on the Army, Navy and Air Forces, to make increases for all three services. That the fear had been occasioned by what was taking place in Germany in the way of increased outlays for war purposes.

I went on to say that what Canada valued above everything else as one of the Nations of the British Commonwealth was the freedom which we all enjoyed and felt was secured by our free association together, and common allegiance to the Common Crown. That sometimes foreign countries might get the impression from the fact that in legislating we spoke of what we were doing as being done only for ourselves, that we might thereby be indifferent to what might happen in other parts. That I thought it was only right to say that if the time ever came when any part of the Empire felt that the freedom which we all enjoyed was being impaired through any act of aggression on the part of a foreign country, it would be seen that all would join together to protect the freedom which we were determined should not be imperilled. I said I felt sure there was no thought of aggression in the mind of any member of the British Commonwealth so far as other countries were concerned. That what we wanted to see prevail was fair play and justice and the avoidance of aggression. I said that the Canadian spirit was best exemplified by what had taken place in the Great War and also at the recent Coronation. There had been no orders or compulsion of any kind; that everything that had been done by Canada had been done voluntarily; that except for there being inadequate accommodation on the ships and in the hotels a very much larger number of Canadians would have crossed for the Coronation. It was this sense of freedom and security which we enjoyed under British institutions which was the real cement of the Empire, and which none of us would wish to see threatened.

Herr Hitler followed these remarks by speaking at some length of the reasons which had caused Germany to arm, of her feeling that she had had on more than one occasion to decide—as a result of the Versailles Treaty—whether her people were to be held in indefinite subjection or whether she would have to assert herself so as to preserve the respect of her people in their own eyes. That France had not disarmed as she should have done, and had Germany not taken notice of the actions of other countries by seeking to strengthen her own position, she could have hoped for no future for herself or her people. He said that to catch up at all to the start which other nations had over Germany, they had to accelerate the pace of arming, and do so on a scale which otherwise would have been wholly unnecessary and unwarranted.

Herr Hitler then said to me in a most positive and emphatic way that there would be no war so far as Germany was concerned. He said he would give me his reasons for so saying. The first was that his real desire was to improve the conditions of the people of Germany; that they were doing and had done a good deal in that direction, and hoped to do more. A war would be certain to undo and destroy all that had been done. In the second place, a war would mean the desolation of Europe; that assuming France and Germany were at war, and that France won, she would discover at the end of the war, while she might have added some peoples from another country to her own, she would, in so doing, have increased only her own problems but apart from that she would have destroyed herself as well as a good part of Germany. Similarly, if Germany were to win, she would do so at the expense of having practically destroyed herself. With instruments of war what they were today, another European war would mean the decimation of Europe. All that war would leave in its wake would be problems of the kind which they were having in Spain today.

He then said that he, himself, and all the members of his Government, had all been through the late war. They knew what war meant, and they did not want others to go through a like experience. He then went on to say that he thought if peoples of any countries were determined to fight, every effort should be made to circumscribe the area of conflict. Herr Hitler said that he did not think England yet realized what Communism meant. That if he had not fought Communism as he did in Germany, the condition of Germany today would be that of Spain at the present time. Herr Hitler also said something about not being able to understand England's attitude on some things, and her unwillingness to co-operate with Germany. At this point I said to him that I thought the Germans did not altogether understand the English, just as I felt, in some things, the English did not understand the Germans. I said that I knew something of each of them, and felt I understood them in their relations with each other perhaps better than they did themselves. I said that we, in Canada, had frequently to be explaining the English attitude on some matters to the Americans, and the American attitude, on some matters, to the English. That our position and association enabled us to understand each of them, and especially to enable us not to mistake their meaning. I then said General Göring had told me that he (Herr Hitler) had been unable to understand why the English should be so annoyed at Baron von Neurath's visit to England being postponed. I said that nothing better could illustrate what I had in mind. I said that if an Englishman who happened to be coming out of his house when it was on fire, and met some people passing by, he would begin to see whether his tie was in order and his coat in its right position lest they might think that he was over perturbed about the situation. That an Englishman very often sought to hide his feelings and others in consequence were liable to mistake them. That England with her vast interest in all parts of the world would never have thought of letting other nations imagine that she had become unduly alarmed over an incident such as that of the *Leipzig*. That had the situation been reversed, England would certainly have had her Minister continue his journey, and would not have given to the world the idea that the matter to her was one of so great international significance.

Herr Hitler took good naturedly what I had said about the English attitude, and said he could understand that. I then went on to say that I hoped the visit would not be unduly postponed; that I was sure it could not do other than great good. Herr Hitler then said that there were interviews and interviews. That an interview such as he and I were having together, exchanging views quite frankly, could not be other than helpful. However, where before an interview took place, expectations were raised with respect to the settlement of a lot of questions which could not possibly be settled at the time of an interview, it was almost inevitable that more harm than good would result from an interview of the kind. Unfortunately, before Baron von Neurath had started out for England, the Press in London had begun to set out different subjects that it was understood were to be discussed, and had raised great expectations in regard to what would take place at the interview. Some of these things could not possibly be settled, and the reaction once it were known that settlements had not been reached, might only leave the last state worse than the first.

He then went on to say there are some things which there is no use discussing, for example, he said, "I might talk to you by the hour or the week about the desirability of Canada leaving the British Empire but all that I could say and all the arguments I could use, would never cause you to alter your determination to remain a part of the Empire. Similarly", he said, "nothing that can be said to me will ever cause me to commit Germany to go to war with regard to some situation that may arise in the future at a time I do not know and with respect to conditions that, for the present, are unknown. I am not like Stalin. I cannot shoot my Generals and Ministers when they will not do my will. I am dependent for my power on the people who are behind me. Without the people I am nothing. The people do not want to be bound by commitments for the future in regard to unknown situations, and they would not support me were I to commit them in advance". I am not quoting Herr Hitler's exact words but what he said was along the lines indicated. Though he did not specifically mention a second Locarno, I thought this was possibly what he had in mind.

At this point, he spoke of the absurdity of what was called "collective security." It only tended to make a European war out of what might otherwise be a much localized affair. At no point in the conversation did Herr Hitler make anything which was in the nature of a threat. He did, however, say something which I did not wholly grasp at the time, about there being some things which should be understood if trouble was to be avoided. What I gathered at the time was that he was referring to the situation on the Eastern borders of Germany and her possible expansion. He said specifically that so far as the question of the colonies was concerned, he had no doubt that this could be worked out satisfactorily in the course of time. That that was not an immediate question. He spoke of the limited area of Germany for purposes of production, and the size of its population, and the need of securing sources of supply and markets. He said something about England not seeking to control German action.

He spoke appreciatively about the action of the Imperial Conference in suggesting that the Versailles Treaty should be separated from the Covenant of the League. He said that most of Germany's problems had grown out of that Treaty. I told him that I had attended Imperial Conferences in 1923, and 1926, as well as this year, and that I had never before found the feeling towards Germany more understanding or better than it was at this last Conference. That while there were many actions on Germany's part which people in England and elsewhere found it difficult to understand, the general feeling toward Germany was, I thought, more friendly than it had previously been. That England's attitude in Europe so far as I had been able to gather, seemed to be that of "an interested spectator". "Interested" from the knowledge that through precipitate action in any part of Europe, situations might be developed which might become menacing to Europe as a whole; that England, and indeed all parts of the world, were interested in preventing anything happening in any part of Europe which might affect the whole world. It was the hope that problems would be solved with time, and caution, and precipitate action avoided, that seemed to me to summarize the British attitude.

I made clear, however, that I had no authority to speak for anyone but was just giving my own personal impressions. Herr Hitler said that he agreed that there was danger in precipitate action, and that Germany had to fear this as well as other countries, and would do what she could to avoid it. He spoke of it being possible to have all difficulties with France amicably adjusted, and of Germany not misunderstanding England's action in increasing her armaments. The one critical note in the course of his remarks was that concerning the alliance formed between France and Russia, and England's sanctioning agreements which were prejudicial to Germany. This was near the end of the conversation. I did not get time to make any response to what was said in this connection. I felt moreover that the subject at this point was one which it was not for me to discuss.

In the course of the conversation, I spoke to Herr Hitler of the impression which my colleagues and I had formed of the Prime Minister, Mr Chamberlain, of how many of us had, in advance, been led to believe we would find Mr Chamberlain very set in his views and rigid concerning certain policies. We were all delighted to find him Liberal and broad-minded in his outlook, and most understanding of human problems. That what he had said in his recent speech in the House of Commons concerning Germany's restraint, et cetera, was just what those of us who had been at the Conference table with him, in confidential discussion, had been led to expect he would say. I thought he had a wide understanding of foreign policy, and that his aim would be to reach understandings which would make for friendly relations between the nations. Hitler said that he was pleased to know this. I concluded the interview by saying I hoped he would not misunderstand my coming by myself without being accompanied by the British Ambassador; that some foreign countries might think that this was an evidence of some tendency toward separation between Canada and Britain. That, as a matter of fact, it was evidence of something quite the contrary. It was evidence of the trust we all had in each other and of the complete freedom of action enjoyed by each part of the Empire in dealing with all matters. That had the British Ambassador accompanied me, they would have had, in Canada, a feeling of subordination so far as our Dominion was concerned. It was the fact that we were all so completely free to settle our own policies that would cause us at all costs to maintain the unity which we enjoyed in the Commonwealth of Nations.

Herr Hitler said that Sir Nevile Henderson had not been in Germany very long, but they all liked him and felt that he had a good understanding of German problems.

At the end of the interview, Herr Hitler presented me with a photograph of himself, mounted in a silver frame and personally inscribed in remembrance of my visit to Berlin. He told me that he had much enjoyed the talk we had had together, and expressed the hope that I would revisit Germany again.

I confess that the impression gained by this interview was a very favourable one. As I told Herr Hitler in the course of the interview, what he said was a relief to my mind because of the very positive manner in which he spoke of the determination of himself and his colleagues not to permit any resort to war. I did feel very strongly that he had big problems within the country which he had to meet. He impressed me as a man of deep sincerity and a genuine patriot. I felt increasingly in the course of my stay that there were conditions in Germany itself which accounted for much that had been done there which it was difficult to understand beyond its borders.

Throughout the interview, Hitler did not appear to be the least excited in anything he said. He spoke with great calmness, moderation, and logically and in a convincing manner. It seemed to me his mind is so absorbed in Germany and in what he wishes to do for the German people, that he is not equally concerned with matters outside Germany which may be far reaching in their effects on Germany itself. His interest in Spain arises unquestionably out of his feelings and fears concerning the spread of Communism.

DOCUMENT 4

Memorandum by Mackenzie King on War Aims, 2 November 1939
(King Papers)

In setting forth Canada's point of view re statements of what we are fighting for, I think it should, above all else, be made a distinctively Canadian point of view. In other words, Canada has been drawn into this war because of certain well known conditions which have occasioned it, all of which are confined to the continent of Europe.

On the continent of North America, there is not even a remote thought of war as between the United States and ourselves, or, indeed, as between any other countries on this continent. And, it might be added, the United States which is as much concerned in the preservation of democracy as Canada is, is not in this war, though Canada is, notwithstanding the fact that as regards Germany, the United States has probably occasioned that country more cause for offence than Canada has in anything she has said or done. These outstanding facts should afford a key to the aims which we in this country should assert as those we are hoping to have effected as a result of Canada's participation in them.

Quite clearly dictatorship is the primary cause of the present war. Behind dictatorship, and making it possible, lies the suppression of free institutions and the methods taken to prevent their development. In other words, what is most needed is an understanding of the conditions which account for the rise of Nazism. These, of course, would include the menace of Communism.

Force, leading to aggression, is the instrument of dictatorship. It will be necessary as a first step to destroy the instrument: where a mad man is rushing around a community with a shot-gun or a sword the first step is to relieve him of the weapons he carries and then to deal with the man himself. If the man himself is mad, he will have to be incarcerated, or dealt with in some even more effective manner. Obviously the overthrow of the regime which has organized the war and perpetrated the acts of aggression which have led to war, is the next step. Insofar as Canada is concerned, it will have to be made clear to the German people that we cannot begin to talk to them so long as they continue to place their reliance on Force and allow the administration which has deprived them of their own liberties to be the ones to dictate the conditions which would govern an abiding peace.

The means whereby British freedom has been secured and maintained will be found in outstanding charters of liberty which form a part of the British

Constitution. These charters did not at the time they were signed purport to establish some order that was entirely new. They rather asserted the existence of certain rights which those who presented them for signature had already belonged to the people [sic], and which they were determined to have recognized. In a similar way our war aims should assert rights which we believe to be fundamental to the preservation of liberty.

The United States Declaration of Independence in which certain fundamental rights are put forth is a parallel to the British Petition of Rights and Bill of Rights. Among British charters of liberty in which fundamental rights of a free people are set forth, in addition to the Petition of Rights and the Bill of Rights, are, of course, the Magna Carta, Habeas Corpus Act, and other acts establishing freedom of assembly, freedom of speech, freedom of worship, etc.

As far as I am concerned, and I believe I can speak for the Canadian people in this, the reason I was prepared to invite Parliament to come to the side of Britain and France in the present war, at the certain sacrifice of Canadian lives and other resources, is that I believed that the liberties which had been secured through years of British struggle, and which are part of the common heritage of the British Commonwealth, would be threatened, imperilled, if not destroyed, by the triumph of Nazism, and the further belief that so long as Nazism was permitted to continue its sway in Germany, we would all not only continue to live under the threat of its power and methods, but would be driven to adopt methods of self-defence which, of themselves, could not do other than work a change in our existing institutions. In other words, in order to successfully oppose force and dictatorship, we would inevitably be driven more and more in that direction ourselves.

I feel this should be made very clear in any statement presented to the world. It is the one really effective wedge that can be driven between the present regime in Germany and the German people themselves. It should be put forward just as soon as possible. It would make clear that what we really desire is freedom. That we believe that the freedom of one nation is bound up with the freedom of another, just as we believe that standards prevailing in one country, if brutal, immoral or menacing, in other respects tend to undermine standards in other nations that are seeking to save their people from evils of the kind.

The basis of all Liberal doctrines is trust in the people. Personally, I am prepared to trust the German people quite as much as those of some other countries provided they are given the right and the power freely to express their own wishes and desires. I agree with Hitler that no peoples desire war themselves, and if their rulers are averse to war, they will never themselves initiate it. This can be made plain to Germany out of the lips of her own present day leaders.

The next thing which I feel should form a part of any representations by Canada is a very clear statement of our reliance upon public opinion to destroy existing dangers, and to preserve freedom, and a clear assertion in this connection that the rights of neutrals are as entitled to respect and to have their wishes known and felt, as those of the belligerents themselves.

In other words, as I expressed it in a report to the Governments at the time of dealing with coal strikes in Southern Alberta which led to the people of the Prairies burning their hay and their vegetables for fuel, private rights cease when they become public wrongs. A quarrel between two peoples, two parties or two countries may be permitted so long as the rights of third parties and third countries are not affected thereby. Whatever is done in seeking to end the present European war must have, as a basis, the effecting of some arrangement which will protect the rights of neutral nations, keep them free of fears by avoiding the possibility of constantly recurring wars.

This means that some machinery will have to be devised which will work toward that end. The machinery of the League of Nations was aimed at this purpose, but it placed its reliance upon the very instrument which it was trying to destroy, namely, coercion and force. Blindly to return to that sort of a remedy is simply to hasten the day for another situation such as the present. If the League of Nations had not placed its reliance upon force, in other words, sought to identify collective security with coercion, sanctions, etc., I am persuaded there would have been no war in Europe, civil or otherwise, from the close of the last war to the present. In the first place, the United States would have been a member of the League. It was the provision in the Covenant which would have committed the United States, as it has committed other countries in advance, to go to war, at some time unknown, in some part of the world at the time unknown, and fight causes at the time also completely unknown, which really caused the United States not entering the League. Similar reasons were the occasion of the withdrawal of other great powers from the League, Germany, Japan, and Italy.

There was, however, a worse consequence than this. Collective security based upon coercion and force had the effect of making that which otherwise have been local wars, into world wars, but what is even worse than that, actually creating the conditions for world wars by making powerful, individual nations which wished to right what, in their minds, were national wrongs, prepare to take on all the membership nations of the League in any war in which they might become engaged. Germany's gigantic military developments have been due to the belief, first, that existing wrongs could not be righted except by the threat or display and the existence of force, and, secondly, by the belief that, as a consequence of the obligations of the League of Nations Covenant, in seeking to remedy a national wrong, Germany had to be prepared to fight all League countries at the same time.

If Geneva had been a forum for the formation of world opinion instead of becoming, as in fact it did, a sort of international war office, all countries would have continued to be represented at Geneva, and there would have been opportunity for conference between representative men of all nations.

The present war has come about through inability to hold a conference. Had Italians, Germans, etc., been mixing freely with representatives of the British Commonwealth, United States, etc., at Geneva, once a year, discussing their grievances and publicly proclaiming them to the world from that particular forum, means would have been found, short of war, to bring about adjustments.

What, therefore, must be aimed at, is making provision for the formation of an intelligent world opinion; above all else, means of impartial investigation of existing wrongs must be provided, and provisions made adequate to insuring this investigation prior to the outbreak of hostilities. In the cases of the invasion of Czechoslovakia and Poland, there was not opportunity for adequate investigation. There was no opportunity given neutral nations to form their own opinion on the merits of the dispute. Had there existed, as between the nations involved, machinery such as is provided, to avoid strikes and lock-outs, in the Canadian Industrial Disputes Investigation Act, or to avoid international conflict as is provided by the International Joint Commission to investigate disputes between the United States and Canada, not one of the acts of aggression which have occasioned the present war would have taken place. If they had taken place, every nation interested in preserving peaceful methods of the adjustment of international differences would have been against the aggressor, and on the side of the nation ruthlessly attacked, and this not merely because of a wrong done one of the belligerent nations, but because every neutral nation would have had its peace threatened, and as this present war already has made sufficiently clear, would have had its whole economic life threatened if not greatly circumscribed.

There are certain evils in the cure of which publicity is much more effective than penalty. Light will destroy germs that darkness helps to propagate. Machinery for letting in the light to the nations concerned, and to all nations with respect to existing grievances is what more than all else is required if the world is to be saved further wars. This machinery obviously will provide that the parties immediately affected are given representation on any tribunal of investigation. The tribunal, however, should have third parties equally represented upon it.

A carefully prepared statement of aims making clear to the German people that this is the kind of thing Great Britain and the British Commonwealth wished to see the basis of any peace, will soon make its appeal to them as it will carry with it from the beginning the kind of power of opinion which will be needed to give it enduring effect.

Any statement should make clear the fundamental Christian truth that no man liveth unto himself, and that no nation liveth unto itself; that we are all our brothers' keepers.

Another aim, therefore, which must be specifically and very clearly stated is that economic nationalism and economic imperialism must end. That, in other words, there must be freedom of communication and commercial intercourse between nations. To this end, the two things in particular that would serve to poison the springs of opinion at the source must immediately cease. Firstly, the exclusion of opinion from without the country as, for example, the prevention of the admission of information either by means of the printed or spoken word, unless it be defamatory in character; and secondly, which is the reverse of the same coin, complete cessation of propaganda both within a country and in word going abroad over the radio, etc., of a character that would prejudice another country, and inflame passions both at home and abroad.

Along with this, of course, should be the strong assertion of the rights of people everywhere to speak their mind freely, to worship freely, and, above all, to have free representative assemblies. I think a condition should be imposed upon Germany—that a plebiscite of her own people must be taken before those in authority shall have the right to invade another country or to declare war. Until a declaration is so made by whosoever may be representing the German people at the time of effecting a truce or peace, there should be no bickering with him. In other words, those who continue to rely upon the sword must perish by the sword.

CHRONOLOGY OF EVENTS, 1935–1940

1935

1 July	Maj.-Gen. E. C. Ashton Chief of the General Staff
3 October	Italy invades Ethiopia
23 October	King Ministry takes office
	Ian Mackenzie Minister of National Defence
2 November	W. A. Riddell proposes oil sanctions at Geneva
2 December	Government publicly repudiates Riddell proposal
9 December	Hoare-Laval plan leaked to press

1936

7 March	Germany invades Rhineland
15 July	League of Nations ends sanctions against Italy
17 July	Civil war in Spain
26 August	Cabinet Defence Committee meets for first time
29 September	Mackenzie King addresses Assembly of League of Nations

1937

5 March	Mackenzie King meets with Roosevelt in Washington
14 May	Imperial Conference opens in London
15 June	Imperial Conference ends
29 June	Mackenzie King meets with Hitler in Berlin
12 December	U.S.S. *Panay* bombed by Japanese

1938

18 January	First Canada–U.S. military staff talks
11 March	Germany invades Austria
17 May	British Air Mission in Ottawa
18 August	Roosevelt speaks at Kingston, Ont.
15 September	Chamberlain flies to Berchtesgaden
29 September	Munich Agreement
21 November	Maj.-Gen. T. V. Anderson Chief of the General Staff

1939

1 January	Joint Staff Committee becomes Chiefs of Staff Committee
	Senior Air Officer becomes Chief of Air Staff
14 March	Germany invades Czechoslovakia
31 March	Britain and France offer Polish guarantee
1 September	Germany invades Poland
3 September	Britain and France declare war on Germany
10 September	Canada declares war on Germany
15 September	Loring Christie Minister to the United States
19 September	Norman McLeod Rogers Minister of National Defence
17 October	Maj.-Gen. A. G. L. McNaughton G.O.C. 1st Canadian Infantry Division
31 October	British Commonwealth Air Training Conference opens in Ottawa
4 November	New U.S. Neutrality Act
10 December	First "flight" of 1st Division sails for Britain
17 December	British Commonwealth Air Training Agreement

1940

26 March	General Election: King Ministry returned
9 April	Germany invades Norway and Denmark
23 April	Mackenzie King meets with Roosevelt in Warm Springs, Ga.
29 April	Mackenzie King meets with Roosevelt in Washington
10 May	Germany invades Belgium and the Netherlands
23 May	C. G. Power Minister of National Defence for Air
10 June	Rogers killed in air crash
11 June	Power Acting Minister of National Defence
22 June	France signs armistice
5 July	J. L. Ralston Minister of National Defence
12 July	Power Associate Minister of National Defence
	Angus L. Macdonald Minister of National Defence for Naval Services
22 July	Maj.-Gen. H. D. G. Crerar Chief of the General Staff
16 August	Mackenzie King meets with Roosevelt at Ogdensburg, N.Y.
17 August	Permanent Joint Board on Defence created
26 August	Permanent Joint Board on Defence holds first meeting
2 September	U.S.–U.K. "destroyers for bases" deal

NOTE ON THE SOURCES

The main, and indispensable, source is the material in the papers of W. L. Mackenzie King, Prime Minister throughout the greater part of the period with which this book is concerned. Second to that, the material in the custody of the Historical Sections of the Armed Forces, up to 1939.

There are two important sources which I was unable to consult. One is the papers of Ian Mackenzie, Minister of National Defence from October 1935 to September 1939; the Mackenzie Papers, deposited at the Public Archives of Canada, are closed to scholars until 1975. The other is the files of the Department of External Affairs, Ottawa; more than any other department of the federal government, it keeps its documents shielded from scholarly scrutiny.

A complete list of the collections of documents on which this book is based is set out below. In each case, the collection is cited by the name under which it appears in the References, followed by the name or location of its present custodian.

Prime Ministers

Bennett Papers (Bonar Law-Bennett Library, University of New Brunswick, Fredericton, N.B.)
King Papers (Literary Executors of W. L. Mackenzie King)

Cabinet Ministers

Lapointe Papers (Public Archives of Canada)
Rogers Papers (Douglas Library, Queen's University, Kingston, Ont.)

Public Servants and Military Officers

Christie Papers (Department of External Affairs, Ottawa)
Crerar Papers, to 1939 (Historical Section, Army Headquarters, Ottawa)
Massey Papers (Rt. Hon. Vincent Massey, C. H.)
McNaughton Papers, to 1939 (Historical Section, Army Headquarters, Ottawa)

Armed Forces

Air Force Records, to 1939 (Historical Section, Royal Canadian Air Force, Ottawa)
Army Records, to 1939 (Historical Section, Army Headquarters, Ottawa)
Naval Records, to 1939 (Office of the Naval Historian, Ottawa)

Other

Dafoe Papers (Public Archives of Canada)
Rowell Papers (Public Archives of Canada)

REFERENCES

I. WAR IN AFRICA

1. O. D. Skelton, "Pros and Cons of Canadian Participation," 24 Aug. 1935, Bennett Papers.
2. Ottawa *Morning Citizen*, 9 Sept. 1935; Quebec *Chronicle-Telegraph*, 9 Sept. 1935.
3. W. D. Herridge to R. K. Finlayson, 20 Aug. 1935. Bennett Papers.
4. Herridge to R. B. Bennett, 30 Sept. 1935, *ibid.*
5. Herridge to Finlayson, 8 Oct. 1935, *ibid.*
6. Herridge to Finlayson, 3 Aug. 1935, *ibid.*
7. R. B. Bennett to H. L. MacNeill, 24 Aug. 1935, *ibid.*
8. *Ibid.*
9. Jean Bruchési, "A French-Canadian View of Canada's Foreign Policy," in *Canada, the Empire and the League* (Toronto, 1936), p. 146.
10. Skelton to N. W. Rowell, 1 March 1932, Rowell Papers.
11. Skelton to Rowell, 21 Oct. 1935, *ibid.*
12. Vincent Massey, *What's Past Is Prologue* (Toronto, 1963), p. 135.
13. Skelton, "Pros and Cons of Canadian Participation," Bennett Papers.
14. Quoted in Nicholas Mansergh, *Survey of British Commonwealth Affairs: Problems of External Policy, 1931–1939* (London, 1952), pp. 192–3.
15. Bennett to Canadian Advisory Officer (Geneva), 9 Oct. 1935 (telegram), Bennett Papers.
16. Canadian Advisory Officer to Secretary of State for External Affairs, 9 Oct. 1935 (telegram), *ibid.*
17. Memorandum by Skelton, 10 Oct. 1935, *ibid.*
18. Skelton to W. A. Riddell, 1 November 1935; Riddell to Skelton, 7 Dec. 1935, King Papers.
19. W. A. Riddell, *World Security by Conference* (Toronto, 1947), p. 106.
20. *Documents Relating to the Italo-Ethiopian Conflict* (Ottawa, 1936), pp. 162–3.
21. Mary McGeachy to J. W. Dafoe, 15 Oct. 1935, Dafoe Papers.
22. *Ibid.*
23. Riddell, *World Security by Conference*, p. 109.
24. Mary McGeachy to Dafoe, 18 Oct. 1935, Dafoe Papers.
25. Riddell, *World Security by Conference*, p. 110.
26. *Documents Relating to the Italo-Ethiopian Conflict* (Ottawa, 1936), pp. 165–6.
27. Riddell, *World Security by Conference*, p. 114.
28. Riddell to Skelton, 11 Dec. 1935, King Papers.

29. Riddell, *World Security by Conference*, p. 114.
30. Quoted in *ibid.*, p. 117.
31. *Ibid.*, p. 118.
32. Quoted in *ibid.*, pp. 118–19.
33. *Ibid.*, p. 119.
34. *Ibid.*, pp. 122–3.
35. *Ibid.*, pp. 123–4.
36. Canada, House of Commons, *Debates*, 1936, vol. I, p. 93.
37. Quoted in Riddell, *World Security by Conference*, p. 130.
38. Canada, H. C. *Debates*, 1936, vol. I, p. 95.
39. *Documents Relating to the Italo-Ethiopian Conflict*, pp. 171–2.
40. T. A. Crerar to J. B. Coyne, 3 Dec. 1935, Dafoe Papers.
41. Quoted in O. D. Skelton, "Canada and the Italo-Ethiopian Conflict", Jan. 1936, King Papers.
42. Crerar to Dafoe, 7 Dec. 1935, Dafoe Papers.
43. Grant Dexter to Dafoe, 17 Dec. 1935, *Ibid.*
44. Mackenzie King to Vincent Massey, 26 Dec. 1935, King Papers.
45. Canada, H. C. *Debates*, 1936, vol. I, p. 98.
46. Diary, 11 Feb. 1936, King Papers.
47. Riddell, *World Security by Conference*, pp. 140–1.
48. Canada, H. C. *Debates*, 1936, vol. I, p. 97.
49. King to Thomas Vien, 11 April 1936, King Papers.
50. Henri Bourassa to King, 19 May 1936, *ibid.*
51. Diary, 11 June 1936, *ibid.*
52. F. H. Underhill, "Canada and Post-League Europe," *Canadian Forum*, Oct. 1936, p. 11.
53. Canada, H. C. *Debates*, 1936, vol. V, pp. 3862–72.
54. "The End Of Collective Security," Winnipeg *Free Press*, 30 June 1936.
55. F. P. Walters, *A History of the League of Nations*, vol. II (London, 1952), p. 684.

II. INNOCENCE ABROAD

1. F. P. Walters, *A History of the League of Nations*, vol. II (London, 1952), pp. 709–10.
2. Skelton to King, 15 May 1936, King Papers.
3. Diary, 15 June 1936, *ibid.*
4. King to Lord Robert Cecil, 23 Sept. 1936, *ibid.*
5. Skelton to King, no date, *ibid.*
6. King to the Duke of Montrose, 10 Aug. 1936, *ibid.*
7. King to Canon B. Heeney, 15 Aug. 1936, *ibid.*
8. Diary, 21 Sept. 1936, *ibid.*
9. Quoted in H. Blair Neatby, *William Lyon Mackenzie King*, vol. II: *The Lonely Heights* (Toronto, 1963), pp. 264–5.
10. League of Nations, Verbatim Record of the Seventeenth Ordinary Session of the Assembly, 29 Sept. 1936, pp. 1–4.
11. King to Bourassa, 2 Oct. 1936, King Papers.
12. King to Peter Gerry, 6 Oct. 1936, *ibid.*
13. King to Lord Tweedsmuir, 2 Oct. 1936, *ibid.*
14. *Ibid.*
15. "When Canada Will Fight," editorial, 30 Sept. 1936.
16. "Mr. King at Geneva," editorial, 1 Oct. 1936.
17. Dafoe to J. A. Glen, 22 Oct. 1936, Dafoe Papers.
18. King to Tweedsmuir, 10 July 1937, King Papers.

19. King to Leighton McCarthy, 7 Nov. 1936, *ibid.*
20. Franklin Roosevelt to King, 21 Feb. 1936, *ibid.*
21. Bruce Hutchison, *The Incredible Canadian* (Toronto, 1952), p. 217.
22. Cordell Hull, *Memoirs*, vol. I (New York, 1948), pp. 527–8.
23. *Ibid*, p. 528.
24. "Memorandum of Conversation with Cordell Hull, Office of the Secretary of State," 5 March 1937, King Papers.
25. King to Tweedsmuir, 15 March 1937, *ibid.*
26. King to Roosevelt, 8 March 1937, *ibid.*
27. King to Tweedsmuir, 15 March 1937, *ibid.*
28. King to Roosevelt, 8 March 1937, *ibid.*
29. King to Roosevelt, 17 March 1937, *ibid.*
30. Quoted in William S. Langer and S. Everett Gleason, *The Challenge to Isolation, 1937–1940* (New York, 1952), p. 22.
31. Quoted in Neatby, *The Lonely Heights*, p. 265.
32. King to Stanley Baldwin (telegram), 13 Dec. 1936, King Papers.
33. J. W. Wheeler-Bennett, *The Nemesis of Power* (London, 1954), pp. 353–4.
34. King to Mrs. G. B. Patteson, 25 June 1937, King Papers.
35. Neville Chamberlain to King, 29 July 1937, *ibid.*
36. In the House of Commons. The speech does not appear in Hansard.
37. W. S. Churchill, *The Second World War*, vol. I, *The Gathering Storm* (Boston, Mass., 1948), p. 250.
38. "Memorandum re Interview with Herr Hitler, Berlin," 29 June 1937, King Papers.
39. King to Hitler, 1 July 1937, *ibid.*
40. King to Anthony Eden, 6 July 1937, *ibid.*
41. *Ibid.*
42. King to Tweedsmuir, 10 July 1937, *ibid.*
43. Speech given over the National Network of the Canadian Broadcasting Corporation, 19 July 1937.

II. APPEASEMENT

1. W. K. Hancock, *Smuts*, vol. I, *The Sanguine Years, 1870–1919* (Cambridge, 1962), p. 512.
2. G. M. Gathorne-Hardy, *A Short History of International Affairs* (London, 1947), p. 418.
3. Diary, 14 March 1936, Massey Papers.
4. King to Massey, 14 March 1936 (telegram), *ibid.*
5. Diary, 15 March 1936, *ibid.*
6. Bourassa to King, 19 May 1936, King Papers.
7. J. B. M. Hertzog to King, 14 March 1936 (telegram), *ibid.*
8. *The Mist Procession: The Autobiography of Lord Vansittart* (London, 1958), p. 529.
9. Canada, H. C. *Debates*, 1936, vol. II, p. 1332.
10. *Ibid.*, p. 1333.
11. Diary, 23 March 1936, King Papers.
12. Quoted in R. MacGregor Dawson, *William Lyon Mackenzie King*, vol. I, *1874–1923* (Toronto, 1958), p. 474.
13. Imperial Conference, 1937, *Summary of Proceedings* (Ottawa, 1937), p. 14, p. 16.
14. Nicholas Mansergh, *Survey of British Commonwealth Affairs: Problems of External Policy, 1931–1939* (London, 1952), p. 89.
15. King to E. M. Macdonald, 11 Nov. 1936, King Papers.

16. King to Tweedsmuir, 24 Aug. 1936, *ibid.*
17. Skelton, "Imperial Conference, 1937", 29 March 1937, *ibid.*
18. King to Viscount Greenwood, 6 Oct. 1937, *ibid.*
19. Crerar to Dafoe, 17 April 1937, Dafoe Papers.
20. Dawson, *William Lyon Mackenzie King*, vol. I, p. 460.
21. Keith Feiling, *The Life of Neville Chamberlain* (London, 1946), p. 303.
22. King to Tweedsmuir, 10 July 1937, King Papers.
23. Quoted in Nicholas Mansergh, *Documents and Speeches on British Commonwealth Affairs, 1931–1952* (London, 1953), pp. 177–8.
24. King to George N. Morang, 29 Sept. 1937, King Papers.
25. King to Greenwood, 6 Oct. 1937, *ibid.*
26. King to Malcolm MacDonald, 2 April 1938. Quoted in Feiling, *The Life of Neville Chamberlain*, p. 349.
27. King to Lady Aberdeen, 29 Sept. 1938, King Papers.
28. Diary, 20 Feb. 1938, *ibid.*
29. Diary, 12 March 1938, *ibid.*
30. King to L. S. Amery, 4 June 1938, *ibid.*
31. Diary, 14 March 1938, *ibid.*
32. Canada, H. C. *Debates*, 1938, vol. IV, pp. 3182–90.
33. King to Tweedsmuir, 10 July 1937, King Papers.
34. J. W. Wheeler-Bennett, *Munich: Prologue to Tragedy* (London, 1948), p. 61.
35. Feiling, *The Life of Neville Chamberlain*, p. 348.
36. King to Lord Runciman, 29 July 1938 (telegram), King Papers.
37. Dafoe to George Ferguson, 1 Sept. 1938, Dafoe Papers.
38. King to Charles Dunning, 3 Sept. 1938, King Papers.
39. King to Lord Tweedsmuir, 6 Sept. 1938, *ibid.*
40. Quoted in Feiling, *The Life of Neville Chamberlain*, p. 357.
41. King to Ribbentrop, 14 Sept. 1938 (telegram), King Papers.
42. Press statement, 17 Sept. 1938.
43. King to Dunning, 19 Sept. 1938, King Papers.
44. King to Tweedsmuir, 20 Sept. 1938, *ibid.*
45. King to Massey, 21 Sept. 1938, *ibid.*
46. United Kingdom, H. C. *Debates*, 1938, vol. 339, col. 21.
49. Quoted in Vincent Massey, *What's Past Is Prologue* (Toronto, 1963), pp. 259–60.
48. Ernest Lapointe to King, 24 Sept. 1938, Lapointe Papers.
49. Quoted in Massey, *What's Past Is Prologue*, p. 261.
50. Quoted in *ibid.*, p. 261.
51. Quoted in *ibid.*, p. 261.
52. Text in Montreal *Gazette*, 28 Sept. 1938.
53. United Kingdom, H. C. *Debates*, 1938, vol. 339, col. 26.
54. King to Lady Aberdeen, 29 Sept. 1938, King Papers.
55. Press statement, 29 Sept., 1938.
56. F. H. Soward *et al.*, *Canada in World Affairs: The Pre-War Years* (Toronto, 1941), p. 113.
57. Ernest Bertrand to King, 3 Oct. 1938, King Papers.
58. "What's the Cheering For?" Winnipeg *Free Press*, 3 Oct. 1938.
59. "Back Stage in Ottawa," *Maclean's Magazine*, vol. LI, 1 Nov. 1938.
60. King to Greenwood, 1 Nov. 1943, King Papers.
61. King to Macdonald, 1 Oct. 1938, *ibid.*
62. Text in the *Globe and Mail* (Toronto), 18 March 1939.
63. Skelton to King, 20 March 1939, King Papers.
64. L. B. Pearson to Massey, 16 July 1939, Massey Papers.

65. Soward, *Canada in World Affairs: The Pre-War Years*, p. 127.
66. Canada, H. C. *Debates*, 1939, vol. III, p. 2043.
67. Canada, H. C. *Debates*, 1939, vol. IV, pp. 2605–13.
68. L. A. Taschereau to King, 1 April 1939, King Papers.
69. King to Hitler, 1 Feb. 1939, *ibid.*
70. Text of message from Hitler to King, transmitted by the German Consul General, 21 July 1939, *ibid.*
71. Senator R. Dandurand to King, 1 July 1939, *ibid.*
72. King to Dandurand, 13 July 1939, *ibid.*
73. King to Lord Riverdale, 20 Nov. 1939, *ibid.*
74. Dr. Paul Schwarz, "A Diplomat Speaks," *Staats-Zeitung und Herold* (New York City), 28 Jan. 1948.
75. *Ottawa Citizen*, 26 Aug. 1939.
76. "Aide-Mémoire from the Consul-General of Poland to the Prime Minister of Canada," 29 Aug. 1939, King Papers.
77. Skelton to King; King to Skelton, 29 Aug. 1939, *ibid.*
78. Text in press release, 27 Aug. 1939.
79. King to Chamberlain, 26 Aug. 1939 (telegram), King Papers.

IV. EMPIRE AND REICH

1. Nicholas Mansergh, *Survey of British Commonwealth Affairs: Problems of Wartime Co-operation and Post-War Change, 1939-1952* (London, 1958), p. 17.
2. Canada, H. C. *Debates*, 1937, vol. I, pp. 1056–7.
3. Memorandum, 29 March 1937, King Papers.
4. Ian Mackenzie to King, 10 April 1937, *ibid.*
5. Field Marshal Sir Cyril Deverell to Maj.-Gen. E. C. Ashton, 7 May 1937, *ibid.*
6. Ashton to Mackenzie, 8 May 1937, *ibid.*
7. King to Mackenzie, 17 May 1937, *ibid.*
8. Memorandum, 15 April 1937, *ibid.*
9. Text in King Papers.
10. Christie Papers.
11. O. D. Skelton to King, 10 June 1937, King Papers.
12. Diary, 10 June 1937, *ibid.*
13. Diary, 11 June 1937, *ibid.*
14. Air Force Records.
15. King Papers.
16. Quoted in F. J. Hatch, "The British Commonwealth Air Training Plan," unpublished paper, Air Force Records.
17. Memorandum by the Joint Staff Committee for the Minister of National Defence, 6 May 1937, King Papers.
18. Memorandum by King, 16 May 1938, *ibid.*
19. Canada, Senate *Debates*, 14 June 1938, p. 553.
20. *Ibid.*, 15 June 1938, p. 565.
21. Sir Francis Floud to King, 22 June 1938, King Papers.
22. King to Floud, 24 June 1938, *ibid.*
23. King to Tweedsmuir, 20 July 1938, *ibid.*
24. Canada, H. C. *Debates*, 1938, vol. VI, p. 4893.
25. *Ibid.*, p. 4897.
26. Memorandum by A.V.-M. G. M. Croil, "Training Scheme of Pilots for the R.A.F.," 19 July 1938, Air Force Records.

27. L. R. LaFlèche to Mackenzie (telegram), 5 Aug. 1938, *ibid.*
28. Memorandum by King, 10 Aug. 1938, King Papers.
29. *Ibid.*
30. John W. R. Taylor, *C.F.S.: Birthplace of Air Power* (London, 1948), p. 157.
31. King to Floud, 31 Dec. 1938, King Papers.
32. Vincent Massey, *What's Past Is Prologue* (Toronto, 1963), pp. 303–6.
33. Quoted in *ibid*, pp. 304–5.
34. Quoted in J. W. Pickersgill, *The Mackenzie King Record*, vol. I, *1939–1944* (Toronto, 1960), pp. 40–1.
35. Skelton to King, 9 Oct. 1939, King Papers.
36. *Ottawa Morning Journal*, 16 Oct. 1939.
37. Grant Dexter to George Ferguson, 7 Nov. 1939, Dafoe Papers.
38. Memorandum by King, 25 Nov. 1939, King Papers.
39. Sir Gerald Campbell, *Of True Experience* (New York, 1947), p. 97.
40. Quoted in Pickersgill, *The Mackenzie King Record*, vol. I, p. 49.
41. Quoted in *ibid.*, p. 52.
42. King to Riverdale, 15 Dec. 1939, King Papers.
43. Pickersgill, *The Mackenzie King Record*, vol. I, p. 52.
44. Memorandum by King, 16 Dec. 1939, King Papers.
45. Memorandum by Col. N. O. Carr, 11 April 1936, Army Records.
46. Memorandum by the Chief of the General Staff, Maj.-Gen. Ashton, 11 July 1936, *ibid.*
47. Memorandum by the Master General of the Ordnance, 26 May 1936, *ibid.*
48. H. Duncan Hall, *North American Supply* (London, 1954), p. 3.
49. King to Hugh Plaxton, 12 Sept. 1936. Quoted in *Report of the Royal Commission on the Bren Machine Gun Contract* (Ottawa, 1939), pp. 17–8.
50. Mackenzie to King, 17 May 1937, King Papers.
51. Col. George Vanier to James Hahn, 11 November 1936. Quoted in *Report of the Royal Commission on the Bren Machine Gun Contract*, p. 25.
52. Col. C. P. Stacey, *Six Years of War: The Army in Canada, Britain and the Pacific* (Ottawa, 1955), p. 26.
53. Col. H. D. G. Crerar to C. P. Stacey, 24 Aug. 1939, Crerar Papers.
54. Memorandum by King, 28 June 1939, King Papers.
55. Memorandum by Massey, 4 Aug. 1939, Massey Papers.
56. G. P. Loggie to Col. Crerar, 7 July 1938, Crerar Papers.
57. Floyd Chalmers to Massey, 1 Aug. 1939, Massey Papers.
58. Quoted in Hall, *North American Supply*, p. 28.
59. *Ibid.*, p. 29.
60. C. G. Power to King, 23 Aug. 1938, King Papers.
61. Memorandum by King, 29 Aug. 1938, *ibid.*
62. Hall, *North American Supply*, p. 31.
63. King to Tweedsmuir, 23 July 1938, King Papers.
64. King to Tweedsmuir, 25 Aug. 1938, *ibid.*
65. R. J. Hammond, *Food*, vol. I, *The Growth of Policy* (London, 1951). p. 15.
66. Memorandum by Skelton, 5 May 1937, King Papers.
67. M. M. Postan, *British War Production* (London, 1952), p. 90.
68. J. Hurstfield, *The Control of Raw Materials* (London, 1955), p. 253.
69. Hall, *North American Supply*, p. 16.
70. *Ibid.*, p. 17.
71. *Ibid.*, p. 17.
72. Harold Crabtree to King, 5 June 1940, King Papers.
73. Memorandum by King, 6 June 1940, *ibid.*

V. REARMAMENT

1. Memorandum by Maj.-Gen. A. G. L. McNaughton, 5 April 1935, McNaughton Papers.
2. Memorandum by McNaughton, 22 Oct. 1935, *ibid.*
3. Quoted in H. Blair Neatby, *William Lyon Mackenzie King*, vol. II, *The Lonely Heights* (Toronto, 1963), p. 332.
4. The Canadian Military Institute, Toronto, *Selected Papers from the Transactions of the Institute*, 1937–38 (no. 33), p. 20.
5. David B. Rogers to Norman McLeod Rogers, 10 March 1939, Rogers Papers.
6. Canada, H.C. *Debates*, 1937, vol. II, pp. 1142–3.
7. Minutes of Fourth Meeting of the Conference of Defence Associations, 14 Feb. 1936, Naval Records.
8. *Ibid.*
9. Diary, 26 Aug. 1936, King Papers.
10. Col. C. P. Stacey, *Six Years of War: The Army in Canada, Britain and the Pacific* (Ottawa, 1955), p. 11.
11. Diary, 10 Sept. 1936, King Papers.
12. King to Canon B. Heeney, 20 Nov. 1936, King Papers.
13. Quoted in Stacey, *Six Years of War*, p. 14.
14. Finlayson to George Drew, 29 Dec. 1936, Bennett Papers.
15. Drew to Finlayson, 4 Jan. 1937, *ibid.*
16. Canada, H.C. *Debates*, 1937, vol. II, pp. 954–65.
17. *Ibid.*, pp. 1142–51.
18. Massey to King, 26 Feb. 1937; King to Massey, 17 March 1937, King Papers.
19. Mackenzie to King, 17 July 1937, *ibid.*
20. Diary, 14 Sept. 1937, *ibid.*
21. Diary, 24 March 1938, *ibid.*
22. Memorandum by A. V.-M. Croil, 14 April 1938, Air Force Records.
23. Maj.-Gen. Ashton to Col. Crerar, 20 Sept. 1939, Crerar Papers.
24. A. V.-M. G. M. Croil to Air Cmdre. E. W. Stedman, 28 Sept. 1938, Air Force Records.
25. Unsigned memorandum, 29 Sept. 1938, *ibid.*
26. Department of External Affairs, Ottawa, to Herbert Marler (telegram), 29 Sept. 1938, *ibid.*
27. A. V.-M. Croil to Air Cmdre. Stedman (telegram), 30 Sept. 1938, *ibid.*
28. "Report of the Minister's telephone conversation with Mr. Christie, at Ottawa, at 10.30 a.m., September 30th, 1938," *ibid.*
29. Department of External Affairs, Ottawa, to Marler (telegram), 1 Oct. 1938, *ibid.*
30. Unsigned memorandum, 1 Oct. 1938, *ibid.*
31. Army Records.
32. Stacey, *Six Years of War*, p. 35.

VI. WAR IN THE WEST

1. Quoted in Louise W. Holborn, ed., *War and Peace Aims of the United Nations* (Boston, 1943), p. 302.
2. United Kingdom, H.C. *Debates*, 1939, vol. 351, col. 946.
3. Quoted in William Langer and S. Everett Gleason, *The Challenge to Isolation, 1937–1940* (New York, 1952), p. 250.

4. King to Chamberlain (telegram), 8 Oct. 1939, King Papers.
5. Memorandum by Skelton, 10 Oct. 1939, *ibid.*
6. King to Chamberlain (telegram), 10 Oct. 1939, *ibid.*
7. Langer and Gleason, *The Challenge to Isolation*, p. 257.
8. Memorandum by Skelton, 27 Oct. 1939, King Papers.
9. King to Tweedsmuir, 16 Oct. 1939, *ibid.*
10. Memorandum by King, 27 Oct. 1939. *ibid.*
11. Quoted in J. W. Pickersgill, *The Mackenzie King Record*, vol. I, *1939–1944* (Toronto, 1960), p. 32.
12. *Ibid.*, p. 7.
13. Memorandum by King, 2 Nov. 1939, King Papers.
14. King to Chamberlain (telegram), 25 Nov. 1939, *ibid.*
15. Quoted in Keith Feiling, *The Life of Neville Chamberlain* (London, 1946), p. 426.
16. W. N. Medlicott, *The Economic Blockade*, vol. I (London, 1952), p. xi.
17. King to Alexander Walker, 4 Sept. 1940, King Papers.
18. Diary, 20 Jan. 1940, *ibid.*
19. Quoted in Pickersgill, *The Mackenzie King Record*, vol. I, pp. 177–8.
20. Memorandum by Skelton, 28 Aug. 1940, King Papers.
21. F. R. Scott, "Lest We Forget," *The Eye of the Needle* (Montreal, 1957), p. 15.
22. A. D. P. Heeney to King, 17 April 1940, King Papers.
23. Memorandum by Skelton, 18 April 1940, *ibid.*
24. Langer and Gleason, *The Challenge to Isolation*, p. 431.
25. *Ibid.*, p. 431.
26. Massey to King (telegram), 2 May 1940, King Papers.
27. Memorandum by Skelton, 2 May 1940, *ibid.*
28. Quoted in Pickersgill, *The Mackenzie King Record*, vol. I, p. 112.
29. Diary, 2 May 1940, King Papers.
30. Memorandum by H. L. Keenleyside, 6 May 1940, *ibid.*
31. Langer and Gleason, *The Challenge to Isolation*, p. 685.
32. Stetson Conn, Rose C. Engelman, and Byron Fairchild, *Guarding the United States and its Outposts* (Washington, D.C., 1964), p. 443.

VII. THE ROAD TO OGDENSBURG

1. Canada, H.C. *Debates*, 1938, vol. III, p. 3179.
2. "Defence Scheme No. 2. Combined Service Plan for the Maintenance of Canadian Neutrality in the Event of a War Between the United States and Japan," 25 Feb. 1938. Army Records.
3. General Staff memorandum, "Unguarded Alaska?" 5 Feb. 1935, *ibid.*
4. General Staff memorandum, "U.S.A., Alaska Highway via British Columbia and Yukon," 11 Feb. 1937, *ibid.*
5. "Memorandum of conversation with President Roosevelt," 5 March 1937, King Papers.
6. H. L. Keenleyside, "The Canada-United States Permanent Joint Board on Defence, 1940–1945," *International Journal*, vol. XVI, no. 1, Winter, 1960–61, pp. 67–9.
7. Christie to King, 16 Oct. 1940, King Papers.
8. Col. Crerar, "Memorandum for C.G.S.," 13 Dec. 1937, Crerar Papers.
9. "Notes on Staff Talks held in 1938 between Staff Officers of U.S. and Canadian Defence Forces," King Papers.

10. King to Mackenzie, 12 Nov. 1938, *ibid.*
11. Diary, 20 Aug. 1938, *ibid.*
12. Christie to King, 16 Oct. 1940, *ibid.*
13. Christie to Skelton, 27 Sept. 1939, *ibid.*
14. "Report on Air Mission to Washington", 3 Sept. 1939, Air Force Records.
15. Sir Gerald Campbell, *Of True Experience* (New York, 1947), p. 99.
16. R. G. Menzies to King (telegram), 7 Sept. 1939; King to Menzies (telegram), 7 Sept. 1939, King Papers.
17. Quoted in William L. Langer and S. Everett Gleason, *The Challenge to Isolation, 1937–1940* (New York, 1952), p. 45.
18. Quoted in *ibid.*, p. 229.
19. Memorandum by Hume Wrong, 29 Sept. 1939; Christie to Skelton, 9 Oct. 1939, King Papers.
20. Whitney H. Shepardson and W. O. Scroggs, *The United States in World Affairs, 1939* (New York, 1940), p. 187.
21. Christie to Skelton, 9 Oct. 1939, King Papers.
22. Langer and Gleason, *The Challenge to Isolation*, pp. 235, 290.
23. Quoted in H. Duncan Hall, *North American Supply* (London, 1954), p. 124.
24. *New York Times*, 5 April 1940.
25. Memorandum by Skelton, 5 April 1940, King Papers.
26. *Ottawa Citizen*, 11 April 1940.
27. Christie to King, 17 June 1940, King Papers.
28. Herridge to Dafoe, 12 July 1940; Dafoe to Herridge, 20 July 1940; Herridge to Dafoe, 24 July 1940; Arthur Meighen to Dafoe, 14 July 1940. Dafoe Papers.
29. Skelton to Herridge, 29 July 1940.
30. Memorandum by Skelton, 25 July 1940.
31. "Memorandum of conversation with President Roosevelt," 23 and 24 April 1940, King Papers.
32. "Memorandum of conversation with Cordell Hull," 28 April 1940, *ibid.*
33. "Memorandum of conversation with President Roosevelt," 29 April 1940, *ibid.*
34. *Ibid.*
35. King to Roosevelt, 3 May 1940, *ibid.*
36. Quoted in J. W. Pickersgill, *The Mackenzie King Record*, vol. I, *1939–1944* (Toronto, 1960), p. 90.
37. *Ibid.*, p. 107.
38. Langer and Gleason, *The Challenge to Isolation*, p. 235.
39. Memorandum by Keenleyside, 23 May 1940, and memorandum by Skelton, 19 May 1940, King Papers: Pickersgill, *The Mackenzie King Record*, vol. I, p. 115.
40. King to Merchant Mahoney (telegram), 26 May 1940; Mahoney to King (telegram), 4 June 1940, King Papers.
41. Winston S. Churchill, *Their Finest Hour* (Boston, Mass., 1949), pp. 145–6.
42. Hall, *North American Supply*, pp. 146 ff.; Edward R. Stettinius, Jr., *Lend-Lease: Weapon for Victory* (New York, 1944), pp. 31–2.
43. Quoted in Pickersgill, *The Mackenzie King Record*, vol. I, p. 127.
44. Quoted in Langer and Gleason, *The Challenge to Isolation*, p. 485.
45. Quoted in *ibid.*, p. 745.
46. Quoted in Churchill, *Their Finest Hour*, p. 356.
47. Quoted in Pickersgill, *The Mackenzie King Record*, vol. I, p. 129.
48. King to Christie (telegram), 12 Aug. 1940, King Papers.
49. Christie to Skelton, 16 Aug. 1940, *ibid.*

50. Quoted in Pickersgill, *The Mackenzie King Record*, vol. I, p. 130.
51. *Ibid.*, p. 133.
52. Quoted in Churchill, *Their Finest Hour*, p. 409.
53. William H. Standley and Arthur A. Ageton, *Admiral Ambassador to Russia* (Chicago, 1955), p. 57.
54. Quoted in Gilbert Norman Tucker, *The Naval Service of Canada*, vol. II (Ottawa, 1952), pp. 62–3.
55. Quoted in Pickersgill, *The Mackenzie King Record*, vol. I, p. 124.
56. Quoted in Nancy Harvison Hooker, ed., *The Moffat Papers* (Cambridge, Mass., 1956), p. 314.
57. Quoted in Col. Stanley W. Dziuban, *Military Relations between the United States and Canada, 1939–1945* (Washington, D.C., 1959), p. 13.
58. *The Moffat Papers*, p. 314, fn. 11; Dziuban, *Military Relations*, p. 14.
59. Quoted in *ibid.*, pp. 314–15.
60. *Ibid.*, p. 319; Dziuban, *Military Relations*, pp. 15–16.
61. Quoted in *The Moffat Papers*, p. 319.
62. Memorandum by Brig. Kenneth Stuart, 15 July 1940, King Papers.
63. *Ibid.*
64. Memorandum by Capt. L. W. Murray, 14 July 1940, *ibid.*
65. Memorandum by Air Cmdre. A. A. A. Cuffe, 14 July 1940, *ibid.*
66. Dziuban, *Military Relations*, p. 18.
67. Quoted in *The Moffat Papers*, p. 344.
68. Langer and Gleason, *The Challenge to Isolation*, p. 704.
69. Dziuban, *Military Relations*, p. 22.
70. Langer and Gleason, *The Challenge to Isolation*, pp. 704–5.
71. Pickersgill, *The Mackenzie King Record*, vol. I, p. 134.
72. King to Roosevelt, 7 Sept. 1940, King Papers.
73. See *The Congressional Record*, 23 Sept. 1940, p. 18857.
74. Lucien Cannon to King, 21 Aug. 1940; Edmund Scheur to King, 21 Aug. 1940; W. J. Lindal to King, 21 Aug. 1940. King Papers.
75. James A. Ross to King, 20 Aug. 1940, *ibid.*
76. Churchill to King (telegram), 22 Aug. 1940, *ibid.*
77. Quoted in Pickersgill, *The Mackenzie King Record*, vol. I, p. 144.

INDEX

(Officers and titled people are listed under the highest rank and title attained during the period 1935–1940.)